Diverging Parties

SOCIAL CHANGE, REALIGNMENT, AND PARTY POLARIZATION

TRANSFORMING AMERICAN POLITICS

Lawrence C. Dodd, Series Editor

Dramatic changes in political institutions and behavior over the past three decades have underscored the dynamic nature of American politics, confronting political scientists with a new and pressing intellectual agenda. The pioneering work of early postwar scholars, while laying a firm empirical foundation for contemporary scholarship, failed to consider how American politics might change or recognize the forces that would make fundamental change inevitable. In reassessing the static interpretations fostered by these classic studies, political scientists are now examining the underlying dynamics that generate transformational change.

Transforming American Politics brings together texts that address four closely related aspects of change. A first concern is documenting and explaining recent changes in American politics—in institutions, processes, behavior, and policymaking. A second is reinterpreting classic studies and theories to provide a more accurate perspective on postwar politics. The series looks at historical change to identify recurring patterns of political transformation within and across the distinctive eras of American politics. Last and perhaps most important, the series presents new theories and interpretations that explain the dynamic processes at work and thus clarify the direction of contemporary politics. All of the books focus on the central theme of transformation—transformation in both the conduct of American politics and in the way we study and understand its many aspects.

BOOKS IN THIS SERIES

Diverging Parties

SOCIAL CHANGE, REALIGNMENT, AND PARTY POLARIZATION

Jeffrey M. Stonecash

*Department of Political Science, Maxwell School,
Syracuse University*

Mark D. Brewer

Department of Government, Colby College

Mack D. Mariani

*Department of Political Science, Maxwell School,
Syracuse University*

A Member of the Perseus Books Group

Copyright @ 2003 by Westview Press, A Member of the Perseus Books Group

Westview Press books are available at special discounts for bulk purchases in the United States by corporations, institutions, and other organizations. For more information, please contact the Special Markets Department at the Perseus Books Group, 11 Cambridge Center, Cambridge, MA 02142, or call (617) 252-5298, (800) 255-1514 or email j.mccrary@perseusbooks.com.

Published in 2003 in the United States of America by Westview Press, 5500 Central Avenue, Boulder, Colorado 80301-2877, and in the United Kingdom by Westview Press, 12 Hid's Copse Road, Cumnor IIill, Oxford OX2 9JJ.

Find us on the World Wide Web at www.westviewpress.com.

Library of Cataloging-in-Publication Data
Stonecash, Jeffrey M.
    Diverging parties: social change, realignment, and party polarization/by Jeffrey M. Stonecash, Mark D. Brewer, and Mack D. Mariani.
        p. cm. — (Transforming American politics)
    Includes bibliographical references and index.
    ISBN 0-8133-4028-4 (hardcover: alk. Paper) — ISBN 0-8133-9843-6 (pbk : alk. Paper)
    1. United States. Congress. House. 2. Polarization (Social sciences) 3. Legislators—United States. 4. Political parties—United States. 5. Representative government and representation—United States. 6. United States—Politics and Government—1989-7. United States—Politics and government—1945-1989. I. Brewer, Mark D. II. Mariani, Mack D. III. Title. IV. Series.

JK1319. S76 2002
328.73'0769—dc21

                                                                        2002003739
                                                                              CIP

Contents

Tables and Illustrations

Figures

Maps

Preface

Conflict between Democrats and Republicans in the House of Representatives at the start of the twenty-first century was greater than it was thirty years before. Members of each party are more likely to join together and vote against the other party. The parties increasingly adopt sharply differing policy positions. Democrats have more liberal voting records than they did thirty years ago, and Republicans have more conservative voting records. Party conflict is pervasive in the House.

In some regards this development is surprising, given current interpretations of American politicians and elections. In recent decades it has been common to argue that the attachment to parties in the electorate has declined and that elections should be seen as candidate-centered, or individualistic. The argument, in brief, has been as follows. Politicians face an electorate in which voters are more likely to be independents. Faced with voters inclined to split their tickets, candidates, and incumbents in particular, focus on using campaign and office resources to enhance their personal visibility. They call attention to their accomplishments rather than entangling their image with that of their party. In this view, members of Congress are seen as primarily concerned with their own fortunes and not those of the party. Yet for some reason members of Congress are voting more and more frequently with their party. That behavior seems odd if politicians want to create an independent image so their electoral fortunes are not tied to national swings of support for Democrats and Republicans.

This book offers an explanation of this increased party cohesion and conflict. The argument, building on the work of Rohde (1991), is that the emergence of greater party cohesion and conflict is largely a product of long-term secular realignment and social change. As a result of these changes, the diversity of constituencies within each party has decreased, while the difference between the electoral bases of the two parties has grown. Realignment has brought the Democrats an electoral base that is less affluent, urban, and non-white. Republicans have acquired an electoral base that is more affluent, suburban and rural, and primarily white. While this gradual realignment was occurring, social change unfolded in ways that accentuated existing differences or added new constituencies that became a further source of differences. Inequality, after declining for several decades, began to increase in the 1970s, leading to constituencies with very real and significant differences about what role government should play in society. At the same time, immigration has resulted in a significant expansion of the "minority" population in the nation. These changes led to constituents with different needs and form the basis of more conflict between the parties.

The basis of analysis that follows is the argument that constituents, how they differ, and in which district they live, matter. Social groups differ in their partisan support. Who composes the population of districts affects partisan outcomes and the subsequent voting patterns of members of Congress. This connection between constituencies and partisan behavior has gotten less attention than it might in recent years, and we think that making that connection central to analyses will help make sense of the growing party polarization. As we will see, House districts vary enormously in their composition and these differences strongly affect which party is likely to win a seat. The result is that parties derive their seats from differing constituents. That leads to conflicting party policy concerns and voting records.

The plan for the analysis is as follows. We will first briefly review the evidence of increased polarization in party voting in recent decades. Following that, Chapter 2 will present an explanatory framework for the subsequent analysis. Because the argument is that the current situation is the consequence of long-term changes, in Chapter 3 we review the realignment changes each party experienced before the 1970s. The current differences in party bases began to emerge long ago, and understanding that history is crucial for understanding the present. Chapter 4 will present the economic and social changes that have occurred since 1970, focusing on the enfranchisement of the black electorate, the rise of inequality, and the dramatic increase in Hispanics. These changes have created new policy concerns and new constituents. The parties have responded by adopting differing positions, which has contributed to continuing realignment of the parties. Chapter 5 examines how the combination of social change and realignment has altered the electoral bases of the parties. Chapter 6 will then assess the implications of all these changes for the polarization of voting in the U.S.

House over the last thirty years. Finally, the framework employed here and the empirical patterns presented have significant implications for the candidate-centered interpretation of elections and politicians, and Chapter 7 will develop those consequences.

1

The Reemergence
of Party Polarization

Republicans and Democrats are finding it harder to work together. While Democrats and Republicans in Congress have always disagreed, their disagreements in the 1990s and early 2000s are more pronounced and more intense than they used to be.[1] The increase in party conflict became particularly evident during the Clinton era. Partisan tensions led to bitter congressional debates, a string of ethical charges, countercharges, and investigations, several government shutdowns, and a House vote to impeach the president of the United States (Drew 1996, 2000). Roger Davidson calls the existing party divisions a "very deep chasm" and argues that we are now "in the midst of the most partisan era since Reconstruction" (*Congressional Quarterly Almanac* 1998, B6).

Greater party division in Congress has been accompanied by a change in the tone of debates on Capitol Hill. Congressional debates, which are televised to the American public via C-Span, frequently break down into shouting matches. An increasing number of members of Congress are reprimanded for engaging in personal insults and un-parliamentary attacks during congressional debates (Jamieson and Falk 2000). Party differences are now expressed in harsh, often personal terms. As Representative Pat Williams, Democrat of Montana, said before he left Congress in 1997, "Not long ago, partisanship was a tool with which one accomplished a policy agenda. Now it's a mechanism whereby one destroys the opponent, embarrasses his family and puts him in jail at the end of the day" (Clines 1998, 3).

The current atmosphere of intense party conflict makes it difficult for members from opposing parties to work together on Capitol Hill. Instead, party leaders attempt to identify clear differences between their party and the other party while using rhetorical attacks and procedural delays to slow or defeat the opposing party's agenda. Republican leaders used these techniques effectively in 1993 and 1994 when Democrats held a majority in both houses of Congress. By sticking together, congressional Republicans were able to defeat President Bill Clinton's first major legislative initiative, a $16 billion economic "stimulus" package. Republicans were also able to delay passage of the Democratic crime bill and to force Democrats to abandon President Clinton's health care proposal without even taking a vote (CQ Annual Report, 1993, 1994). Though unified, Republicans were not able to prevent Democrats from passing tax increases in 1993. But by forcing Democrats to pass the bill without any Republican votes, Republicans were able to portray Democrats as a "tax and spend" party during the 1994 campaign.

After Republicans gained the majority in Congress in November 1994, it was the Democrats' chance to play spoiler. Democrats turned up the rhetorical heat during congressional debates on the "Contract with America," the set of ten policy commitments that the House Republicans made during the 1994 election. Democrats derided them as the "Contract *on* America" (*Congressional Record*, February 22, 1995, H2030) and a "War on the Poor" (February 24, 1995, H2219). Democrats aimed their fire at Republican Speaker Newt Gingrich in particular (Drew 1996), but intense conflict between the parties continued even after Gingrich announced his resignation in late 1998.

Though the parties were divided on a wide range of issues, the deepest divisions emerged over the tax issue. In proposing tax cuts in 1999 and 2000, Republicans fought for cuts in the personal income tax, arguing that any budget surplus, if left in Washington, would invariably be spent to increase the size of government. In their view, the federal government was already too big and any surplus that existed should be "returned to the people who earned it" in the first place. Democrats disagreed, arguing that tax cuts would squander the surplus and prevent needed spending increases on popular programs like Social Security and Medicare. They also argued that too much of the tax cut went to the affluent. In 1999, 97 percent of House Democrats voted against the Republican tax cut proposal, while 98 percent of Republicans voted in support. According to Gebe Martinez, House Democrats used the vote to "create a record . . . that puts the differences between the parties in stark contrast" (Martinez 1999, 1777). In 2000, Republicans tried again, this time attaching a minimum wage increase to their tax cuts in the hopes of attracting some measure of Democratic support. Congressional Republicans remained remarkably unified, with 99.5 percent voting in favor of the 2000 tax cut. Yet Democratic unity did not falter significantly. Eighty percent of House

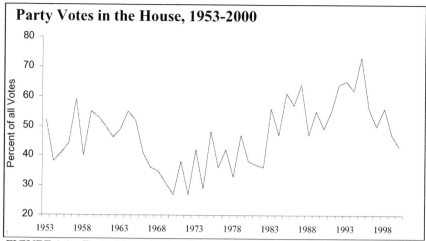

FIGURE 1.1   Party Votes in the House, 1953-2000

Democrats voted against the bill, even though it included a minimum wage increase that would benefit many of their core constituencies.

Finally, early in 2001, with the Republican George W. Bush president, and Republicans in control of both houses, Republicans ignored Democratic objections and passed a tax cut in excess of one trillion dollars, to be phased in over a decade. Republicans again emphasized the importance of putting more money in the hands of those who earned it and would spend it and restraining the flow of revenue to government. Democrats complained about most of the benefits going to the affluent. The differences and divisions between the parties were clear.

Even a national crisis could not suppress the party conflicts that exist. Following the September 11, 2001, terrorist attacks there was considerable comment that the nation was united and that bipartisan policymaking would prevail. Faced with a slumping economy, Congress sought to create a legislative package to stimulate business activity. The divisions between the parties quickly emerged. The House Republicans passed a bill that provided most of the tax benefits to corporations as refunds for previously paid taxes and that accelerated tax cuts for the more affluent. The Republicans' argument was that returning taxes in this way would prompt more spending. Democrats, in control of the Senate, passed a very different package. Theirs provided tax "rebates" to those low-income individuals who did not pay taxes and did not get the benefits of an earlier rebate program for taxpayers. The Democrats also sought to provide more funds for unemployment compensation and health insurance for those without it. Democrats argued that this plan would put money in the hands of the most needy, who would be most likely to spend the funds.[2] The disagreement about what to do was so significant that party leaders in the two houses simply chose not to do anything during the 2001 session, despite the evidence of economic problems.

The Trend in Party Conflict

The current tendency of the parties to unite to vote against each other differs from the more muted partisanship of the 1960s and 1970s. During that period, Congress took up a number of bills involving the issue of whether the national government should play a greater role in society. Many of these bills prompted considerable opposition because they redistributed authority between the federal government and the states or granted new rights and benefits to specific groups. Should the federal government intervene to make sure that blacks had the same rights as others? Should the federal government establish and manage a national health care program for senior citizens? Should the federal government require that women have the same opportunities as men in school sports programs? Should there be a federal commission to ensure equal employment laws are enforced? Table 1.1 shows the extent of party differences on three key pieces of legislation during this era: the Civil Rights Act of 1964, Title IX, a bill requiring equal opportunity in sports for women in educations institutions, and the Equal Employment Act of 1972. Each of these bills created conflict over a redefinition of rights and the role the national government in providing these rights.

Party Differences on Legislation, 1960s-1970s and 1999-2000				
Legislation	Democrat		Republican	
1960s — 1970s	Yes	No	Yes	No
Civil Rights Act, 1964	184	102	108	26
Title IX Act, 1972	127	103	91	74
Equal Employment Act, 1972	184	57	119	53
1999 — 2000				
Tax Cut, 1999	6	203	217	4
Minimum Wage-Tax Cut, 2000	41	167	215	1
Source: Various editions of <u>Congressional Quarterly Reports</u>				

TABLE 1.1   Party Differences on Legislation, 1960s-1970s and 1999-2000

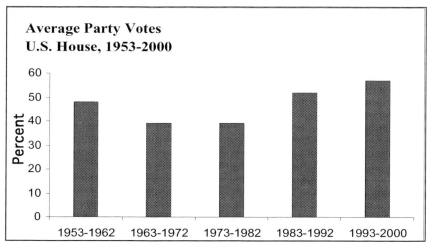

FIGURE 1.2   Average Party Votes U.S. House, 1953-2000

As Table 1.1 indicates, divisions within the parties were more important than divisions between the parties. A majority of both parties voted for the legislation, but there were significant divisions within each party on these bills. In each case a substantial bloc from each party defected and voted in opposition to the majority of their own party. These votes from the 1960s and 1970s are very different from the strict party line votes on President Clinton's major initiatives in 1994 and 1995. They also differ from the party divisions on the Republican's proposed tax cuts in 1999 and 2000, presented in Table 1.1. The difference between the eras can be stated more precisely. The parties divided on some issues during the 1960s and 1970s. Likewise, the parties have experienced internal divisions from time to time during the 1990s.[3] Nonetheless, the examples in Table 1.1 illustrate the general trend. Differences between the parties have been with us for some time, but those differences have become more pronounced in the last two decades.

Diverging Parties: Party Voting and Party Unity

To systematically track changes in conflict, it is valuable to examine congressional divisions using a wide array of votes rather than a handful of examples. One common measure of party division is the percentage of party votes that take place in the House. Party votes are those roll call (recorded) votes where a majority of Republicans vote in opposition to a majority of Democrats (Ornstein et al. 2000; Fleisher and Bond 2000a, 3; Rohde 1991, 8). A high percentage of party votes indicates that the parties regularly oppose each other on legislation, while a low percentage

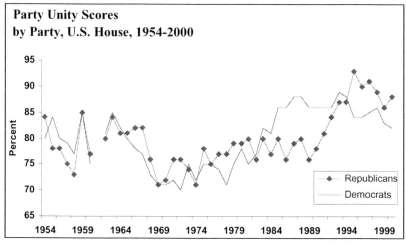

**Party Unity Scores
by Party, U.S. House, 1954-2000**

FIGURE 1.3   Party Unity Scores by Party, U.S. House, 1954-2000

means that the parties oppose each other less frequently. Figure 1.1 indicates the percentage of House votes that were party votes from 1953 to 2000.[4] Party voting decreased in the late 1960s and 1970s and then increased dramatically from the early 1980s through the mid–1990s, reaching a high of 73 percent in 1995.

After a steady rise from 1970 through 1995, the percentage of party votes dropped, reaching only 47 percent in 1999 and 43 percent in 2000. Some of this decline may have been because Republicans wanted to postpone dealing with some controversies. During 1999 and 2000 Republicans controlled the House of Representatives by a very small margin. Following their seat losses in the 1996 and 1998 elections, Republican leaders used the rules and their control of the agenda to push controversial (and potentially losing) issues off the House floor (Bettelheim 2001). Some conflicts were simply shifted to House committees or conference committees, while other conflicts were avoided altogether. The emergence of massive budget surpluses may also have contributed to a decline. Potentially divisive conflicts could be avoided–at least for the time being–by increasing spending for all sides. Republican leaders may also have been trying to avoid extensive partisan battles with President Clinton in the year leading up to the 2000 presidential election.

Time will tell whether the decline in party voting in 1999 and 2000 is an indication of declining partisanship or a temporary lull in continued party conflict. Nonetheless, it is important to keep recent trends in perspective. Party voting levels in 1999 and 2000 averaged 45 percent, which is still distinctly higher than levels of 20 to 30 percent that prevailed in the 1960s and early 1970s. Recent levels of party voting seem low, but only in comparison to the very high levels of party voting of 1995. When averaged out across a ten-year period (Figure 1.2), the long-term trend for party votes is clear: The percentage of party votes over the last ten years was higher than for any other ten-year period in the last half-century.[5]

Party unity scores are a second and related measure of party polarization. Party unity scores measure the percentage of the time that an individual member of Congress votes with his or her party on a vote (*CQ Almanac* 1998, B19; Rohde 1991, 9). While party votes tell us how often the two parties oppose each other, party unity scores give us an idea of the intensity of the party divisions on those votes. Members with high party unity scores are the most loyal partisans, while those with low party unity scores are the most likely to vote with the opposing party against their own party's position.

Figure 1.3 represents the average party unity scores for Republican and Democratic members of the House from 1954 to 2000.[6] For both parties, the trends in party unity resemble the trends we see in party votes. Average party unity drops somewhat in the 1960s and early 1970s and then climbs to high points in the 1980s and 1990s. In contrast to the more dramatic decline in the percentage of party votes, party unity scores dip only slightly in the late 1990s. Democratic and Republican party unity scores largely parallel one another. The only exception is that Democratic unity comes earlier, climbing more steeply in the 1980s, while Republican unity has its biggest gains in the 1990s. For both Democrats and Republicans, the average party unity score was highest in the 1980s and 1990s and lowest in the late 1960s and early 1970s. Scores on both party votes and party unity indicate that in recent years Republicans and Democrats in the House were more likely to vote differently and to stick together on those votes (Patterson and Caldiera 1988; Rohde 1991; Bond and Fleisher 2000).

Ideological Divisions

Knowing that the parties are polarized does not tell us much about *how* the parties differ from one another. The parties could vote differently on relatively minor issues. This raises the question: Are voting divisions a sign of real differences in the parties' political values or are they merely a consequence of political posturing and petty squabbling between the parties?

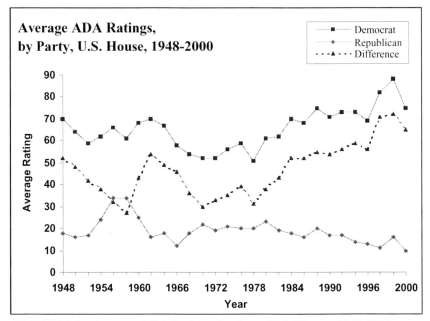

FIGURE 1.4   Average ADA Ratings by Party, U.S. House, 1948-2000

Another way to measure divisions is to assess the ideological position-ing of party members. In American politics, we generally categorize po-litical ideologies along an ideological spectrum of liberalism and conser-vatism. Liberals, in the most basic sense, believe that the government should take a more active role in regulating the economy, providing a safety net, and ensuring equity in society. In contrast, conservatives gen-erally believe that the government should have a more limited role and that society is better off when decisions about economics and values are left to free markets.[7]

While this ideological continuum is useful for organizing differences, there is a long history of concerns about whether analyses based on a sin-gle liberal-conservative dimension oversimplify the complexities of con-gressional voting behavior. As early as 1958, Duncan MacCrae made the case that congressional voting alignments do not fit neatly into a liberal-conservative pattern. Instead of looking at things in liberal or conserva-tive terms, MacRae suggested that voting alignments be studied across numerous policy areas (1958). In later research, Aage Clausen found that there were different patterns of influence, with different voting align-ments emerging across different policy areas (Clausen 1973; Clausen and Van Horn 1977; Schneider 1979). Others have picked up that theme, suggesting that unidimensional treatment of voting alignments does not explain as much of the variance as do treatments that take into account multiple dimensions (Smith 1981; Wilcox and Clausen 1991; Koford 1989). Others, however, disagree and present evidence that congressional voting behavior can be analyzed through a single liberal-conservative dimension. Jerold Schneider, for instance, argued that multiple dimensions might have been needed to explain congressional behavior during the 1950s and 1960s, but that by the 1970s, a single liberal-conservative dimension was dominant (1979). Poole and Rosenthal also examined congressional voting behavior in the 1950s. Using spatial models to gauge the accuracy of other measures, they found that "many of the multiple dimensions claimed in previous research can be interpreted in a single liberal-conservative dimension" (1985, 383). In a later, longitudinal study of congressional voting, Poole and Rosenthal argue that most congressional voting behavior from 1789 to 1985 can be explained through a single dimension (1991, 230). With that in mind, we will focus on a single measure of liberal–conservative differences, while cautioning that this somewhat oversimplifies the nature of differences among members.[8]

Americans for Democratic Action (ADA) Ratings

ADA ratings are often used as a measure of the ideology of members of Congress (Shaffer 1982, 1989; Frymer 1994; Fleisher 1993; Taylor 1996). The ratings are assigned to individual members of Congress by Americans for Democratic Action (ADA), a liberal interest group,[9] based on a select number of votes taken in each session of Congress.[10] The votes are chosen to reflect the ADA's position on core liberal issues. Members of Congress with high ADA ratings are considered liberal, while those with low ADA ratings are considered conservative. While ADA scores are not perfect measures of ideology, they do correlate with other efforts to measure ideology and appear to provide a reasonable indication of the positions members take.[11]

Figure 1.4 presents the average ADA rating of Republican and Democratic members of the House of Representatives from 1948 to 2000.[12] Across this entire period, House Democrats were (on average) considerably more liberal than House Republicans. For Democrats, ADA ratings dropped through the 1960s and early 1970s before steadily increasing through the 1980s and 1990s. How dramatic were these shifts? The average ADA score for House Democrats dropped 18 points from 1962 to 1972 and then increased 30 points between 1978 and 1998. For House

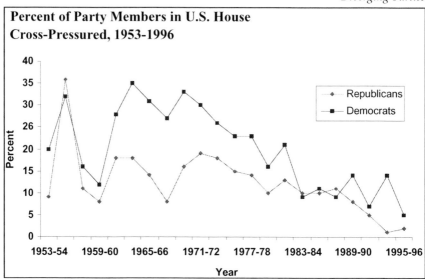

FIGURE 1.5   Percent of Party Members in U.S. House Cross-Pressured, 1953-1996

Republicans, their average ADA ratings drifted upward in the 1950s, then the trend reversed by the early 1960s. From that point onward, House Republicans have been distinctly conservative. The average ADA rating for House Republicans was remarkably stable from the 1960s through the 1980s, hovering around 20. During the 1990s, the average ADA rating for House Republicans dropped even lower, as House Republicans voted even more conservatively.

By 1999, Republicans were extremely conservative and Democrats extremely liberal. The dotted (middle) line on Figure 1.4 tracks the difference between Republicans' and Democrats' ADA ratings. As measured by ADA ratings, the ideological distance between the parties is greater at the beginning of the 2000s than at any point in the previous five decades. Another widely used measure, DW-NOMINATE scores, indicates the same pattern (Poole and Rosenthal 1991, 1997, 115–145; Jacobson 2000a, 13, 2000b).

Fleisher and Bond, using data based on conservative interest group scores as well as ADA ratings, also concluded that ideological divisions between the parties are increasing. They assigned members of Congress an ideological score based on their voting record, and then compared members' scores with each party's average ideological score. When a member's score was closer to the average score of the opposing party than their own party, that member was listed as a "cross-pressured"

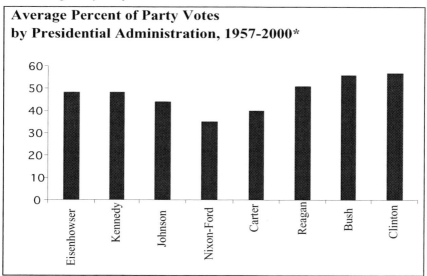

FIGURE 1.6 Average Percent of Party Votes by Presidential
            Administration, 1957-2000

member (Fleisher and Bond 2000b, 164–168; Bond and Fleisher 2001).[13]
These members are cross-pressured because they are likely to be pulled
in one direction by their own party affiliation and in the other direction
by their ideological similarity to members of the other party. The number of members categorized as cross-pressured declined dramatically in
the 1980s and 1990s. Figure 1.5 illustrates the decline of these cross-
pressured members as a percentage of each party's total membership in
the House.[14]

Conclusion

The parties are diverging from one another, both in terms of voting and
in terms of ideology. The general pattern of divergence is fairly consistent. In the 1960s and 1970s, the parties moved closer together. During
this period, members from opposing parties voted together more often
and became more ideologically similar. Beginning in the late 1970s and
early 1980s, the parties began to diverge. The parties became more likely
to vote in opposition to one another, more internally unified, and more
ideologically distinct from one another.

The trend toward increased party division intensified during the
1990s, with partisan divisions reaching modern highs in the 1990s.[15] The
intensity of party divisions in the Clinton era makes it tempting to view

partisanship as an outgrowth of conflict between particular political personalities (Bill Clinton and Newt Gingrich, for example). However, it is very clear that the trend of increased partisanship pre-dates the Clinton era. Figure 1.6 illustrates the trends over the course of every presidential administration from Eisenhower to Clinton.[16] As the graph makes clear, the average annual percentage of party votes during the Clinton administration (48 percent) was not significantly higher than that of the Bush administration before it (47 percent).[17]

Congressional decisionmaking today takes place within the context of these deep party divisions. While cross-party coalitions still occur from time to time, intense conflict between the parties is now the norm. The crucial question is *why* the parties have diverged from one another. We think that diverging constituencies explain this growing difference, and in the following chapter, we offer an explanation of the sources of this polarization.

Notes

1. This partisan resurgence is well documented in the literature. See, for instance: Rohde (1991; 1992), Dodd and Oppenheimer (1989), and Davidson and Oleczek (1990, 39-64). For an overview of the persistence of partisanship through the 1990s, see Lucas (1999). For an overview of the resurgence of partisanship in the electorate see Aldrich (1999) and Bond and Fleisher (2000). On the intensity of party conflict in the 1990s, see also Rosenbaum (1996), Alvararez and Schmitt (2000).

2. David E. Rosenbaum, "Package of G.O.P. Tax Cuts Is Approved by House Panel," *New York Times,* October 13, 2001, A10; Richard W. Stevenson, "Lawmakers' Votes on Economic Legislation Will Test Talk of Bipartisanship," *New York Times,* October 24, 2001, A12; Gretchen Morgenson, "An Economic Stimulus Bill With Corporations in Mind," *New York Times,* October 27, 2001, C1; Richard W. Stevenson, "Democrats' Recovery Plan Moves Forward in Senate," *New York Times,* November 9, 2001, A22; Adam Clymer, "With Sagging Economy as Ally, Democrats in Congress Go on the Attack," *New York Times,* November 11, 2001, A32; Adam Clymer, "House G.O.P. Rejects Stimulus-Bill Summit," *New York Times,* November 14, 2001, B7; Adam Clymer, "Stimulus Bill Prompts Insults But No Action," *New York Times,* November 16, 2001, A16.

3. Consider, for example, the issue of trade during the Clinton administration. President Clinton relied on a coalition of Republicans and Democrats to pass trade agreements such as NAFTA and GATT. This cross-party coalition on trade emerged again in 2000, when a coalition of Republicans and Democrats joined to pass legislation to give permanent Normal Trade Relations status to China and to support China's entry into the World Trade Organization (WTO). See Schmitt (2000).

4. *Congressional Quarterly Almanac,* 1998; *Congressional Quarterly Weekly Report,* January 6, 2001, 67; Ornstein, Mann, and Malbin (2000).

5. Data compiled from *Congressional Quarterly Almanac*, 1998; *Congressional Quarterly Weekly Report*, January 6, 2001, 67; Ornstein, Mann, and Malbin (2000). Figures represent the average party vote score for the U.S. House of Representatives over a ten-year period.

6. Ornstein, Mann, and Malbin (2000); *Congressional Quarterly Weekly Report*, January 6, 2001, 67. There is no data available for 1961.

7. These definitions of liberalism and conservatism are, of course, extremely simplified. A more thorough review of the development and dimensions of liberalism and conservatism can be found in Dolbeare and Medcalf (1993). See Chapter 3 in particular.

8. To further complicate matters, what policy positions signify the ideological position of liberal and conservative may shift over time, sometimes dramatically. What is a liberal position today might tomorrow be described as a conservative position (Dolbeare and Medcalf 1993, 30). One example of this shift might be seen in the shift in the debate on tax credits for the working poor in our society. In the 1970s, conservatives viewed tax credits for the working poor as a "negative income tax" that would be a more responsible alternative to welfare programs. By the 1990s, however, many conservatives were opposing these tax credits, viewing the Earned Income Tax Credit (EITC) as another form of wasteful government spending. Thus, over time, liberals and conservatives switched positions on the issue. Many conservatives were now opposed to the tax credits, and liberals, who were initially skeptical of the program because they feared it would undermine the existing welfare system, were the program's biggest defenders. The conservative shift on the EITC was noted by Speaker Newt Gingrich, who criticized the program because he thought it undermined normal market incentives and raised marginal tax rates (*Congressional Record*, October 17, 1995, E1952). Republican Representative Joel Hefley of Colorado also criticized the EITC as "pork," saying that "90 percent of the benefit checks go to those who pay no income taxes in the first place–including illegal aliens and prisoners" (*Congressional Record*, October 12, 1995, H9900).

As a result of the shifting meaning of liberal and conservative, it is difficult to measure congressional ideology with great precision. This is particularly true when attempting to examine that behavior over long periods of time. While no measure of ideology is likely to be precise, we can nonetheless compare some basic conceptions of liberal and conservative policy preferences to how members vote on the House floor. With this information, it is possible to develop a rough measure of where members stand ideologically in relation to one another.

9. According to the ADA website, the ADA has published voting records for members of Congress since its founding in 1947.

10. In 1999, for instance, ADA ratings were based on twenty roll call votes.

11. We should be cautious about putting too much faith in any one measure of ideology, including ADA ratings. While ADA ratings are widely used, there are at least four general concerns raised about them. First, ADA ratings are based on a small selection of votes (Burden, Caldiera, and Groseclose 2000), which include a disproportionate number of close votes. As a consequence, some scholars fear that ADA ratings exaggerate ideological extremism (Fowler 1982; Snyder 1992a and

1992b). Second, the votes selected by the ADA for the ratings change from year to year, making it impossible to compare legislators' ADA scores across time (Burden, Caldiera, and Groseclose 2000; Smith 1981). Third, ADA ratings fail to account for congressional decisionmaking that takes place off the floor, presenting a truncated agenda upon which to base congressional ideology and ignoring committee reciprocity that affects roll call votes (Fowler 1982; Vandoren 1990; Hall and Grofman 1990). Fourth, it is argued that ADA ratings are "contaminated" by outside forces like constituents, the economy, and party (Jackson and Kingdon 1992; Hill, Hanna, and Shafqat 1997; Carson and Oppenheimer 1984; Burden, Caldiera, and Groseclose 2000; Vandoren 1990).

While we agree that ADA ratings are not perfect, we do believe they provide a valid and easily understandable gauge of congressional ideology. Despite its limitations, ADA scores have been shown to be sound measures of congressional ideology (Shaffer 1989; Smith, Herrera, and Herrera 1990; Krehbiel 1994) that are remarkably stable over time (Herrera, Epperlein, and Smith 1995; Smith, Herrera, and Herrera 1990). ADA scores are, according to Burden, Caldiera, and Groseclose, "still the most comprehensive and road-tested measures available" (2000). We disagree with the idea that a changing selection of votes makes it impossible to compare ADA scores across time. In fact, the changing selection of votes allows ADA ratings to reflect changes in the policy positions of American liberalism across time (Shaffer 1989, 34-35). The policy positions selected by the ADA for its annual ratings provide researchers with a good–albeit imperfect–measure of liberalism at a particular place in time.

For our purposes it is absolutely vital that ADA scores capture much more than the personal ideology of individual members of Congress. We are interested in the *public* ideology of legislators, which is the product of a mix of personal, constituency, and party pressures, among others (Shaffer 1989). ADA scores may or may not be an appropriate measure for personal ideology, but we believe them to be a good measure of the public ideology of legislators. They are of additional value because they are drawn from roll call votes, public actions that are observable to constituents and the parties, rather than less observable (and less measurable) activity in committee, caucus, or elsewhere.

Finally, the same broad pattern of ideology divergence found in the ADA ratings is reflected in other measures of congressional ideology as well. Many scholars have made adjustments to the ADA ratings by omitting absences (Taylor 1996), combining ADA ratings with other ratings (Fleisher and Bond 2000), or creating new indices based on advanced mathematical techniques (Groseclose et al. 1999). Others have created new indices based on advanced mathematical techniques (Groseclose, Levitt, and Snyder 1999; Carson and Oppenheimer 1984; Jackson and Kingdon 1992). DW-Nominate scores, which rely on spatial models, show that ideological polarization declined somewhat in the 1950s and 1960s, held steady in the 1970s, and increased substantially in the 1980s and 1990s (Jacobson 2000a, 10–15). Andrew Taylor, who adjusted ADA scores to account for presidential influences in voting, found that since the 1970s the Democratic Party in the House has become more liberal and the Republican Party more conservative (Taylor 1996). These alternative measures of ideology–along with Bond and Fleisher's research on "cross-pressured" members (Figure 1.5)–serve to reinforce the general conclusions drawn from ADA ratings (Figure 1.4).

Thus, multiple measures of congressional ideology point to a Congress with two parties that are more ideologically polarized from one another than thirty years before. Republicans and Democrats are not only more divided in terms of votes, they are also more divided in terms of broader political values. There are fewer Republicans who are ideologically sympathetic to their Democratic colleagues and vice versa. A similar pattern of polarization can be observed in the Senate as well (Poole and Rosenthal 1984; Rohde 1992; Berke 1999; Bond and Fleisher 2000; Ornstein et al. 2000; Alvararez and Schmitt 2000). The virtual disappearance of conservative Democrats and liberal Republicans means that ideological coalitions created of members from both parties no longer exist.

12. ADA ratings for 1946–1994 are taken from Tim Groseclose's web site of http://wesley.stanford.edu/groseclose/. We then acquired the ADA ratings for the years 1995–1999 at http://www.adaction.org/. We use the unadjusted ADA scores rather than the adjusted scores. The reasons for that choice are explained in the Appendix, "Unadjusted and Adjusted ADA Scores."

13. Joseph Cooper and Gary Young make a distinction between cross-partisanship (the degree of intraparty division) and bipartisanship (the degree that members of both parties vote the same way). While the distinction is useful, for our purposes we use cross-pressured in a more inclusive sense to include both bipartisan and cross-partisan votes (that is, all votes that are not "party votes"). See Cooper and Young (1997), 246-274. See page 254 in particular.

14. Compiled from data presented in Fleisher and Bond, 2000b.

15. Schraufnagel argues that if a more comprehensive index of conflict is created, conflict is now much higher than it was in the 1950s and 1960s. He combines the ideological voting records of members from Poole and Rosenthal, party unity scores, and the percentage of support for presidential proposals for each party and calculates the extent to which the parties differ (2001). This index reaches the highest levels during the 1990s.

16. Data compiled from *Congressional Quarterly Almanac*, 1998; *Congressional Quarterly Weekly Report*, January 6, 2001, 67; Ornstein, Mann, and Malbin (2000). Figures represent the average party vote score for the U.S. House of Representatives over the four- or eight-year term of a presidential administration. Roll call votes in the Januarys following the quadrennial presidential election were credited to the incoming administration (for example, Bill Clinton's average scores cover a period from January 1993-December 2000). The Nixon and Ford administrations are taken as a whole, with the score reflecting the average annual percentage of party votes from January 1969 through December 1976.

17. This is not to say, of course, that individual political figures did not contribute to the partisanship of the era. They clearly did. As evidence presented later indicates, partisan conflict on votes reached modern highs during the Clinton era. The *New York Times* editorial board, for instance, argued that the primary cause of legislative disagreement between Republicans and Democrats was Republicans "extreme dislike of President Clinton." See "Getting Along in Congress," *New York Times*, March 1, 1999, A20. While we agree that many–if not most–congressional Republicans did dislike Clinton, we believe that the source of disagreement

between the parties goes much deeper. The point we wish to emphasize here is that increasingly intense party conflict began earlier and helped shape the partisanship of the Clinton era.

2

Explaining Increasing Conflict

Party conflict has increased in the House of Representatives in recent decades. Democrats and Republicans in the House have generally disagreed in the past, but their disagreements are now more pronounced and more intense.[1] The concern of this analysis is why party conflict has increased. The analysis that follows is based on three simple organizing propositions: districts and their nature are central to understanding conflict, districts differ in population composition, and these differences affect partisan success and result in divergent electoral bases. These differences in electoral bases lead to political conflict.

The Basis of the Analysis

The first proposition is that members are elected from districts and any explanation of House-member behavior must begin with districts and their populations. District level analyses were once relatively common (Turner 1951; MacRae 1952; Froman 1963; Mayhew 1966; Shannon 1968; Turner and Schneier 1970), but with the emergence and availability of national survey data sets, analyses focusing on districts and their composition as a source of member behavior have become less common. The argument of this analysis is that, while national surveys of individuals are very valuable for indicating *national* behavior and trends, they neglect the role of the spatial distribution of the population across districts and the impact of changes in the composition of American society. These national surveys are of limited utility for telling us why *members* differ.

The second proposition is that districts differ (Drier et al. 2001, 3–24). Some House districts are rural, almost completely white, and voters are relatively conservative. Voters in these districts are not enthusiastic about welfare and other government assistance programs, and they generally are less supportive of government programs. Other House districts are densely populated, urban, largely minority in composition, and less affluent. These populations are relatively liberal and in great need of a broad array of programs, such as food stamps and housing assistance. They are generally much more supportive of and positive about a significant role for government in society.

These differences in turn affect which party is likely to win elections (Brady 1988; Stonecash and Lindstrom 1999). Republicans are likely to win the first type and Democrats the second. This results in parties with divergent electoral bases. Each party will then derive its support from constituents with different needs and views about government. This creates House parties with some clarity in their electoral bases, and these party members in turn advocate policies that reflect the needs of their constituents. Given their different constituencies, Democratic and Republican party members propose different policies and find themselves opposing each other. As they continue to oppose each other, the sense of difference increases, and party members pressure each other to join together, resulting in even greater polarization. In sum, district constituencies shape election outcomes and member voting behavior on issues. Varying districts electing different party candidates leads to conflict.

The Role of Secular Realignment

At the center of this explanation about the source of conflict are district constituencies and their relationship to partisan outcomes. While that relationship may appear simple and obvious, it has not always been clear. Indeed, this book tells a story of gradual political and social change that has created a stronger relationship between district constituencies and partisan outcomes compared to what prevailed from the 1950s until the 1970s. The emergence of party polarization is because the electoral base of each party has evolved from being fairly diverse to being more uniform. This is a product of realignment, a change in what party differing constituencies elect, and sustained change in the composition of American society. These changes have taken decades to occur. This polarization has occurred in the House and Senate. The analysis here focuses only on the House because the connection between diverse district constituencies and party polarization is easier to see in the House.

The process of realignment will be reviewed in some detail in Chapters 3 and 5, but an initial summary may be useful at this point. In brief, the parties for much of the 1900s were collections of conflicting constituencies. Then each party gradually acquired new constituents who conflicted with existing constituents, creating conflict and tension within each party. Over a considerable length of time some constituents shifted their party loyalty to the other party, reducing the tensions within each party. These electoral moves generally do not occur quickly, because the historical attachment of constituents to a party may be strong and abandoning one's party is not easy. But gradually there is a "sorting out," and parties find themselves with different and more coherent constituencies than in prior decades (Key 1959). That leads to more homogenous party electoral bases and more inclination of party members to vote with each other and against the other party (Rohde 1991; Aldrich 1995; Aldrich and Rohde 2001).

To be more specific, the Democratic Party has gradually shed its conservative wing to become more liberal and the Republican Party has gradually shed its liberal wing to become more conservative. In the early 1900s the Democratic Party was based primarily in the conservative South and the Republican Party was based primarily in the more liberal North. The Democratic Party was restrained from being liberal because of its reliance on the South. The Republican Party was limited in its conservative inclinations because of its reliance on the more liberal North. As a consequence of various within-party conflicts, the areas outside the South moved more Democratic over time, resulting in a Democratic Party with more of its base in liberal areas of the country. The conservative South moved steadily Republican after World War II, and as the Republican Party shed its liberal base in the Northeast and Midwest, it became a more consistently conservative party. These trends have changed the parties' electoral bases and their policy concerns.

These changes evolved gradually, with each party adding new constituents and losing old constituents over time. The additions and losses happened simultaneously, and there were eras when the evolving changes left each party with very diverse electoral bases. The 1960s and 1970s, in particular, were a time when the parties were in the midst of these transitions. Each party had a highly diverse electoral base, resulting in relatively low unity of party voting. The much-noted reemergence of party conflict and polarization is because this process of change continues to unfold and create more homogeneous party electoral bases.

The votes on the Medicare Act of 1965 illustrate the tensions within each party while this transition was occurring. This bill involved the creation of a national insurance program for seniors. While politically attractive for most members because it helped seniors, the bill involved the

Internal Tensions and Party Voting: The Medicare Bill				
	Democrat		Republican	
Percent of District Urban	Number	% Yes	Number	% Yes
0 - 59	121	75.2	69	37.7
60 - 79	51	84.3	27	55.6
80 plus	123	94.3	39	59.0
Total	295		135	

TABLE 2.1   Internal Tensions and Party Voting: The Medicare Bill

expansion of the national government and it entailed an intrusion of government into the private sector. Government would now become involved in reimbursing the private health care sector and would inevitably be drawn into evaluating services and billing. The bill was supported by liberals and opposed by conservatives.

The parties opposed each other, with most Democrats supporting the legislation and most Republicans opposing it. But the more interesting matter involved the divisions within each party, which were evident in the vote. The tensions within the parties stemmed from the fact that urban districts tended to be more liberal than rural districts. Table 2.1 presents the number of party members from districts with varying levels of urbanization, along with how those members voted on the bill. Within the Republican Party, 69 of its 135 seats, or 52 percent of its seats, came from districts that were less than 60 percent urban. These members voted against the bill. The party also had many members (49 percent) in more urban districts, and these members voted for the bill. In this case, having a less or more urban constituency resulted in a split within the party. The Democratic Party voted strongly in support of Medicare, but it also had internal tensions associated with urbanization. Forty-two percent of its seats came from the most urban districts and 94 percent of these members voted strongly in favor of the bill. Those members in the least urban districts (121 of 295 or 41 percent of its seats) were less supportive and only 75 percent voted for the bill. Those with rural districts were less supportive of this program, even if it was for seniors, and were more likely to feel pressures to defect from the party. In both parties urbanization differences revealed tensions within the party that pulled members away from the majority in the party.

The argument of this book is that since the 1970s each party's diversity has declined, reducing internal conflicts and making more unified party voting more likely. The party bases continued to evolve because the changes initiated within each party inevitably led to new policy concerns that attracted some and alienated others. This sorting out has continued for at least three decades and is unlikely to be over.

The Role of Social Change

The source of party polarization involves more than just the re-sorting of an existing and stable population. At the same time the parties were acquiring different constituents and advocating different policies, American society was changing in ways that further contributed to the emerging polarization. Beginning in the 1970s, two broad changes began that have significant political implications. First, inequality in the distribution of income, job-related conditions, and access to opportunities increased. Second, immigration steadily increased the prevalence of non-whites in American society. Together these changes have resulted in an electorate more diverse in its needs and attitudes about the proper role of government. While the parties were developing more distinct electoral bases and differing policy positions, social change was creating diverging electoral needs that made the policy debates between the parties more relevant to the electorate.

These changes have changed the composition of House districts in a way that can only be regarded as remarkable, compared to 1970 data. The society is different from what existed in 1970, and that is reflected in the distribution of types of districts. These changes created more of a basis for the parties to diverge in their concerns and electoral bases. As Fenno summarizes it:

> the roots of the institutional-level change toward polarized partisanship lie *outside* the institution. They lie out in the country, in the districts where the grassroots representational relationships between each individual member and his or her constituents are pursued, shaped and maintained (2000, 151).

The Role of Diverging Electoral Bases on Party Cohesion

Party realignment and social change have had their own effect on the dynamic of party interactions. As party members acquire differing constituencies and are concerned with different policy positions, their sense of differentiation from each other increases. Their inclination to work together with other members of their own party and to vote together is

The Sources of Diverging Party Electoral Bases:
Realignment and Social Change and The Democratic Party
(Assuming 100 seats are elected)

% Non-white	Party Alignment: Democratic Success			Percent Distribution of All Districts			Sources of Party Seats (# of seats from group)		
	Initial	After	Δ	Initial	After	Δ	Initial	After	Δ
0 — 9.9	45*	35	-10	60+	30	-30	27	11	-16
10 — 19.9	50	50	0	20	30	10	10	15	+5
20 plus	55	65	10	20	40	20	11	26	+15
	*Percents read across			+Percents sum down			48	52	

TABLE 2.2   The Sources of Diverging Party Electoral Bases: Realignment and Social Change and the Democratic Party

likely to increase and lead to even greater polarization. This in turn leads party members to pressure members from atypical districts to go along with the party on major policy conflicts, creating greater divergence between the two parties. Differences reinforce each other and push party members further apart. The combination of realignment, social change, and pressures for party solidarity lead to higher levels of polarization than existed thirty years ago.

An Overview

The changes of relevance are presented as examples in Tables 2.2 and 2.3. Table 2.2 provides a hypothetical example of how the electoral bases of a party are changing. In this example, the Democratic Party is used. The Republican Party patterns would be just the opposite of those shown. In the first set of three columns the concern is realignment, or how party success by the district trait of percent non-white changes over time. The first column ("initial") indicates party success before change, and the second column ("after") indicates party success after realignment. Before change, Democrats won 45 percent of districts with 0–9.9 percent non-whites and 55 percent of districts with 20 percent or more non-whites. After realignment, with the Democratic Party more closely identified as concerned with the needs of non-whites, Democrats do not do as well in largely white districts (winning 35 percent of seats), but do better in districts with 20 percent or more non-whites. The party's relative success is now more closely connected with the composition of the population of the district.

At the same time, social change is altering the distribution of the types of districts from which members are elected. Initially 60 percent of all House districts were 0–9 percent non-white, but afterward only 30 percent

Party Bases and Party Loyalty						
	Sources of Party Seats			Party Loyalty		
% Non-white	Initial	After	Δ	Initial	After	Δ
0 — 9.9	27	11	-16	60	80	20
10 — 19.9	10	15	+5	70	85	15
20 plus	11	26	+15	80	90	10

TABLE 2.3   Party Bases and Party Loyalty

are in this category. Initially 20 percent were 20 percent or more non-white and subsequently 40 percent of all districts are in this category.

Finally, the combination of these changes shifts the electoral base of the party. Initially the party won 45 percent of the sixty seats that were 0–9.9 percent non-white, or twenty-seven seats. This meant twenty-seven of the Democrats' forty-eight seats came from this type of district. After the change the party derives eleven of its fifty-two seats from this type of district. Before realignment and social change, the party derived eleven seats from the districts that were 20 percent or more non-white districts (55 percent of twenty districts). After change, it derives twenty-six seats of its fifty-two seats from districts with 20 percent or more non-white. The reliance on districts with a substantial non-white population has increased. The combination of realignment and social change can produce a significant shift in the sources of party seats. Given a two-party system, these changes will leave the remaining seats to the Republican Party and result in a significant increase in that party's reliance on largely white districts. Together, realignment and social change have interacted to shift the sources of party seats and create electoral bases that differ more from each other.

Finally, the change in the relative source of party seats is likely to affect party voting. Table 2.3 provides another hypothetical example of party change. It indicates the percentage of times party members vote with their party initially and after change. Those members who constitute the majority of the party (from the 20 percent or more non-white districts) will become more dominant and opposed to the dominant group within the Republican Party. As party policy differences increase, the members from the dominant types of districts are likely to pressure members from those districts not dominant (the 0–9 percent non-white districts for

Democrats) to go along with the party in conflicts with the Republicans. If that pressure is successful, then the members from the less typical districts, who may naturally have less party loyalty than other members will increase their party loyalty more than others, increasing the overall party polarization. Their party loyalty will still be less than that of others, but their change may well reflect the extent to which increasing party differences result in greater party solidarity and more members voting with the party positions. If all three of these changes occur–realignment, social change, and subsequent greater willingness to vote with the party–then party polarization will increase.

The Implications for Interpreting Elections

The concern here is with the sources of party polarization. This explanatory framework, however, has implications beyond just explaining that trend. Much of the current interpretation of congressional elections, to be reviewed in Chapter 7, is built around the view that campaigns are candidate–centered. This view of elections suggests that the emergence of greater party polarization is, in many ways, a surprise.

> The result [of changes in party organizations and new issues] was the growth of candidate-centered politics, wherein candidates personalized campaigns and elections, running not as members of long-lived teams, but as individuals who would behave independently in office. Members of Congress were particularly adept at developing electoral techniques that enabled them to personalize their electoral coalitions. Increasingly, they were able to avoid association with their party's larger issues of national policy. Instead, they were able to win on the basis of their personal characteristics, their personal policy positions, their record of service to the district, and the great resource advantages that enabled them to discourage strong challengers and beat those whom they could not discourage. (Fiorina 2001, 145)

From this perspective, the dominant factors shaping election outcomes are the presence of an incumbent in the race, his or her general attractiveness, the incumbent's style in interacting with the electorate, and candidate resources (Gaddie and Bullock 2000, 7). Incumbents who "work the district" with frequent visits and "pork-barrel" appropriations for local programs win by larger margins. Incumbents who use the perks of office–district mailings, staff to attend to constituent problems–win by larger margins (Jacobson 2001, 21–39). Incumbents who raise more campaign funds from interest groups and build up campaign fund balances scare off strong challengers and win by more (Herrnson 2001, 150–170; Jacobson 2001, 40–43). The argument is that incumbents can successfully focus on creating high name recognition and a positive image that makes them relatively safe from challenges.

The implication of this interpretation is that constituencies and issues are not central to election outcomes and the subsequent voting behavior of members (Salmore and Salmore 1989, 39–62). Members of Congress are presumed to achieve electoral success primarily through visibility and district benefits, and not by their issue connections with constituents. In fact, the connection of members to their constituents, other than in terms of visibility, is largely neglected as relevant in the candidate-centered interpretation of electoral outcomes. The candidate and his or her resources, broadly defined, are regarded as more important.

This framework does not provide a basis for explaining why party members are increasingly aligning voting with their party and against the other party (Fiorina 2001, 149). Indeed, if members are concerned with their own images, visibility and independence, then they should be less inclined to regularly align themselves with the party. The image of members as strong partisans would entangle them in a national party image and reduce their unique image. In short, a candidate-centered view does not suggest that party divisions should be increasing.

The explanation offered in this book has significant implications for how we interpret elections. The candidate-centered framework has come to dominate how we see elections to the House. The presumption is that candidate resources shape outcomes, with constituents fading into the background. The argument offered here constitutes a challenge to that framework. As Chapter 7 will discuss, constituencies have a major effect on which party wins elections. There are approximately forty-five races out of 435 each election year that are competitive, in which the quality of the candidate and his or her resources can play a significant role in determining an election outcome. In most districts, however, the composition of the district is of primary influence. The implication of our work is that constituencies need to be restored to a central role in understanding election outcomes, rather than presuming outcomes are a product of candidate resources such as name recognition, staff, and campaign funds. Further, as the analysis in Chapter 7 will indicate, much of the evidence that provided the basis for forming a candidate-centered explanation–the presumed growth of margins of victory of incumbents–did not occur.

Incorporating constituencies and connecting them to the voting records of members will help us understand the sources of party polarization in the House. Focusing on this connection will also help us understand the factors shaping House elections, and it will suggest that the role of resources has probably been significantly overemphasized in the study of House elections. Getting to this final interpretative implication, however, will take us some time. We begin with a review of the origins of party realignment that began some time ago.

Notes

1. This partisan resurgence is well documented in the literature. See, for instance, Rohde (1991; 1992), Dodd and Oppenheimer (1989), and Davidson and Oleszek, (1990, 39–64). For an overview of the persistence of this partisanship through the 1990s, see Lucas (1999). For an overview of the resurgence in partisanship in the electorate as well as Congress, see Aldrich (1999) and Bond and Fleisher (2000).

3

The Origins of Increased Party Polarization

Party differences have increased in the U.S. House of Representatives since the 1970s. While the rise in polarization is relatively recent, the sources of this development are not. For both parties, the origins of this increased polarization began early in the twentieth century. The premise of this book is that the current high levels of party polarization are primarily a result of increased homogeneity within the respective electoral bases of the Democratic and Republican parties in the House. Building on the claim first advanced by Rohde (1991, esp. 40–65, 162–167; see also Aldrich and Rohde 2001), we argue that as the diversity within each party's constituency base decreases and the difference between each party's electoral base increases, polarization between the parties will increase. As we will show over the next four chapters, this dynamic aptly describes what has happened to both the Democrats and Republicans in the House of Representatives. Intra-party diversity has declined dramatically, inter-party differences have grown, and polarization has risen accordingly.

These developments, however, did not occur overnight. Throughout the twentieth century, the constituency bases of both parties have been gradually but thoroughly reorganized. Three broad changes in American society and electoral politics have combined to drive this sorting-out process. First, the role of regionalism in American electoral politics has changed. At the beginning of the twentieth century the American party system was almost completely regional in nature, with the Democrats dominating elections in the South and the GOP controlling contests in the remainder of the nation (David 1972, 33; Schattschneider 1960, 76–83; Sundquist 1983, 134–169). Such absolute sectionalism, where geographic region of the nation largely determines which party will be victorious, no longer exists in American politics, at least at the national level. Both parties are now competitive in congressional races throughout all regions of the country (Berkman 1993, 58–61).

While competition within regions has increased, region still has some relevance in defining the electoral bases of the parties. Over the course of the twentieth century, the regional centers of gravity within both parties in the House have shifted considerably. For the Republicans, the shift has been from the older industrial centers of the Northeast and Midwest to the Sunbelt areas in the South and Southwest. The center of gravity for House Democrats, in turn, has moved from the rural South to the previously Republican-dominated urban areas of the Northeast and Midwest (Bensel 1984, 274; Berkman 1993, 57–58). These shifts have significantly altered the constituency bases of each party, and thus the positions advocated and actions taken by each party respectively in the House of Representatives.

The second major change in American electoral politics that has affected polarization in the House also involves alterations in the constituency bases of both parties. The parties now differ significantly in terms of the types of districts that they represent. As the regional character of House elections has declined, other factors have come to play an important role in determining which party will win in a particular district. Specifically, district characteristics such as median family income, the percentage of the population that is non-white, and the level of urbanization now have higher correlations with partisan success in House races. Increasingly, Democratic candidates win in districts that are low income, have a relatively high percentage of non-whites, and are urban. Republicans now dominate elections in districts that are relatively affluent, largely white, and rural or suburban. The rise in importance of these district characteristics for electoral success has contributed to greater differences between the parties in the House, and thus to increased polarization.

Finally, as this sorting out has occurred, the United States has witnessed significant change in the composition of its society over the last thirty years. Income inequality has increased substantially (Levy 1998, 1988). Previously disenfranchised segments of population have secured the right to vote due to changes in electoral law and mobilization efforts (Alt 1994; Stanley 1987; Timpone 1995). Geographic segregation by race and class, always high in American society, has become even more prevalent as affluent whites have continued their flight to the suburbs, while those who are less affluent and/or non-white remain behind in the cities (Jackson 1985; Massey and Denton 1993, Teaford 1993, 1979). Changes in immigration laws and patterns have resulted in a significant increase in the percentage of Americans who are non-white, the vast majority of whom are settling in urban areas (Briggs 1992; Carlson 1994; Massey 1995). The result of these changes is greater homogeneity within districts, and greater difference between districts (Gimpel 1999, 13–14, 326). Because different parties represent different types of districts, polarization in the House has increased.

As noted at the outset of this chapter, each of the developments discussed above occurred gradually over the course of the twentieth century. Because of their importance in explaining in the partisan conflict that currently exists in the House of Representatives, each development merits a careful examination. To some, events that occurred over one hundred years ago may not seem relevant to the current political environment. However, in this case understanding the past is central to understanding why conflicts were muted relative to what they might have been. Regional loyalties were so strong that social and economic divisions that might have developed were diminished. To fully understand the high levels of polarization that characterize the present-day House, it is first necessary to examine the situation from which we have changed. This chapter begins such an examination.

The House Parties in the Early Twentieth Century

From the end of Reconstruction (1877) until 1892, the Democrats and the Republicans were relatively evenly matched in terms of strength at the national level. Both parties won the presidency, and both controlled the House at various times during this period (David et al. 1960, 32–33; Degler 1964, 41; Rossiter 1960, 80). This situation came to an abrupt halt with the realignment of 1894–1896. The results of the elections held during these years radically reordered the American political landscape. What could be termed a stalemate in partisan strength at the national level was rapidly transformed into Republican domination (Kleppner 1987, 89). In the largest-ever transfer of seats between parties, the Republicans turned a ninety-four seat deficit in the House of Representatives into a 132-seat majority in the elections of 1894 (Degler 1964, 41–42). The GOP retained control of the House in 1896, and the party's presidential candidate, William McKinley, defeated Democrat William Jennings Bryan by an overwhelming margin. The end result of the realignment of 1894–1896 was the dominance of the Republican Party. With the exception of the years from 1910–1918, when a serious rift within the GOP allowed the Democrats to recapture both Congress and the presidency, the Republicans controlled national-level American politics from 1896 until the advent of the New Deal (Brady 1988, 84; Burnham 1965; David et al. 1960, 33, 39–40; Degler 1964, 42; Kleppner 1987; Sinclair 1982, 18; Sundquist 1983, 134–181).

What caused the shift to the Republicans during the mid–1890s? Certainly the Panic of 1893, a large-scale downturn in the economy that we would today call a recession, played a significant role. As the party in power during the onset of the panic, the Democrats were largely blamed for the economic bad times and punished accordingly by voters in the 1894 elections (Degler 1964, 47; Goldman 1979, 114; Sundquist 1983, 138–146, 159–160). However, this was not the only reason for the repudiation of the Democratic Party. More important for our purposes are the shifts in party constituencies that took place during this realignment. As stated above, the parties were relatively evenly matched prior to the 1894–1896 period. The Democrats dominated the South, and the Republicans had an advantage in the Midwest, but most of the rest of the country saw vigorous competition between the two parties (Sundquist 1983, 161). In urban areas outside of the South, the Democrats usually held a slight advantage, while in more rural areas (again, outside of the South) the Republicans had a slim edge (Rossiter 1960, 86–88; Sundquist 1983, 163).

This all changed in 1896. With the effects of the Panic of 1893 still lingering, many voters were concerned with economic issues. This was particularly true of urban workers in the industrial centers of the Northeast and Midwest. Despite campaign rhetoric of being for the "common man," William Jennings Bryan, the Democratic presidential candidate, offered little in the way of substantive programs to benefit labor. On the other hand, his Republican opponent, William McKinley, heavily courted the labor vote. With his promise of a "full dinner pail," McKinley was able to win over the majority of America's industrial workers. Moreover, Bryan was a representative of the Southern and Western wings of the Democratic Party. As such, he was the embodiment of an agricultural way of life and of evangelical Protestantism. These qualities hurt Bryan in urban areas of the Northeast and Midwest, where many immigrants shared neither his emphasis on farm issues nor his religious background. These factors resulted in a massive swing of urban areas to McKinley and the Republicans (Burnham 1965; Degler 1964, 47–50; Kleppner 1987; Sundquist 1983, 162–168). Of the eighty-two American cities with a population of 45,000 or more in 1896, only twelve went for Bryan, and seven

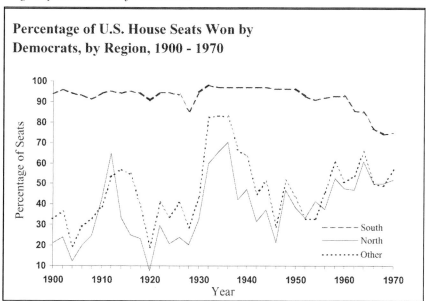

FIGURE 3.1   Percentage of U.S. House Seats Won by Democrats, by
             Region, 1900-1970

of these were in the South (Degler 1964, 48). And it was not just in urban
areas that the Republicans gained. Throughout all of the Northeast and
Midwest, the Republicans fared extremely well, solidifying their hold on
states where they had previously held an advantage and gaining an edge
in states that had previously been competitive or Democratic. Only in the
South did the Democrats remain the dominant party (Black and Black
1987, 233; Degler 1964, 49; Sundquist 1983, 158–161).

The remarkable regional character of the party system produced by the
realignment of 1894–1896 can be seen in Figure 3.1. The Democrats dominated House elections in the South, while the Republicans controlled the
vast majority of seats in the rest of the nation. Figures 3.2 and 3.3 show
this regionalism in different ways, presenting the proportion of House
seats for each party by region from 1900–1970. From 1900–1932, a majority of Democratic House members came from the South, except for the
years in which the Republicans were split internally. During this same period, the GOP House party was dominated by members from Northern
districts.

The crucial matter is what regionalism meant for the composition of
each party. As a party with its strength based largely in one region during the early decades of the century, the Democrats experienced little internal tension or dissent. They were a relatively homogeneous and united

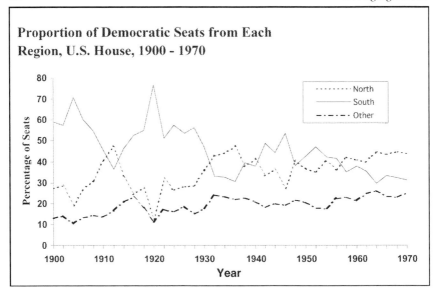

FIGURE 3.2   Proportion of Democratic Seats from Each Region, U.S.
House, 1900-1970

minority party, with a focus on agricultural issues and maintaining a society where only whites had influence. The Republicans, on the other hand, were much more diverse. They represented a region, the North,

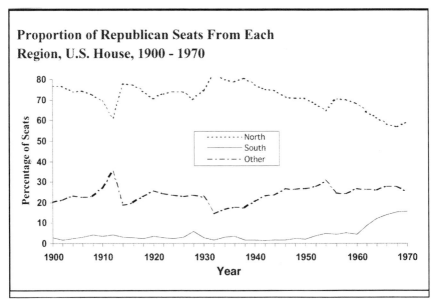

FIGURE 3.3   Proportion of Republican Seats from Each Region, U.S.
House, 1900-1970

with considerable diversity. This diversity was reflected in their membership. Among their House membership, the Republicans had representatives from urban and rural districts, industrial and agricultural districts, old stock and immigrant districts, Northern and Midwestern districts. This heterogeneity resulted in periodic tensions within the party, but the GOP was able, for the most part, to hold together and govern as the majority party. This situation would not last. The tensions within the Republican Party would emerge and eventually lead to a significant shift in the base of the party. The Democrats would also develop their own tensions and experience change.

The Parties During the 1920s and 1930s

A large portion of the Republicans' urban success in the realignment of 1894–1896 was due to the fact that they had been able to attract many immigrant-stock, largely Catholic voters. This feat is particularly impressive in light of the long-standing attachment of these primarily Catholic immigrants to the Democratic Party before 1896 (Burner 1968, 15–17). While many of these immigrant voters returned relatively quickly to their traditional support of the Democrats (Sundquist 1983, 167–168), the Republicans were able to retain enough support among these groups to continue winning the majority of House seats in urban areas through 1920 (Degler 1964, 52). Despite this continued success in urban areas, and their continuance as the majority party in the House, the tensions between urban and rural and old stock and immigrant elements within the Republican Party were never far from the surface.

Table 3.1 illustrates this point. This table presents the vote in the House on the Volstead Act, the enabling legislation for the Eighteenth Amendment to the Constitution, establishing national Prohibition. As can be seen from the table, both parties supported the Volstead Act by more than a two-to-one margin. However, both parties also contained a significant bloc of dissenters. This dissent came primarily from members in the North, the location of the majority of urban and immigrant stock districts. As anti-Prohibition sentiment grew throughout the 1920s, the Democrats were able to use this development to their advantage in the North, while Republicans from this region increasingly found the views of their constituents at odds with the position taken by their party (Kyvig 1979, xiii).

It was also during the 1920s that these tensions within the Republican Party began to show in the electoral arena. Throughout the decade, the vote totals of Republican House candidates in urban areas declined

Party Differences on the Volstead Act (1919), By Region				
Region	Democrat		Republican	
	No	Yes	No	Yes
North	39	8	39	115
South	11	84	1	4
Other	2	24	8	49
Total	52	116	48	168

Source: Vote taken from *Congressional Record*, July 22, 1919 (p. 3005). Partisan affiliation of members taken from the *Congressional Directory* of the 66th Congress, 1st Session (1919: 133-140).

TABLE 3.1   Party Differences on the Volstead Act (1919), by Region

(Eldersveld 1949, 1193–1195; Ewing 1947, 80–82; Lubell 1956, 35). The party's support for industrial elites and its WASP (White Anglo-Saxon Protestant) heritage continually clashed with the working class Catholic background of many urban dwellers.

Beginning in 1922, the Democrats were increasingly able to recapture seats in the cities, especially in the Northeast, for the first time since the early 1890s (Burner 1968, 103–106). As the success of the Democrats in urban House elections rose, they too began to experience internal dissent and tension. In much the same manner as happened in the Republican Party, the Northern wing of the party, with its support based largely in urban, heavily ethnic areas, began to clash with the Southern and Western wings of the party, whose support bases were largely rural and old stock. The two elements of the Democratic Party increasingly disagreed on which policies to pursue and on which direction the party should take.[1]

These disputes were laid bare at the 1924 Democratic National Convention. The Northern, urban wing of the party and the Southern/Western, rural wing of the party battled it out for ascendancy within the party. The Northern wing, wanting a presidential nominee who reflected the interests of their largely urban and ethnic constituents, pushed New York State Governor Al Smith—a Catholic, the grandson of Irish immigrants, and a confirmed "wet" on the issue of Prohibition—as the party's choice. The Southern/Western wing of the party was completely opposed to Smith, who was an anathema to their rural and old stock constituents based on both his personal characteristics and political views. They instead wanted one of their own, William G. McAdoo—son-in-law of Woodrow Wilson and a diehard "dry" on Prohibition whose attempt for the nomination was backed by both the Ku Klux Klan and the

Anti-Saloon League—to be the party's nominee for president. In perhaps the most acrimonious national party convention ever, the two wings of the party fought for supremacy. After 103 ballots, by far the most ever needed by an American political party to choose a presidential nominee, neither side could claim victory and a compromise candidate, John W. Davis, was selected as the party's presidential nominee. Neither side was pleased with the outcome, and the Democrats left their convention with an almost complete division existing between the two wings (Allswang 1971, 95; Bernstein 1960, 75–76; Burner 1968, 103–141; Goldman 1979, 153–157; Hicks 1960, 92–97; Huthmacher 1959, 84–99).

By the end of the 1928 national convention, it was clear that the Northern, urban wing had come out on top (Allswang 1978, 5; Bernstein 1960, 77). The Northern wing was able to push Al Smith through as the party's presidential nominee despite the objections of the Southern wing (Allswang 1971, 96–97; Burner 1968, 190–192).[2] The nomination of Smith by the Democrats significantly eroded the power of the Southern members within the party. Never again would Southern Democrats be as dominant in the selection of the party's presidential nominee. In subsequent elections the South declined as a source of votes for winning contestants for the Democratic presidential nomination at contested conventions. From 1896 to 1924, Southern delegates contributed an average of 32 percent to the eventual winner's vote total. From 1928 to 1956, this contribution declined to just 16 percent (David et al. 1960, 397–398). This loss of power on the part of the South to decisively influence the party's presidential nominee was institutionalized in 1936 at the Democratic National Convention when the two-thirds rule was abrogated.[3] In the words of Huthmacher, it was clear that the Democrats were under "new management" (1959, 152).

At the national level, Smith lost badly in 1928. However, with Smith as their candidate, the Democrats made further inroads into urban areas and substantially increased their vote totals in the cities. Smith was able to mobilize the immigrant stock population of the cities as no presidential candidate had been able to previously (Andersen 1979, 9; Degler 1964, 51–52). Smith substantially increased Democratic vote totals in cities outside of the South, winning many cities by large margins and making significant gains over previous Democratic candidates in those he did not win (Bernstein 1960, 78–79; Burner 1968, 228; Degler 1964, 53–57; Endersveld 1949, 1194; Lubell 1956, 33–43; Sundquist 1983, 192–194). The move of the cities into the Democratic camp in the 1928 election was so substantial that Lubell termed it the "Al Smith Revolution" (Lubell 1956, 36).[4]

The landslide victories enjoyed by Franklin Roosevelt and many Democratic House candidates in urban areas in 1932 solidified the Democrats' grip on the cities of the Northeast and Midwest. In 1932, 1934, and 1936, urban areas went overwhelmingly Democratic (Bernstein 1960, 508–513). The ranks of Democratic voters in the cities expanded dramatically, as millions of citizens voted Democratic for the first time and stayed Democratic.[5] From 1927 to 1935, the Democrats went from holding approximately one-third of the House seats in urban, industrial districts to about two-thirds (Brady 1988, 101). Roosevelt and the New Deal completed what Al Smith had started. Urban areas in the North moved decisively into the Democratic column (Allswang 1971, 166–167; Degler 1964, 57; Lubell 1956, 29–60; Turner and Schneier 1970, 119). They had been transformed into a "network of Democratic bastions" (Sundquist 1983, 214–215).

Parties and the Aftermath of the New Deal Realignment

The results of the New Deal Realignment that took place from 1928–1936 began to change the internal dynamics of both political parties. By the 1930s the Republicans were once again firmly established as the party of old stock, Protestant, non-urban, and more affluent voters outside of the South, while the Democrats (in the North) had established themselves as the party more supportive of the interests of immigrant stock, non-Protestant, less affluent, and urban voters (Allswang 1971, 103–108; Sundquist 1983, 168). The Democrats also maintained, and even strengthened, their hold on the South (Bartley 1976, 255; David 1972, 46–47). The Democrats went from being an almost exclusively Southern-based party to a national party, with approximately equal segments of the party's House delegation based in Northern urban districts and the Solid South (Brady 1988, 102; Sinclair 1982, 19). These changes marked the beginnings of a shift from Southern and rural constituencies to Northern and urban constituencies (Rubin 1976, 117; Turner and Schneier 1970, 117–120, 132). The Republicans consolidated their hold on rural districts outside of the South, but lost much of their urban base. The urban districts that remained Republican were largely located on the fringes of cities, middle class and suburban in nature. The locus of power began to move from the urban areas of the Northeast to suburban and rural areas outside of the South, although the magnitude of the shift was not as large as occurred within the Democratic Party. The GOP now had little chance in central city districts (Turner and Schneier 1970, 120–132).

These shifts in electoral bases were by no means complete. As Figures 3.1–3.3 clearly show, elements of the old alignment remained, and even regained some of their prominence in the 1940s as Republicans regained seats for approximately a decade. The Republicans, despite their inability to win many urban districts, still drew a substantial percentage of their seats in the House from the Northeast. Democratic success outside of the South declined somewhat during this decade, with Southern members once again constituting a plurality of the party's caucus in the House. However, the complete regional nature of the old party system had been cracked (outside of the South), and the constituency bases of each party were somewhat different than what they had been before the New Deal.

Combining different constituencies created tensions within each party. The New Deal realignment created the unlikely combination of representatives from Northern urban areas and Southern rural areas in the same Democratic Party, and it is not surprising that Democratic members of the House did not always see eye to eye during the 1930s and 1940s. Some potential areas of disagreement between the two groups of Democrats, such as agricultural policy, are relatively obvious. Democrats from the still largely agrarian South were more supportive of proposals designed to benefit agricultural interests than were their Northern, more urban counterparts (Sinclair 1982, 26–29; Turner and Schneier 1970, 125, 176–177). However, a majority of the Northern Democrats also voted in favor of pro-agricultural policies in the 1930s and 1940s, and thus agricultural policy was not a major area of disagreement within the party (Sinclair 1982, 29, 67–69).

Other tensions that began to develop within the party during the 1930s and 1940s were perhaps less obvious, and certainly more substantial. During Roosevelt's first term as president, the Northern and Southern wings of the Democratic Party in the House were strongly united in their support of the president, with Southern Democrats exhibiting an even higher level of liberal voting behavior than their Northern counterparts (Reiter 2001, 112–113). Democratic House members from both regions were highly supportive of the administration's proposals dealing with social welfare policy and government management of the economy (Sinclair 1982, 51–65). However, this situation began to change rather dramatically after FDR's first term. Southern Democrats became increasingly concerned about Roosevelt's continued expansion of the welfare state, and his desire to permanently institutionalize many of the social welfare programs instituted during the Depression (Garson 1974). Southern Democrats adopted increasingly pro-business views after 1937, and they became more and more disconcerted with the ever-widening scope of national government involvement in the economy (Garson 1974; Turner and Schneier 1970, 176). Meanwhile, the support of non-Southern House Democrats for these policies remained strong (Sinclair 1982, 51–72).

One specific policy area that did divide Northern and Southern Democrats in the House during this era was organized labor. Indeed, the split between the two wings of the party on labor issues led Mayhew to state that: "A case can be made that labor issues have divided the Democratic Party by section more clearly and consistently than any other issue except race," (1966, 109). Northern members, with a large portion of their electoral support coming from urban, industrial workers, were strongly supportive of legislation that was favorable to organized labor. Southern members, given their region's long history of antipathy toward labor unions, almost complete lack of unionization, and relative absence of industrialization, were vehemently against pro-labor measures (Garson 1974; Katznelson et al. 1993; Sinclair 1982, 56–58; Turner and Schneier 1970, 126–128, 176). Northern and Southern Democrats were so diametrically opposed on the matter of organized labor that only one other issue could possibly produce a larger split within the party.

That issue, of course, was civil rights. As Key has argued, the political system and culture of the American South was largely based on the subjugation of blacks (1949), and Southern representatives were adamantly opposed to any efforts to extend civil rights to African-Americans. On the other hand, Northern Democrats were in an entirely different situation. The New Deal realignment had brought Northern blacks (who, unlike Southern blacks, were able to vote) into the Democratic Party (Bernstein 1960, 511; Carmines and Stimson 1989, 32–34; Lubell 1956, 100–102). Blacks, who had previously supported the Republicans because of their heritage as the party of Abraham Lincoln and emancipation, made up an increasingly important part of the constituencies of many Northern House Democrats after 1932. Because of this, many Northern Democrats felt compelled to be responsive to the demands of blacks, including their calls for protection and extension of their civil rights (Sinclair 1982, 37–38, 49). This pressure on Northern Democrats increased as large numbers of blacks continued to move from the South into the North (Judd and Swanstrom 2002, 140–145; Rubin 1976, 109–110). As legislation aimed at ensuring the civil rights of African-Americans began to appear in the House during the late 1930s, Northern and Southern Democrats consistently and sharply divided, with the Northern members favoring and the Southern members opposing these bills (Brady 1988, 111; Katznelson et

Party Differences on Anti-lynching Legislation (1940), By Region				
Region	Democrat		Republican	
	No	Yes	No	Yes
North	3	86	7	110
South	95	1	0	3
Other	24	21	2	28
Total	122	108	9	141

Source: Vote taken from *Congressional Record*, January 10, 1940 (pp. 253-254). Partisan affiliation of members taken from the *Congressional Directory* of the 76th Congress, 3rd Session (1940: 147-154).

TABLE 3.2   Party Differences on Anti-Lynching Legislation (1940), by Region

al. 1993; Sinclair 1982, 37–42). The division within the party became even more intense as civil rights issues became more prominent in the 1940s (Bensel 1984, 225). The divide was so great that Lubell termed the situation a "civil war inside the Democratic Party" (1956, 9). An example of this divide is provided in Table 3.2, which presents the vote in the House, broken down by party and region, on legislation designed to outlaw the practice of lynching. Northern Democrats were almost unanimous in their support of the bill, while Southern Democrats were even more solidified in their opposition. Such a pattern within the House Democratic caucus was the norm with regard to all civil rights legislation from the 1920s through the 1960s.

The Republican Party in the House was also marked by some internal tensions during the 1930s and 1940s. Members from Northeastern urban districts tended to be more supportive of social welfare legislation than were their colleagues from rural districts. The more urban representatives were also slightly more supportive of legislation favorable to industrial workers, although the party as a whole was decidedly anti-labor (Sinclair 1982, 56–59). A division within the party also existed on agricultural issues, with Republicans from rural areas, particularly in the Midwest, being much more supportive of policy designed to benefit farmers than were urban Republicans from the Northeast (Sinclair 1982, 68–69; Turner and Schneier 1970, 200). Perhaps the biggest division within the GOP occurred on issues relating to foreign affairs. Throughout the 1930s and 1940s, Republican House members from rural districts located in the interior of the nation were consistently less supportive of U.S. involvement in foreign affairs than were Republicans from Northeastern and Pacific districts (Sinclair 1982, 45–47; Turner and Schneier 1970, 197–201).

While these divisions did exist within the Republican Party, they were not nearly as large as those exhibited by the Democrats (Turner and Schneier 1970, 120, 199–200, 206). This does not mean, however, that the differences within the GOP were insignificant. In many ways they represented a substantial alteration of the pattern of internal Republican Party differences that existed prior to the New Deal. Before the Great Depression, the Northeast was the center of Republican orthodoxy, with party mavericks hailing from the Midwestern and Western states. Post-New Deal this alignment was reversed. The Northeastern Republicans were the liberal (relative to other House Republicans) party insurgents, while Midwestern members had become the party's conservative regulars (Rae 1989, 6; Sinclair 1982, 58–59).[6] This development would become increasingly important to the party in the 1960s and beyond.

1950–1970: The Blossoming of Internal Party Tensions

The 1950s and 1960s saw the tensions and divisions within the parties increase dramatically. Once again, conflict was more pronounced within the Democratic Party. At the 1948 Democratic National Convention northern delegates succeeded in adding a strong civil rights plank to the party's platform. The platform endorsed the civil rights legislation that Democratic President Harry Truman had sent to Congress in 1948, and explicitly called for congressional action to secure equal rights in voting, employment, personal security, and military service. The civil rights plank split the convention (David et al. 1960, 376; Goldman 1979, 191). Southern delegates were outraged. North Carolina was the only Southern delegation to give Truman even a single vote for the presidential nomination (Garson 1974, 280). The entire delegation of Mississippi and part of the Alabama contingent walked out of the convention. Garson nicely summarized the view of many Southern Democrats in the aftermath of the 1948 convention: "The Democratic Party, then, no longer represented the South's interests. It had become dominated by intellectuals, self-seeking labor leaders, and most poignant of all for white southerners, insensitive Negroes. These groups, demurred Dixie's politicians, now enjoyed so much influence within Democratic councils that southerners had been relegated to an almost emblematic position," (Garson 1974, 234). Some Southerners were so upset at the actions of the national Democratic Party that they formed their own party, the States' Rights Democrats, or, as they came to be known, the Dixiecrats. In the 1948 presidential election the Dixiecrats, with South Carolina Governor

Strom Thurmond as their nominee, captured 22 percent of the popular vote in the South, winning the four Deep South states of Mississippi, Alabama, Louisiana, and South Carolina (Black and Black 1987, 262; Carmines and Stimson 1989, 34–35).

The tension that had been simmering within the Democratic Party since the 1930s over civil rights now boiled over into full-blown conflict. The Northern wing of the party had made it very clear that the future direction of the Democratic Party was going to include an effort to secure civil rights for blacks. The Southern wing made it equally clear that they would fight this effort every step of the way. Eventually, something would have to give.

The Democrats managed to win the presidency in 1948, despite losing the electoral votes of the four Southern states. But Truman's margin was very slim, and the closeness of the election caused the two warring elements of the Democratic Party to attempt to temporarily put aside their differences with the goal of maintaining the presidency. Illinois Governor Adlai Stevenson, the party's presidential candidate in both 1952 and 1956, made a conscious effort to appease members of the Southern wing of the party during his campaign speeches (Carmines and Stimson 1989, 35–36). The efforts to bring the South back into the Democratic fold were successful, and in 1952 and 1956 all of the Southern states gave their electoral votes to the Democrats. However, the Democrats lost the presidency in both of these years and, more important, cracks were beginning to show in the Solid South at the level of the mass electorate.

General Dwight D. Eisenhower was the Republican presidential candidate in 1952. Revered as a national hero for his efforts in World War II, Eisenhower provided the GOP with a very attractive candidate. In 1952 and again in 1956 Eisenhower was able to attract higher percentages of the popular vote in South than had any previous Republican candidate (Black and Black 1987, 262–263; Pomper 1963). In 1960, the Democrats nominated John F. Kennedy for president. Kennedy, like Al Smith before him, was a Catholic and the South as a region had traditionally been home to a strong anti-Catholic bias. Given Kennedy's Catholicism, combined with the fact that the 1960 Democratic platform once again contained a strong pro-civil rights plank, it is not surprising that many white Southerners abandoned their traditional party allegiance and voted Republican (Converse 1966b, 115–122; Pomper 1963; Prendergast 1999, 143–145). As the Republican percentage of popular vote increased in the region throughout the 1950s, it was clear that the political environment was changing in the heretofore solidly Democratic South.

Party Differences on 1964 Civil Rights Act, By Region				
Region	Democrat		Republican	
	No	Yes	No	Yes
North	6	121	3	81
South	86	8	15	0
Other	10	54	8	27
Total	102	283	26	108

Source: Vote taken from 1964 CQ Almanac, p. 636-37.

TABLE 3.3   Party Differences on 1964 Civil Rights Act, by Region

Interestingly, even though the Republicans were increasing their percentage of the popular vote in the South, they were not opposed to civil rights for blacks. They were, after all, the party of Lincoln and emancipation and had long been supportive of civil rights (Carmines and Stimson 1989, 36–37; Sinclair 1982, 40–41). This stance continued throughout the 1940s and 1950s. In 1957 President Eisenhower, even though he did it reluctantly, sent federal troops into Little Rock, Arkansas, to enforce school desegregation. The 1960 GOP platform was just as strongly in favor of civil rights as its Democratic counterpart. Clearly, the Republican Party was not against civil rights for blacks (Carmines and Stimson 1989, 36–39). Substantively, the party did not provide a viable alternative for those Southerners wishing to bolt the Democratic Party because of its position on race issues. Because of that, most Southerners remained within the Democratic Party, leaving the party with continuing tensions.

This all changed in 1964. In that year, the Democrats, led by the Northern wing of the party and Lyndon Johnson, a president from the South, passed the Civil Rights Act of 1964, the most sweeping civil rights legislation in American history. As Table 3.3 indicates, Southern Democrats were heavily opposed, while Northern Democrats and those from the rest of the country voted heavily in favor of the legislation. It was clear that a final showdown within the Democratic Party on civil rights had come. The vote also indicated a developing tension within the Republican Party. Northern Republicans voted heavily in favor of the bill, while all Southern Republicans voted against it.

Into this situation stepped Barry Goldwater, a senator from Arizona who was the leader of a growing conservative movement within the Republican Party. He had opposed the 1964 Civil Rights Act, not on the grounds of racism or bigotry, but based solely on his conservative principles. Goldwater was strongly against the involvement of the federal government in state and local affairs; he believed that states and localities should be allowed to manage their own business. This stance made Goldwater particularly attractive to white Southerners who opposed federal government action on civil rights (Carmines and Stimson 1989, 44–45; Kazin 1995, 226).

The Republican Party's nomination of Goldwater in 1964 provided a firm differentiation between the parties on the issue of civil rights. It also allowed for an unmistakable ideological distinction between the two parties. Under the direction of Johnson and the Northern wing of the party, the Democrats had clearly reinforced their image as the more liberal party, favoring a strong and active federal government, despite the wishes of the party's Southern wing. With Goldwater as their nominee, the Republicans marked themselves as the conservative party, advocating a limited role for the national government and autonomy for states and localities. Liberals and conservative voters, both in the North and in the South, were presented with clear alternatives in the choice of which party to support.

Goldwater's nomination also marked a significant turning point in the internal dynamics of the Republican Party. The traditional conservative wing of the party, located since the New Deal primarily in the Midwest, combined with the rapidly growing conservative movement in the South and West to take control of the party. The liberal wing of the GOP, located mainly in the Northeast, was clearly at odds with the rest of the party. After 1964 the Northeastern wing of the party never controlled the direction of party affairs (Rae 1989, 46). Goldwater moved the Republican Party further to the right of the political spectrum, particularly on race issues, where the party has remained (Carmines and Stimson 1989, 55). Looking to build on the success of Eisenhower, the Goldwater campaign also adopted the now famous "Southern strategy" in an attempt to lure disaffected whites from the Democratic ranks (Carmines and Stimson 1989, 45; Rae 1989, 69).

The Southern strategy worked, at least in terms of getting Southern whites to vote for Goldwater. The Goldwater campaign elevated Republican success in the South to previously unseen levels. Goldwater won the electoral votes of five southern states (Mississippi, Alabama, Georgia, Louisiana, and South Carolina) that had not supported the GOP candidate since Reconstruction and ran very competitively throughout the rest of the region (Carmines and Stimson 1989, 45; Kazin 1995, 226). It was not only at the presidential level that Republicans were successful in the South in 1964. In the Deep South, the GOP captured 48 percent of

**Growing Democratic Reliance
on Urban Districts, 1921 - 1964**

Year	Total Democrats	# In Metro Districts	Percentage
1921	130	31	23.8
1930-31	160	46	28.8
1937	322	149	46.3
1944	214	93	43.5
1948	187	77	41.2
1953	213	108	50.7
1959	282	142	50.4
1964	258	153	59.3

Source: Turner and Schneier, Party and Constituency, 118. They classify members as to whether they are in a district that is over 50 percent metropolitan. As a note of caution, they do not explain how this classification is conducted, or list which districts fall into this category.

TABLE 3.4   Growing Democratic Reliance on Urban Districts, 1921-1964

the popular vote in House elections, 13 percentage points higher than its previous best (Cosman 1967, 15). The outcomes of these elections resulted in Republicans comprising a majority of the Alabama House delegation and the first House Republicans from Georgia, Mississippi, and South Carolina (Bullock 1988, 562–563; Cosman 1967, 15).

While they fared very well in the South, Goldwater and the Republicans were trounced throughout the rest of the nation, and especially so in the North. Johnson's victory over Goldwater represented one of the largest landslides in presidential election history. In the Northeast, home of the party's liberal wing, House Republicans were especially hard hit. Here, both conservative and liberal Republican House members met with defeat.[7] The Democrats made dramatic inroads in the Northeast, significantly increasing the northern component of the party's House caucus (Bullock 1988, 572; Rohde 1991, 7). The party now had a much larger base among urban districts. Table 3.4 indicates the transition the Democratic Party had undergone in forty years in its reliance on urban districts. In 1921 24 percent of the party's districts were urban. By 1964 this number was 59 percent. The party was primarily urban, but there was still 40 percent from less urban areas. The end result of the 1964 elections was that both congressional parties now had increasingly diverse memberships.

At the same time these partisan developments were taking place, changes were occurring in Southern society. The South, which had long been socially and economically distinct, was becoming more like the rest of the nation (Petrocik 1987). For most of its history the South was a largely rural society, but urbanization was now rapidly increasing. Industrialization too was making advances in the South, displacing in some part the region's traditional agrarian economy. Educational levels were increasing, as were family income levels. Both of these demographic characteristics in the South were rapidly becoming comparable to those that existed in the rest of the country (Black and Black 1987, 23–72; McKinney and Brookover Bourque 1971). All of these trends were helped along by the large migration of non-Southerners into the South and by the inevitable generational replacement of old Southerners by their progeny (Black and Black 1987, 16–22). In addition, the large-scale migration of blacks out of the South and into the North continued. This decreased the percentage of the Southern population that was black while at the same time increasing the percentage of blacks in the North (Black and Black 1987, 12–15). All of these changes served to weaken the traditional distinctiveness of the South.

The societal changes discussed served to further alter the electoral bases of both parties. Class politics had long been subordinated by racial politics in the South (Key 1949). The increases in urbanization, industrialization, and affluence in the South began to change this situation. A political cleavage based on social class similar to that which existed in the North began to develop in the South, resulting in a rise in Republican identification among Southerners even prior to the parties taking separate stands on the issue of civil rights. Those with higher levels of education and family income were becoming increasingly likely to vote Republican (Converse 1966a, 221–222; Cosman 1967, 22; Heard 1952, 154–156; Matthews and Prothro 1964, 109; Prothro, Campbell, and Grigg 1958, 133, 139; Brewer and Stonecash 2001). Pomper noted the increasing success Republican House candidates were having in affluent districts (Pomper 1963). After the events of 1964 served to differentiate the parties on civil rights, both economic and racial conservatives could relate to the attraction of the Republican Party (Carmines and Stimson 1989, 185; Cosman 1967, 22–23; Sundquist 1983, 269, 290).

Changes were also occurring in the North. The continued movement of blacks into the North made them an increasingly important part of

Northern Democratic members' constituencies. As the Republican Party became increasingly conservative during the 1950s and 1960s (Rae 1989, 29–91), more and more Northern districts with liberal constituencies sent Democrats to Congress. This happened on a large scale in both 1958 and 1964. As the Northern wing of the party gained in importance within the Democratic Party, the party became even more liberal (Rohde 1991, 162–163). In turn, the decline in importance of the Northeastern wing within the Republican Party led to increased conservatism within the GOP (Berkman 1993, 67–73).

The primary focus of this chapter has been the changing internal dynamics of both parties' House delegations from the early 1900s through the 1960s. However, the actions and positions of the parties' presidential candidates have also been much discussed in this chapter. This leads to an important point. By no means are we suggesting that the changes that occurred within both parties during the twentieth-century were driven only by factions of the congressional parties. Indeed, given much of what has been discussed in this chapter, it is highly likely that the partisan transformations in question were fueled by presidential politics. Certainly presidents and presidential candidates were central figures in many of the changes described here. Al Smith and FDR were critically important to the development of a Democratic base in Northern urban areas. Harry Truman was a key figure in the alienation of many Southerners from the Democratic Party, and Dwight Eisenhower was the first Republican presidential candidate to attract a significant number of these disgruntled Democrats. And of course, Barry Goldwater and Lyndon Johnson were extremely important in presenting the American public with a clear ideological distinction between the parties. We are not arguing that the House parties were responsible for the alterations of the American party system. We are, however, arguing that the House parties have been both significantly affected by and responsive to these changes.

These changes in the parties' bases resulted in a high amount of tension and confusion within both parties. Prior to the New Deal realignment, Southern members had comprised the most loyal segment of the House Democratic caucus, being the group most likely to support party positions. Northern members were the least loyal, the group most likely to go against the party position. After 1936, this began to change. Northern Democrats gradually became the most loyal segment of the party, with Southern representatives increasingly playing the role of party mavericks. A similar shift occurred in the Republican House conference in the aftermath of the New Deal realignment, as members from

Changing Party Loyalty, by Percent Metropolitan, 1930-31 and 1964		
Year and Percent Metropolitan	Average Indices of Loyalty	
1930 - 31	Republican	Democratic
0 - 25.0	80.4	92.7
25.1 - 50.0	86.4	90.1
50.1 - 75.1	86.5	85.4
75.1 - 100	90.7	82.0
1964		
0 - 25.0	79.3	60.0
25.1 - 50.0	76.6	65.5
50.1 - 75.1	70.2	75.8
75.1 - 100	65.6	81.3

Source: Turner and Schneier, <u>Party and Constituency</u>, 123.

TABLE 3.5   Changing Party Loyalty, by Percent Metropolitan, 1930-1931 and 1964

Northeastern districts went from being the most loyal to the most likely to abandon the party position. Midwestern and Western members shifted from being the least supportive of party positions to the most supportive, where they were joined by the slow but steadily increasing number of Southern Republicans (Sinclair 1982; Turner and Schneier 1970). The dominant constituency bases of both parties were changing. Members whose constituents held views contrary to the dominant position within each party were increasingly forced to defect and vote against the party on measures before the House. By the 1960s the diversity in the voting records of members within each party, and particularly for Democrats, was far greater than it had been at any other time in the 1900s (Smith and Gamm 2001, 251).

Table 3.5 presents evidence on the shift that had occurred. Districts are first classified as to what percentage was living in a metropolitan area in 1930–31 and in 1964. The average loyalty level for members within each party in these districts is then calculated. The percentages indicate how frequently members in categories of districts voted with their party. In

1930–31 the Republican Party received its greatest loyalty from members from the most urban districts. By 1964, with the party losing seats in Northern urban districts, the center of gravity was shifting West and South and to more rural districts. Urban Republican members in 1964 had the lowest levels of loyalty, as they struggled to work with the more conservative members from less urban districts. Democrats underwent a shift in the opposite direction. In 1930–31 the party's most loyal members came from rural districts, and members from urban districts were the least loyal. By 1964 this pattern had reversed, and the most loyal members were those in more urban districts.

Because each party still possessed a relatively sizable minority wing in the late 1960s, diversity and tensions within the parties were high. Thus, party polarization was low. The 1970s would witness a continuing process of tension resolution and constituency-base sorting within each party. However, before moving to review the political changes that unfolded after 1970, it is first necessary to examine the some of the fundamental social changes that American society has experienced over the last four decades, and discuss the impact of these changes on partisan conflict in the U.S. House.

Notes

1. For a good discussion of the tensions within both parties during the 1920s see Huthmacher 1959, 77–116.

2. Smith's nomination in 1928 was largely a foregone conclusion even before the convention began (Bain 1960, 232; Hicks 1960, 203). A number of factors contributed to the relative ease with which Smith was able to secure the nomination in 1928. Many Democrats were concerned about the damage done to the party by the divisive 1924 Convention, heard by the American public on the radio, and were determined to avoid such a situation in 1928 (Congressional Quarterly 1985, 88). This certainly aided Smith in his drive for the nomination. Smith also began to cultivate support for 1928 soon after the 1924 general election, sending envoys to meet with various state party elites and working to place allies in positions of power within the national party organization (Goldman 1979, 159–160). In a move designed to appease Southern party members, Smith engineered the selection of a Southern city—Houston—as the site of the convention (Bain 1960, 232; Goldman 1979, 160). William McAdoo, Smith's primary opponent in 1924, was tainted with the stain of the Teapot Dome scandal and regarded by many party members as impossible to nominate Hicks 1960, 203; Noogle 1962, 137–141). McAdoo's formal withdrawal as a candidate in 1927 left Smith without any real opposition, and paved his way to the nomination (Bain 1960, 231–232; David et al. 1960, 117; Goldman 1979, 160).

3. The two-thirds rule, which required that presidential and vice presidential candidates receive at least two-thirds of the convention delegates' votes to win the nomination, was instituted by the Democratic Party at its first national convention in 1832. The practical effect of the rule was to enable a minority faction of the party to block the nomination of a candidate found unacceptable by the minority in question. Over time the Southern wing of the party became the champion of this rule, viewing it as an assurance that no candidate with views in opposition to the unique characteristics of Southern society could be nominated for the presidency by the party (Bass 1988, 305; David et al. 1960, 208, 211). Various calls for the removal of the rule repeatedly met with Southern opposition, and the rule was retained. In 1936, however, Franklin Roosevelt was coming off a landslide victory in 1932 and was determined to eliminate the two-thirds rule. Roosevelt was successful, and the rule was abrogated by voice vote without any serious debate (David et al. 1960, 211; Rubin 1976, 116). Even among Southern delegates, the opposition was not uniform. Many Southern delegates were pleased with Roosevelt's performance as president and were supportive of the rule change. The state delegations from Arkansas, North Carolina, and Louisiana voted in favor of abrogation (Bass 1988, 311). The effect of the rule change was to prevent the South (or any other minority faction) from blocking candidates it found unacceptable. The abrogation of the two-thirds rule is another example of the power shift within the Democratic party from the Southern wing to the Northern and urban wing of the party (Bass 1988, 314; Reiter 2001, 114–115; Rubin 1976, 116). In the prophetic words of North Carolina Senator Josiah W. Bailey, "The abolition of the two-thirds rule will enable Northern and Western Democrats to control the party, nominate its candidates, and write its platforms," (Bass 1988, 314).

4. For a dissenting view on whether it was Al Smith who permanently attracted urban areas to the Democratic Party, see Clubb and Allen 1969.

5. For a discussion about whether the majority of these new Democrats were mobilized from previously non-voting segments of the population or were converted from Republican or other party allegiance, see Andersen 1979 and Sundquist 1983, 229–239.

6. As Clausen wrote (1973, 87–118), this pattern continued in the 1950s and early 1960s.

7. Some disagreement exists within the literature on whether conservative or liberal Republicans suffered more as a result of the 1964 House elections. Sinclair (1982, 114) claims that conservative Republicans were hardest hit in the 1964 election. Carmines and Stimson (1986, 88–89; 1989, 76–77) present evidence that it was more liberal Republicans who lost in 1964.

4

Social Change
and Political Implications

The electoral bases of the parties were steadily shifting in the years leading up to the 1970s. As those electoral alignments evolved, the composition of the electorate was also changing in ways that would have important political effects. Blacks, who had been excluded from the political process, obtained the right to vote, and in the South they were becoming a significant factor in elections. Large numbers of new constituencies, mainly Hispanic, were also entering America via immigration. These new constituents were dramatically altering the composition of many House districts. At the same time, economic change was affecting segments of the electorate in very different ways. Inequality in the distribution of income, which had declined in the post–1946 era, began to steadily increase in the 1970s. These changes created a more diverse society and provided the basis for greater divergence of the electoral bases of the political parties. This diversity has not spread evenly across House districts. Districts vary enormously in their populations, creating the basis for diverging parties. Each of these developments deserves some explanation.

The Emergence of Black Voters in the South

The role of blacks in American politics has changed significantly in the last fifty years. They have gone from political insignificance to becoming a significant constituency in many House districts. They have become more important through registration and migration to other districts. They are liberal, supportive of greater government activism and of the Democratic Party. Their political emergence and diffusion across the United States has added an invariably liberal component to the U.S. electorate and had a great deal to do with the growing differences between the parties.

The Fifteenth Amendment (1870) extended voting rights to blacks throughout the United States. The amendment prohibited the denial of the franchise based on "race, color, or previous condition of servitude." While blacks were briefly able to take advantage of this right, Southern whites balked at allowing blacks to vote, resorting to subterfuge, fraud, and in many cases lethal violence to prevent blacks from casting ballots (Grofman, Handley, and Niemi 1992, 5–8; Kousser 1992, 141–145). With the end of Reconstruction in 1877, Southern whites regained control of their own political affairs, and by the 1890s, blacks were effectively disenfranchised throughout the vast majority of the South (Zimmerman 1995, 289; Davidson 1992, 10–11; Grofman, Handley, and Niemi 1992, 10). The almost complete disenfranchisement of Southern blacks remained largely intact for the next fifty years. There were pockets of the South where blacks could and did vote, but these were very few.

Efforts to give blacks the right to register were persistent during the 1900s, but progress was slow. Civil rights groups, most notably the NAACP, led the efforts to regain the franchise for blacks. They were successful in getting the Supreme Court to declare the Grandfather Clause[1] unconstitutional in 1915, but this victory failed to result in any appreciable increase in black voting (Davidson 1992, 11–12). In 1940, only 250,000 blacks were registered to vote in the South, a total that represented only 3 percent of the eligible black electorate (Timpone 1995, 437; Davidson 1992, 12; Stanley 1987, 97). The result was that many Southern districts had large contingents of black voters, but they had no impact on who was elected from these districts. The Southern Democrats elected from these districts were conservative and responsive to white voters, who were preoccupied with maintaining segregation. The demographic profiles of these districts had little connection to the actual electorate dominating the districts.

The first victory of any real magnitude in the effort to regain black voting rights in the South came in 1944. Since the 1880s Southern politics had been essentially one-party politics. The only meaningful elections took place in Democratic primaries, which the parties declared as being for whites only, thereby denying blacks the right to participate in the only elections that mattered (Stanley 1987, 88). In 1944, the U.S. Supreme Court declared the white primary unconstitutional in the case of *Smith v. Allwright*. With the end of the white primary, black voting began to rise in the South (Alt 1994, 355; Davidson 1992, 12; Stanley 1987, 97; Campbell and Feagin 1975, 132–133). In 1947, just three years after the decision in *Smith*, 595,000 blacks were registered to vote in the South, bringing the

Table 4.1 Black Presence and Registration,
Southern States, 1960 and 1970

State	% State 1960	% Registered 1960	1970
Alabama	30.0	13.7	66.0
Arkansas	21.8	38.0	82.3
Florida	17.8	39.4	55.3
Georgia	28.5	29.3	57.2
Louisiana	31.9	31.1	57.4
Mississippi	42.0	5.2	71.0
North Carolina	24.5	39.1	51.3
South Carolina	34.8	13.7	56.1
Tennessee	16.5	59.1	71.6
Texas	12.4	35.5	72.6
Virginia	20.6	23.1	57.0
South - total	22.7	29.1	62.0
Remainder of nation	6.7		

Sources: The black percentage of the population in 1960 for Southern states is taken from the *Statistical Abstract of the United States: 1962*. The registration figures are taken from the *Statistical Abstract of the United States: 1971*, p. 365.

TABLE 4.1   Black Presence and Registration, Southern States, 1960 and 1970

total to 12 percent of the eligible electorate. By 1956 the total number of African Americans registered had increased to over 1.2 million, or 25 percent of those eligible (Timpone 1995, 437; Stanley 1987, 97; Garrow 1978, 7, 11; and Matthews and Prothro 1963, 27).

Significant barriers to black participation in electoral politics still remained, however. Among the most onerous of these barriers were the poll tax, the literacy test, lengthy residency requirements, and early and somewhat complicated registration procedures. As Stanley and others have noted, these barriers depressed the electoral participation of lower status whites as well. The mechanisms, however, were aimed primarily at preventing blacks from voting, and local election officials had significant leeway in interpreting or bending the rules to allow for white electoral participation (Stanley 1987, chapter six). Extra-legal mechanisms gave wide discretion to local officials who controlled registration and voting and used economic and physical intimidation to deter blacks from participating. These powers played a large role in keeping the levels of registration and voting among southern blacks at low levels (Alt 1994, 355–258; Grofman, Handley, and Niemi 1992, 22–23; Stanley 1987, chapter six). As Table 4.1 indicates, in 1960 blacks constituted a significant proportion of the population in most Southern states, but their registration rates were relatively low.

As the 1960s dawned, the national political climate was shifting to support dismantling of the barriers to black electoral participation in the South. The Democratic Party outside of the South was increasingly in favor of black enfranchisement in the South, and the burgeoning civil rights movement was successfully moving national public opinion in favor of the guarantee and protection of voting rights for African-Americans (Zimmerman 1995, 290). The ratification of the Twenty-Fourth Amendment in 1964 outlawed the use of the poll tax in federal elections, and the Supreme Court abolished the use of the poll tax in all elections in 1966 (Alt 1994, 356; Stanley 1987, 92–93). The civil rights movement was successful in promoting grassroots efforts to secure black voting rights. The Voter Education Project conducted voter registration drives throughout the South beginning in the early 1960s and registered large numbers of black voters, especially in the Rim South and urban areas (Timpone 1995, 426). The percentage of blacks registered to vote in the South rose from 29 percent in 1960 to over 43 percent in 1964 (Timpone 1995, 437; Stanley 1987, 97; Campbell and Feagin 1975, 133). By 1970, 62 percent of Southern blacks were registered to vote, as Table 4.1 indicates.

The most important action in guaranteeing Southern blacks the right to participate in electoral politics came in 1965 with the passage of the Voting Rights Act. This act is widely acknowledged as one of the most important and effective pieces of federal legislation ever enacted. According to the United States Commission on Civil Rights (USCCR), "Its passage and enforcement have been responsible for substantial increases in the number of blacks registered, voting, and elected to office" (USCCR 1975, v). The Voting Rights Act suspended the use of literacy tests in determining eligibility to vote (abolishing them completely in 1975 amendments) and authorized the use of federal registrars to register black voters in areas where black registration was below certain levels. It also allowed for the presence of federal election observers at the polls in the areas covered by the act's "trigger" mechanisms.

Black Registration in the South, 1940-1996

Year	Number	Percent	Blacks as % Registered voters
1940	250,000	3.0	NA
1947	595,000	12.0	NA
1952	1,009,000	20.0	NA
1956	1,238,000	24.9	NA
1960	1,463,000	29.4	10.6
1964	2,164,000	43.0	13.2
1968	3,112,000	60.3	16.5
1972	3,577,000	62.9	16.6
1976	4,149,000	62.3	16.1
1980	4,254,000	55.8	14.6
1984	5,597,000	65.7	16.7
1988	5,842,000	63.7	21.6
1992	6,314,000	64.5	18.1
1996	6,742,000	64.1	18.3

The number of blacks registered has been rounded off to the nearest thousand. The figures listed for 1971 are generated from 1971 data for some states (AL, AR, GA, MS, TN, TX, and VA) and 1972 data for others (FL, LA, NC, and SC). The percentage of blacks in the registered electorate is not available prior to 1960 because many Southern states did not keep voter registration records. The figures given for the raw number and percentage of blacks registered in prior to 1960 are estimates cobbled together from various sources, and thus must be viewed with some caution, as Matthews and Prothro (1963, 25-27) and Garrow (1978, 7, 11) note. Source: 1940-1956 Matthews and Prothro (1963, 27) and Garrow (1978, 7, 11). 1960-1984 Stanley (1987, 97), Timpone (1995, 437), and *Statistical Abstract of the United States* 1974 (436), 1984 (253), and 1990 (264). 1988-1996 Bureau of the Census, Current Population Report P-20, No. 440 (36-40); CPR P20-466 (23-30); and CPR P20-504u (23-30).

TABLE 4.2   Black Registration in the South, 1940-1996

These actions were highly successful in increasing registration and voting among Southern blacks (Timpone 1995, 434–435; Alt 1994, 368–369; USCCR 1975, 33–36; Hood III, Kidd, and Morris 2000; Davidson 1992, 21; Grofman, Handley, and Niemi 1992, 22–23; Carmines and Stimson 1989, 48–50; Stanley 1987, chapter six; Campbell and Feagin 1975, 133–135). After passage of the Voting Rights Act there were large and rapid gains in both the registration and turnout of Southern blacks, as the data in Tables 4.1 and 4.2 indicate. To be sure, registration levels were already rising, and other factors such as the registration drives of the Voter Education Project and the galvanizing effect of the racially charged 1964 presidential election played an important role in increasing black registration and turnout (Timpone 1995; Carmines and Huckfeldt 1992, 117),[2] but it is also clear that the Voting Rights Act was crucial in pushing change along.

Regardless of the assignment of causality, it is evident that Southern blacks made remarkable advances in electoral participation during the 1960s. In the years immediately following 1965, Southern blacks

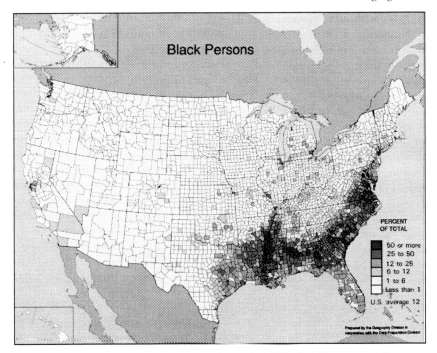

MAP 4.1   Black Persons, Percent of Total. SOURCE: Bureau of the
           Census

increased their voting rate more rapidly than did any other major social
group in the United States (Bullock 1981, 666). These increases drastically
altered the political environment of the South. Almost overnight the composition of the electorate was fundamentally changed. During the 1980s
and 1990s blacks constituted 18–21 percent of the Southern electorate, and
in many districts they were a much larger percentage of the population.
Parties and their candidates and officeholders had new constituents to respond to, with new agendas and different partisan appeals (Carmines
and Huckfeldt 1992, 117). Southern electoral politics was irreversibly
changed.

The emergence of blacks as an electoral force has been crucial to the
politics of the South. Map 4.1, created by the Census Bureau using 1990
data, indicates the concentration of blacks in counties of the nation. Even
as the South has experienced greater urbanization and affluence, it is still
a region in which blacks have a very significant presence. While much
has been made of the rise of the Republican Party in the South, it is important to note that blacks are a substantial portion of many House districts in the region, they are registered at levels equal to whites, and, as

we shall see, those districts elect Democrats. The political consequences of this will be examined in more depth in the next chapter. The point to be made here is that while the black population in the United States has spread beyond the South, blacks remained spatially concentrated in certain areas, specifically urban areas in the North and select areas in the South. They continue to be a presence and they now are registered and vote in significant numbers.

Rising Immigration and Greater Diversity

Another development that has proven to be of major importance for American electoral politics is a major increase in immigration. By 1997, one-fifth of the American population—55 million people—was either immigrants (27 million) or the U.S.-born children of immigrants (28 million) (Rumbaut, Foner, and Gold 1999, 1258). This influx has been a relatively recent phenomenon. Of the 27 million Americans who are of foreign birth, 90 percent have arrived since 1960, and 60 percent have arrived since 1980 (Rumbaut, Foner, and Gold 1999, 1259). The decade of the 1980s saw the largest number of foreign-born people settle in the United States (Briggs 1992, 3). Over the last forty years, the United States has once again become the recipient of a large number of immigrants.

Of course, the United States has a long history of immigration to its shores. From the 1840s through the 1920s, foreign immigration substantially contributed to the nation's rapidly growing population. However, immigration slowed to a trickle with the passage of the Immigration Act of 1924. This legislation, passed because of worries about too much immigration, placed the first cap on immigration to the United States at approximately 150,000 per year, with the possibility of a few thousand more because of special exemptions (King 2000, 229–230; Gimpel and Edwards 1999, 94; Briggs 1992, 57). Perhaps more important, the act established national origin quotas, setting limits on the number of immigrants who would be allowed from each country. Motivated in large part by the desire to preserve the WASP make-up of the American population, the quota system overwhelmingly favored the nations of Northern and Western Europe while severely restricting access for immigrants from other parts of the world (King 2000, 5–6; Carlson 1994, 214–216). Of the 150,000 visas to be issued each year, 82 percent were reserved for those emigrating from Western and Northern European nations. The nations of Southern and Eastern Europe were allotted 14 percent, while the remaining 4 percent went to the rest of the Eastern Hemisphere with the

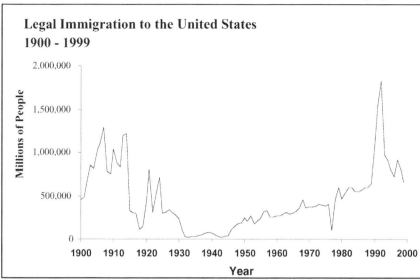

FIGURE 4.1   Legal Immigration to the United States, 1900-1999

exclusion of Asia, from which almost all immigration was already barred (Briggs 1992, 57–58).

Although the Immigration and Nationality Act of 1952 provided some modification of the 1924 Act (most notably by allowing small amounts of immigration from Asian nations and by giving preference to aliens with needed job skills), the limits on both total immigration and individual nations stayed for the most part intact (King 2000, 232; *Congressional Digest* 1996, 130; Briggs 1992, 57). As late as 1965 three nations from the favored part of Europe—Great Britain, Germany, and Ireland—were allotted 70 percent of the available immigration visas (King 2000, 229–230). Because of the conditions and restrictions imposed by the 1924 Act, combined with the Great Depression and World War II and its aftermath, immigration to the United States was significantly reduced until the 1970s (King 2000, 229; Massey 1995, 635–638; Briggs 1992, 4).

During the late 1960s, the forty-year-long drought of immigration to the United States came to an end. For the first time since the 1920s, immigration to the United States topped the 3 million mark (Fallon 1996, 149; Massey 1981, 57). The primary cause of this reversal was the Immigration and Nationality Act Amendments of 1965.[3] The first major change to American immigration policy since 1924, the 1965 amendments radically altered the relocation of foreign peoples to the United States. In keeping with the heightened concern for equality that characterized the

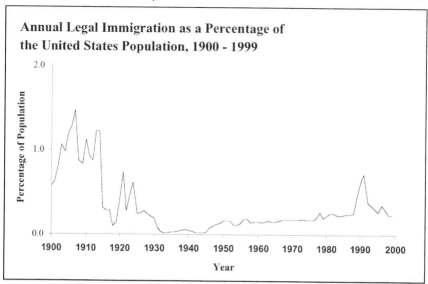

FIGURE 4.2   Annual Legal Immigration as a Percentage of the U.S.
Population, 1900-1999

mid–1960s, the 1965 legislation abolished the national-origins quota system and placed the residents of all nations on equal footing with regard to immigration eligibility. National-origin preferences were replaced by an emphasis on family reunification as the primary criteria for admittance to the United States (King 2000, 243–246; Briggs 1992, 7–8, 103–110; Keely 1971, 159). The cap on total immigration was also raised to 290,000 per year, with the potential to be pushed much higher by more generous exemptions (Briggs 1992, 109–110; Keely 1971, 159).

Figures 4.1 and 4.2 provide an overview of the record of immigration during the 1900s, expressing immigration in terms of the total number and as a percentage of the population. Figure 4.1 indicates the recorded number of entering immigrants for each year, while Figure 4.2 presents what percentage immigrants are of the U.S. population for each year. Total immigration has been increasing in recent years, though the immigration in any given year has not constituted a large percentage of the U.S. population. Over the last several decades, the number of immigrants arriving in a particular year has rarely constituted more than 0.5 of a percent of the total population. The impact on the composition of American society has come from the cumulative effect of the relatively steady levels of immigration each year.

These numbers understate the total immigration into the country, because they do not include illegal immigration. Although attempts to

determine the number of undocumented aliens are obviously specula-
tive, a 1992 study by the Immigration and Naturalization Service placed
the total at 3.2 million. Informed observers estimate that 300,000–500,000
people immigrate illegally each year (Gimpel and Edwards 1999, 12–13;
Fallon 1996, 158). When the estimates of illegal entries are combined
with the figures for legal entrants, the total number of immigrants arriving in the United States each year is much greater.

With the enactment of the Immigration Reform and Control Act of
1986, a large percentage of these illegal entrants were made eligible for
permanent residence status through a variety of amnesty programs.
Between 1989 and 1994, almost 2.7 million undocumented aliens were
granted permanent residence under these amnesties, further adding to
the legal immigration totals (Fallon 1996, 158; Briggs 1992, 160–161).

Additional legislation has further served to increase immigration totals. In 1990 Congress passed and President George Bush signed the
Immigration Act of 1990. The primary feature of this legislation was a
substantial increase of the total immigration cap. Upon taking effect in
October 1991, the law raised the total immigration cap to 700,000 per year
for 1992–1994 and 675,000 per year thereafter. Additional exemptions
were built into this legislation, opening the possibility that the actual
yearly totals may significantly exceed the stated limits (Gimpel and
Edwards 1999, 185–199; Briggs 1992, 233 238). The bottom line is that, as
the 2000s started, the United States was in the midst of an extended period of high immigration, the likes of which has not been seen since the
early part of the 1900s (Briggs 1992, 1). Table 4.3 summarizes all these legislative changes.

In some ways this recent pattern of immigration resembles that of a
century ago. Large numbers of people, many of them relatively poor and
of low education by American standards, are arriving in the United
States each year in search of economic opportunity. In other ways, however, current immigration is much different than that of previous eras.
Before 1960, the overwhelming majority of immigration to the United
States consisted of white Europeans. During the 1950s only 25 percent of
legal immigrants were from South America and the Caribbean. During
the 1980s and 1990s 47 percent of all legal immigrants were from South
America and the Caribbean (U.S. Immigration and Naturalization 2000,
20–22). The vast majority of current immigrants are Hispanic and Asian,
with these two ethnic groups accounting for over 80 percent of total legal
immigration since 1960 (Gimpel 1999, 16; Gimpel and Edwards 1999,
6–9; Rumbaut, Foner, and Gold 1999, 1259; Massey 1995, 639; Carlson

Table 4.3: Significant Twentieth Century
Immigration Legislation in the United States

Legislation	Effects
Immigration Act of 1924	Established the first numerical cap on immigration, approximately 150,000 per year. Also put in place the national origins quota system, setting limits on the number of immigrants that could come from each country. Immigration from the nations of Northern and Western Europe was heavily favored under this quota system.
Immigration and Nationality Act of 1952	Largely continued the policies of the Immigration Act of 1924, including the national origins quota system. Did allow some limited immigration from Asian nations. Also established a preference for immigrants with needed job skills.
Immigration and Nationality Act Amendments of 1965	Abolished the national origins quota system. Established family reunification as the primary preference category under American immigration policy. Placed the first limit on immigration from the Western Hemisphere, 120,000 per year out of a total cap of 290,000. Continued preferences for those potential immigrants with specific job skills.
Immigration Reform and Control Act of 1986	Created a general amnesty program for illegal immigrants who had been in the United States continuously since 1982, and for certain undocumented agricultural workers. Established penalties for employers who knowingly hired illegal aliens.
Immigration Act of 1990	Increased the immigration ceiling to approximately 700,000 per year, with numerous exemptions. Tripled the number of visas allotted to employment needs.

Source: Gimpel and Edwards 1999, 95; Congressional Digest 1996, 130, 160; Greenblatt 1995, 1067.

TABLE 4.3   Significant Twentieth-Century Immigration Legislation in the United States

1994, 214, 217; Cain, Kiewiet, and Uhlaner 1991, 390). The new immigrants are racially and/or ethnically distinct from the white majority of the American population. When these differences are combined with the relative poverty of the recent arrivals, the increase in immigration is changing the composition of American society and affecting electoral politics.

In a representative democracy with its legislature elected from geographically based districts, population changes produce political change (Gimpel 1999, 3; Suro 1998, 5). This is especially true when the new additions to the population tend to locate primarily in certain areas, as is the case with the immigrants who have arrived in the United States since the 1960s (Rumbaut, Foner, and Gold 1999, 1259; Gimpel and Edwards 1999, 14–15; Massey 1995, 632–633). The vast majority of the new immigrants are located in large urban areas, primarily in central cities

(Carlson 1994, 226; Waldinger 1989, 211–214). According to the 1990 Census, 90 percent of Hispanic Americans and 94 percent of Asian Americans live in urban areas (Carlson 1994, 230). Certainly not all members of these groups are post–1960 immigrants, but it is likely that a large majority of them are. Moreover, a substantial portion of the new immigrants settle in the urban areas of selected states, such as California, Texas, New York, Florida, Illinois, and New Jersey (Frey 1996, 744; Carlson 1994, 226–230). This serves to further increase the concentration of the immigrant population. Immigrants do not register and vote immediately, but as time passes they do, and their presence in the population becomes important politically.

In addition, there is evidence that the arrival of these immigrants in an area results in some out-migration on the part of whites who reside there, further increasing the concentration of the immigrant population (Gimpel 1999; Frey 1996, 2000). As both Frey and Gimpel relate, these two segments of the population have different motivations for determining where to live. Immigrants locate mainly in port-of-entry cities, where previous members of their social group have already settled and where established social networks exist. White out-migrants, on the other hand, tend to relocate away from immigrant areas and into areas populated mostly by whites. The end result of these dual population movements is increased geographic segregation by race and ethnicity within the United States. Segregation by class increases as well, due to the fact that many immigrants have low income levels, much lower than the whites who are leaving (Gimpel 1999; Frey 1996). In a society that has always been characterized by high levels of economic and racial segregation, evidence suggests that the increased immigration of the last forty years is contributing to heightened levels of separation.

Map 4.2, created by the Census Bureau, indicates that Hispanics are heavily concentrated in the states in the Southwest part of the nation. This concentration of Hispanics is of particular importance because of their record of voting Democratic. While there was a time when it was assumed that the Sunbelt would be a solid electoral base for the Republican Party (Phillips 1969, 7; Sale 1975; Galston 1985; Reddy 1991), it is now difficult to see this area as a solid Republican electoral base. The concentration of the Hispanic population in urban areas in these states provides the Democrats with a significant potential electoral base in the region.

Table 4.4 presents more precise data on the impact of Hispanics in some states. The table includes states with the highest percentage of Hispanic population. In California, Arizona, and Florida, Hispanics are now

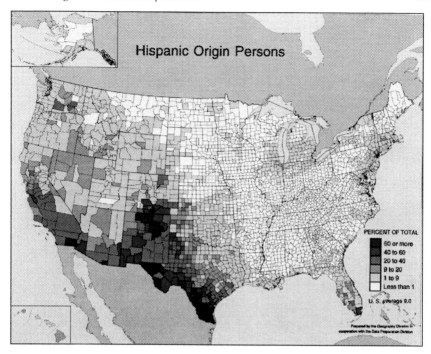

Hispanic Origin Persons

PERCENT OF TOTAL

60 or more
40 to 60
20 to 40
9 to 20
1 to 9
Less than 1

U. S. average 9.0

Prepared by the Geography Division in cooperation with the Data Preparation Division

MAP 4.2   Hispanic-Origin Persons, Percent of Total. SOURCE: Bureau of the Census

approximately a third of all residents. Change in some of these states will be examined in more detail in Chapter 5.

Of course the fact that a large number of immigrants now reside in the United States does not necessarily mean that they will have an electoral impact. Many of these new immigrants are children under the age of eighteen, and thus unable to vote. Many have yet to become naturalized, and therefore cannot vote because they are not citizens. Undocumented aliens lack even the permanent resident status that would allow them to become citizens. In addition, many of the new immigrants possess low levels of income and education, two characteristics that tend to result in low political participation. Thus it is not surprising to learn that many immigrant areas are marked by low voter turnout (Gimpel 1999, 329–331; Jackson 2001; Ramirez 2001). However, this situation will gradually change. As did the immigrants before them, America's newest arrivals will eventually become citizens, register, and vote. In many areas this progression is already well under way. Their numbers and their geographic concentration make it very likely that recently arrived immigrants will affect American electoral politics in significant ways (Gimpel 1999, 332; Suro 1998, 299–301).

Table 4.4: Regional and State Presence of Hispanics
1990 and 1999[*]

Region	1990	1999
Northeast	7.4	9.5
Midwest	2.9	3.8
South	7.9	10.9
West	19.1	22.7
States		
California	25.8	32.7
Arizona	38.2	39.6
New Mexico	18.8	22.3
Texas	12.9	14.3
Florida	25.5	29.2
New York	12.2	15.9
Illinois	12.3	15.5

[*] The 1990 data are taken from the 1994 City and County Data Book (Bureau of the Census, 1996), "Table A States – Population Characteristics." P. 3. The 1999 data are from the following web page: http://www.census.gov/population/projections/state/stpjpop.txt

For more detailed information, see Population Paper Listing #47, "Population Projections for States, by Age, Sex, Race, and Hispanic Origin: 1995 to 2025." The totals for Hispanics and blacks are from: http://www.census.gov/population/projections/state/stpjrace.txt

Series Projections. For more details, see PPL #47, "Population Projections for States, by Age, Sex, Race, and Hispanic Origin: 1995 to 2025."

TABLE 4.4   Regional and State Presence of Hispanics, 1990 and 1999

The Fortunes of the Electorate:
Growing Economic Divisions

While the composition of the electorate has been shifting, the economic experiences of the American population have also been diverging in ways that create the basis for differing electoral bases. The crucial change has

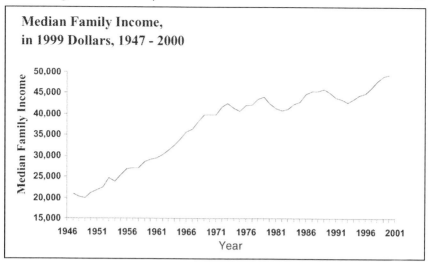

FIGURE 4.3 Median Family Income, in 1999 Dollars, 1947-2000

been in the distribution of income and wealth. After steady declines in inequality from the mid–1940s through the 1970s, inequality began to steadily increase. In the 1970s the economy began to change in ways that produced economic gains for the more affluent and more educated, while those with less education experienced declines. Economic rewards were distributed in a divisive way. The change was a product of several trends.

The growth of income, after sustained increases from the late 1940s through the 1960s, slowed dramatically beginning in the 1970s. Median family income, corrected for inflation and expressed in 1999 dollars, increased from $20,886 in 1947 to $44,097 in 1979. Since then there has been only modest growth, and by 2000 family income had increased, over twenty years, by just $5,000 to $49,237. The trend in family income is shown in Figure 4.3.[4]

It was not just that income growth began to slow. Change in the economic situation of families was accompanied by significant changes in how many families earned their income. Between 1979 and 1999, families at all income levels were working more hours (Uchitelle 1999, sect. 3, 1). Since the 1970s average weekly earnings for *individual workers* have declined (Miringoff and Miringoff 1999, 99–100). Many families have been able to maintain stable *family* incomes only because more women have joined the labor force and provide a growing portion of family income (Danziger and Gottschalk 1995, 76–81). In 1950 the percentage of women in the labor force was 23; by 1960 it was 30 (Kreps and Leaper 1976, 76). By the mid-1990s it was almost 60 percent (Hayghe 1997, 42).

Table 4.5: Percentage Change in Income by Income Groups and Era[1]		
Income Group	Era and Percentage Change	
	1949 - 1969	1973 - 1991
Lowest	457.1	-19.0
2	168.4	-8.1
3	130.8	-1.1
4	114.6	4.1
5	106.3	9.6
6	102.2	12.7
7	99.8	15.6
8	94.9	17.8
9	92.8	20.8
Highest	102.2	21.5

[1] Source: Danziger and Gottschalk 1995, 53. Incomes are first grouped from lowest to highest, and then broken into groups of tenths. The percentage increases in incomes within each category, from the beginning to the end of the era, are then computed. The same differences were reported when the years of 1947-79 and 1980-97 were compared (Allen 1999, 57).

TABLE 4.5   Percentage Change in Income by Income Groups and Era

As median family income grew and then stagnated, the distribution of income also experienced a significant shift. Inequality decreased from the 1940s to 1970 and then has increased steadily since then (Levy 1988, 13–16; Samuelson 1997, 71). While this shift in the trend is important in itself, perhaps more important are the changes that are the basis for the growing inequality. Table 4.5 compares the growth in incomes for the earlier era with the most recent one. For this table, family incomes at the beginning of an era (for example, 1949) are first ranked from lowest to highest. They are then grouped by tenths, from the lowest to the highest. At the end of the era (1969) family incomes are again ranked and grouped. The change from 1949–1969 within the groups is then calculated, and percentage change is determined.

Table 4.6: Average Pre-Tax Income by Income Group (1997 dollars)				
	1979	1989	1997	% Δ 79-97	$ Δ 79-97
Lowest fifth	$11,800	$11,700	$11,400	-3.4	- $400
Second fifth	27,100	27,300	28,600	5.5	1,500
Middle fifth	41,400	42,700	45,100	8.9	3,700
Fourth fifth	56,800	61,900	65,600	15.5	8,800
Highest fifth	109,500	138,000	167,500	53.0	58,800

Source: Isaac Shapiro, Robert Greenstein, and Wendell Primus, Pathbreaking CBO Study Shows Dramatic Increases in Income Disparities in 1980s and 1990s, Center on Budget and Policy Priorities, Washington, D.C., May 31, 2001, p. 10.

TABLE 4.6   Average Pre-Tax Income by Income Group (1997 Dollars)

From 1949 to 1969 incomes increased for all income levels, and the greatest increases were received by those with the lowest incomes. In contrast, from the early 1970s until 1991 increases in income were experienced only by those in the upper income categories. The growth in inequality in American society has come about because after 1969 those in the lowest income levels experienced actual declines in real income, and those at the top experienced real growth in income. The most significant changes began in the early 1980s, when the demand for unskilled labor declined sharply and the demand for highly educated workers increased (Levy 1998, 46–49). The same pattern of declining incomes for the less affluent and real increases for the more affluent continued throughout the 1990s (Shapiro and Greenstein 1999; Johnston 1999; Ryscavage 1999, 45–80). Table 4.6 indicates how the levels of income by income quintiles changed over time for the last two decades of the 1900s. Those in the bottom quintiles have experienced almost no growth, while those in the top two categories have experienced considerable growth, further increasing inequality.

These income inequalities have been accompanied by greater inequality in other areas. Those with less income are less likely to have health care (Miringoff and Miringoff 1999, 93), or to participate in a pension system. Those with less income are less likely to be able to afford the cost of attending college. Indeed, from the early 1970s through 1995, the real cost of attending college has steadily increased (Commission on National Investment in Higher Education 1996, 10) and support from government to help defray the costs of higher education has declined. State governments now provide less tax revenue support and devote smaller portions of their budgets to higher education than they did twenty years ago (Mortensen 1995, 1). The inequalities of the distribution of income have come to play a significant role in affecting who is likely to get a college degree. Children have also been affected, and from 1970 to the late 1990s, the percentage of children living in poverty increased. The United States now has a higher percentage of children in this situation than most other industrialized nations (Miringoff and Miringoff 1999, 80–85).

Economic Change and Implications for Diversity Among House Districts

All these inequalities have enormous potential to structure political conflict. Some segments of the population are experiencing economic stress, while others are enjoying affluence. The important matter is whether the parties choose to focus on these changes and make them a political issue (Teixeira and Rogers 2000). The extent to which the parties have done so and the implications for political alignments will be taken up in the next chapter. Suffice it to say that these economic changes have resulted in substantial segments of the population having very different economic needs, which carry the potential for polarized perceptions about the need for government action.

If these social and economic changes are distributed unevenly across districts, that will create greater diversity among districts, which, when filtered through the representative process, will make conflicts more a part of political discussions.

There is evidence that inequality and segregation among communities has increased. It is largely the affluent and whites who move to the suburbs (Jackson 1985, 231-271; Judd and Swanstrom 1998, 194–205). The movement of the affluent, combined with zoning laws that act to exclude the less affluent (Danielson 1976, 27–106), has lead to greater racial (Orfield and Yun 1999) and class segregation within metropolitan areas (Massey and Denton 1993, 24–88; Jargowsky 1996, 989–991; Rusk 1995, 27–37). In the last two decades the effort to separate populations has increased even further with the emergence of "gated" communities, or communities with walls around them and gates used to screen those without proper identification. By 1997 it was estimated that 20,000 such communities existed, encompassing over 3 million housing units (Blakely and Snyder 1997, 7). Differing economic circumstances are not distributed equally within communities or House districts. Some districts have a relatively affluent population, while others have populations with much lower incomes (Drier et al. 2001, 1–12).

In summary, the changes discussed here have considerable potential to reshape House districts. Blacks have become relevant in the South and many have moved to urban areas. Immigration has increased, particularly among Hispanics, and they have located primarily in seven states where they have become a significant presence. Over this time, economic inequality has increased.

Changes in House Districts

The important matter for House elections and the political parties is how these changes have affected House districts. The Bureau of the Census releases information on the demographic profile of each district each decade, making it possible to examine the distribution of districts by various traits across decades. Table 4.7 presents the distribution of districts since the 1960s for median family income, the income in the middle of each district's distribution, the percentage of the district that is non-white, and urbanization levels.[5] The data on median family income are adjusted for inflation, so figures are presented in terms of constant purchasing power.[6]

The diversity among districts is crucial because it creates very different collections of constituencies to which the parties can appeal. If all districts were similar, then members of Congress would face very similar electorates, and there would be less likelihood of the parties' having different electoral bases. For each indicator a measure of dispersion around the mean is also presented. The extent of dispersion tells us what possibilities there are for differing electoral bases to develop. Whether they do develop depends on the stances the parties pursue, and how the electorate reacts, matters to be discussed in the next chapter. The first issue, however, is the extent of dispersion. A higher number indicates more diversity among districts.[7]

For income a clear pattern emerges. From the 1960s through the 1980s the national average for the median family income for districts increased slightly and the dispersion among districts decreased. The change from the 1980s to the 1990s is, however, very different. The average median family income increased significantly from 1980 to 1990, but the gain was not experienced uniformly. Some districts did not gain, while in others there were significant gains. The result was that dispersion increased, and during the 1990s dispersion was greater than it had been in any earlier decade. The coefficient of variation was around 20 in the 1970s and 1980s, but increased to 26 during the 1990s.

The 2000 census reveals further change. The Bureau of the Census released some 2000 demographic data using districts drawn in the early 1990s, before the reapportionments to be done by 2002.[8] The distributions

Diverging Parties

Changing Distributions of Median Family Income,
Percent Non-White, and Percent Urban, House Districts, 1960s - 2000
(% in each category, by decade)

Apportionment for Decade of:

Family Income	1960s	1970s	1980s	1990s	2000 data
				1990s	
0 - 29,999	20.7	9.0	6.4	5.1	2.9
30 - 34,999	13.1	14.4	16.3	10.8	5.7
35 - 39,999	22.8	21.2	25.8	17.9	9.1
40 - 44,999	19.1	21.6	26.2	20.9	7.1
45 - 49,999	14.3	15.9	11.0	14.0	13.8
50 - 54,999	6.9	10.6	8.5	10.6	11.9
55 - 59,999	2.3	4.4	3.5	6.0	10.5
60 - 64,999	.7	2.3	1.8	5.5	13.3
65,000 +	.2	.7	.5	9.2	25.7
Mean	$ 38,484	41,720	40,844	46,236	55,555
Coefficient of Variation	24.4	21.5	19.8	26.0	27.2

Percent Non-White					
0 - 9	64.8	61.6	44.8	40.6	22.5
10 - 19	13.1	18.5	24.9	24.6	26.7
20 plus	22.1	19.9	30.3	34.9	50.8
Mean	11.5	12.2	16.6	19.5	25.1
Standard deviation	13.6	14.6	16.4	18.5	19.3

Urbanization Percent					
0 - 69	45.8	45.5	44.1	39.8	
70 - 89	13.1	19.1	21.4	24.4	
90 plus	22.1	35.4	34.5	35.9	
Mean	11.5	67.8	73.3	73.4	
Standard deviation	13.6	24.6	23.0	22.9	

Note: All median family income data from districts are expressed in terms of 2000 dollar values. Figures from 1960, 1970, 1980, and 1990 are converted to 2000 values using the Consumer Price Index.

TABLE 4.7   Changing Distributions of Median Family Income, Percent Non-White and Percent Urban, House Districts, 1960s-2000

for districts for the 2002–2010 elections will differ after new district lines are drawn, but using existing data for 1990s districts allows us to assess change across the last decade. Incomes generally increased during the 1990s, but the dispersion across districts also increased, rising to 27.1. The increasing inequality in incomes experienced by individuals is also occurring across districts. This pattern occurs for the nation as a whole and also within all three regions of the nation.[9]

The distribution of districts by race has also changed considerably. During the 1960s 65 percent of House districts were 0–9 percent non-white. By the 1990s 41 percent of districts were in this category, and the 2000 data indicate that only 23 percent of districts were in this category. Correspondingly, there has been a rise in the percentage of House districts with 20 percent or more non-whites.[10] In the 1960s 22 percent of House districts contained 20 percent of non-whites or more; by the 1990s 35 percent of House districts were in this category; and in 2000 51 percent were in this category. The number of districts with 20 percent or more non-whites was 88 in the 1970s, 152 in the 1990s, and 221 in 2000. The indicator of diversity, the standard deviation, has also steadily increased. Urbanization levels, while also increasing, have changed by a lesser amount. The average level of urbanization has increased since 1960, and there are more districts that are 90 percent or more urban.

The important matter is how these traits are related. If these traits are related, then it results in sets of districts with concentrations of differing groups of constituents. If, for example, urbanization is related to the presence of non-whites, then the resulting overlap of urbanization and non-whites can create groups of districts that provide differing bases for the political parties. Table 4.8 indicates the relationship between level of urbanization and the percentage of non-whites for House districts since the 1960s. In the 1960s urbanization increases were not associated with the presence of non-whites. There were not more relatively non-white districts as urbanization increased, as non-whites were as likely to be rural as urban. By the 1990s a clear relationship had developed. Among the less urban districts, 63 percent were primarily white (0–9 percent non-white). The more rural districts are now primarily white. Among those districts that are 90 percent or more urban, 54 percent have a population that is 20 percent or more non-whites. The non-white population is now primarily urban.

The 2000 census data indicate an even stronger relationship. By 2000, using the districts drawn in the early 1990s, 56 percent of districts with 20 percent or more non-whites were in heavily urban areas. In the 1960s only 31 percent of these districts were heavily urban areas. The difference is because blacks and other minorities migrated to urban areas and because immigrants are moving to urban areas. The presence of non-whites has a stronger association with lower incomes than it did in the 1960s and 1970s.[11]

The ultimate concern is how social change is affecting the diversity of the electorate and the potential for diverging electoral bases for the House

The Urbanization-Non-White Connection:
House District Distributions, 1960s - 2000

Urbanization %	Percentage of Non-Whites			
	0 - 9	10 - 19	20 plus	Correlation
1960s				
0 - 69	66.5	9.3	24.2	.03
70 - 89	74.3	14.9	10.8	
90 plus	55.7	19.7	24.6	
1970s				
0 - 69	66.7	12.6	20.6	.18
70 - 89	79.5	15.7	4.8	
90 plus	46.1	27.3	26.6	
1980s				
0 - 69	62.8	15.5	21.7	.32
70 - 89	41.6	42.2	16.2	
90 plus	24.0	25.9	50.1	
1990s				
0 - 69	63.0	13.9	23.1	.42
70 - 89	36.8	35.9	27.4	
90 plus	17.3	28.9	53.9	
2000 Census data for Non-White % - 1990s districts				
0 - 69	48.6	22.0	29.5	.51
70 - 89	12.3	44.3	43.3	
90 plus	.6	19.9	79.5	

Note: The table indicates, for each level of urbanization, the distribution of districts by percentages of non-whites. The concern is whether higher levels of urbanization are associated with more districts that have relatively high percentages (20 % or more) of non-whites. The first concern is, within each decade, the presence of more non-white districts increases as urbanization increases. The second concern is whether that relationship changes and increases over time. The last set of results relies on urbanization levels from the 1990 census and non-white percentages from the 2000 census. Urbanization levels for House districts is not available on the Census Bureau web page, so only non-white figures can be used. Since urbanization has not changed by much over time, the presumption is that relative stability of urbanization has occurred, and it is safe to use the 1990 data. Source: data compiled by the authors.

TABLE 4.8   The Urbanization-Non-White Connection: House District
Distributions, 1960s-2000
Non-White and Percent Urban, House Districts, 1960s-2000

parties. Table 4.9 indicates the extent of diversity among House districts for the 1970s, a time of relatively low polarization, compared to districts

The Urbanization-Non-White Connection: House District Distributions, 1970s - 2000

Urbanization %	Percentage of Non-Whites		
	0 - 9	10 - 19	20 plus
1970s			
0 - 69	30.4	15.2	16.3
70 - 89	5.8	3.0	9.7
90 plus	9.4	.9	9.4
1990s			
0 - 69	25.1	9.0	6.2
70 - 89	5.5	8.7	10.3
90 plus	9.2	6.7	19.3
2000 Census data for Non-White % - 1990s districts			
0 - 69	19.3	8.7	11.7
70 - 89	3.0	10.8	10.6
90 plus	.2	7.1	28.5

Note: The numbers represent the percentage of all districts (435) within each category. The percentages sum to 100. Source: data compiled by the authors and data taken from the Census Bureau web page.

TABLE 4.9   The Urbanization-Non-White Connection: House District Distributions, 1970s-2000

for the 1990s. The numbers are the percentage of the 435 districts within each category for each decade.

In the 1970s most House districts were less urban, and when districts had 20 percent or more non-whites, most of them were in less urban areas. Thirty percent of all House districts were less urban and 0–9 percent non-white. Only 9 percent of districts were heavily urban (90 percent or more) and 20 percent non-white. By the 1990s significant change had occurred. Almost as many districts were heavily urban and 20 percent or more non-white (19.3 percent in the 1990s) as were those primarily white and less urban (25.1 percent in the 1990s). Using the 2000 census data there are more heavily urban and 20 percent or more non-white (28.5 percent, or 124 districts) than primarily white and less urban (19.3 percent or 84 districts). To the extent that demographics result in differing constituencies with different policy concerns, there are now sets of very different districts that can provide electoral bases for the parties.

Change Within States

Amidst these general changes, the nature of change has varied across the states. Changes by race have been particularly varied. In some cases states have lost seats, even while increasing the number of seats with a substantial non-white population. In other states the population has increased, accompanied by considerable increase in the prevalence of non-whites. Table 4.10 presents the extent of change for several of the more populous states.

Over the last several decades New York has experienced little population growth, and with the rest of the nation growing, the state has lost House seats. In the 1960s the state had forty-two seats, and by the 1990s the state had lost ten seats. While it was losing seats, it also experienced a significant change in its non-white population. From the 1960s to the 1990s the state lost nineteen heavily white districts and picked up four districts with 20 percent or more non-whites. The 2000 census data indicate that the number of such districts increased to eighteen of thirty-one.

Over the same time, Florida, Texas, and California were experiencing enormous population gains. Change played out differently in the three states, however. In Florida, the state went from one House district with 90 percent whites in the 1960s to twelve districts in that category in the 1990s. The 2000 data indicate that trend was abruptly reversed, and there is once again only one district with 90 percent whites. In contrast, Texas and California experienced remarkable increases in the proportion of their population that was non-white. Texas picked up seven districts, but it experienced an increase of fourteen seats with 20 percent or more of non-whites following the 1990 census. The 2000 census indicates that twenty-four of thirty seats fall in that category. In California the change was even more dramatic, with the state gaining fourteen seats, but seats with 20 percent or more non-white went from five to thirty-five following the 1990 census and to forty-nine of fifty-two following the 2000 census. All these states had more seats with 20 percent or more non-whites in the 1990s compared to the 1960s, but in New York, Texas, and California the increases were very substantial.

In other states change came about not through population growth, but because, during each decade's reapportionment, state legislatures rearranged district boundaries in ways that affected the significance of non-

Distribution of House Districts by the Percentage Non-White, 1960s - 1990s and 1990 Districts Using 2000 Census for Existing Districts						
The Nation	Decade of Apportionment and % distribution					
% Non-white	1960s	1970s	1980s	1990s	2000 data	
0 - 9	64.8	61.6	44.8	40.6	22.5	
10 - 19	13.1	18.5	24.9	24.6	26.7	
20 plus	22.1	19.9	30.3	34.9	50.8	
	Decade of Apportionment and # of Districts					
By State	1960s	1970s	1980s	1990s	2000 data	Change
New York						
0 - 9	30	25	15	11	5	-25
10 - 19	6	7	8	11	8	2
20 plus	5	7	11	9	18	13
Total	41	39	34	31	31	
Florida						
0 - 9	1	2	5	12	1	0
10 - 19	7	11	9	6	15	8
20 plus	4	2	5	5	7	3
Total	12	15	19	23	23	
Texas						
0 - 9	9	10	3	2	0	-9
10 - 19	8	9	11	8	6	-2
20 plus	6	5	13	20	24	18
Total	23	24	27	30	30	
California						
0 - 9	33	32	5	2	0	-33
10 - 19	1	7	15	15	3	2
20 plus	4	5	25	35	49	45
Total	38	44	45	52	52	

TABLE 4.10   Distribution of House Districts by the Percentage Non-White, 1960s-1990s and 1990 Districts Using 2000 Census for Existing Districts

whites. In some states major efforts were made to create districts with substantial proportions of non-whites. These efforts often reflected the desire of Democrats to increase the probability of a minority candidate's winning a seat. There was also support from Republicans who wanted to pack minorities into fewer districts, thus creating more primarily white districts and increasing the chances of Republican success. This occurred in Georgia and North Carolina, presented in Table 4.11. During the 1960s through the 1980s each state had a relatively stable number of districts with 30 percent or more of non-whites. Then, following the 1990 census, the states both redistricted and created fewer districts with 30 percent or

**Stable Relative Populations: the Shifting Racial
Composition of House Districts, In Georgia and North Carolina**
(the percentage non-white per district)

District number	Georgia					North Carolina				
	60s	70s	80s	90sI	90sII	60s	70s	80s	90sI	90sII
1	38	35	34	25	32	45	36	36	58	51
2	39	37	37	59	40	49	41	41	24	30
3	37	32	36	20	27	29	27	29	23	22
4	31	15	15	19	42	23	24	21	23	24
5	27	44	66	65	64	23	14	17	16	15
6	41	20	16	10	9	23	21	22	9	22
7	9	7	7	15	14	38	33	37	29	33
8	27	31	36	23	32	25	20	22	27	32
9	7	6	6	6	5	12	22	25	11	12
10	33	33	26	20	39	12	11	11	6	8
11				66	13	7	7	7	9	7
12									58	37
Number <= 20	2	3	4	6	4	4	3	3	5	4
Number > 30	6	6	5	3	6	3	3	3	2	5

TABLE 4.11   Stable Relative Populations: The Shifting Racial Composition
of House Districts, in Georgia and North Carolina

more non-whites, and more districts with 20 percent of less. These district lines were challenged in court and were eventually redrawn. The final district results for the 1990s are included. The redrawn lines produced a restoration of the number of districts in each state that had a significant presence of non-whites.

While some states, such as New York, were losing seats, they were experiencing an increase in the number of districts with a significant non-white presence. Others, such as California and Texas, were experiencing both an increase in seats and an increase in the number of districts with a significant non-white presence. Finally, states like Georgia and North Carolina were struggling with how to use apportionment to affect the representation of a more stable non-white presence. While the process of change has played out differently across the states, the net result has been a significant increase in the percentage of districts that have 20 percent or more non-whites.

Social change is clearly changing the composition of House districts and is shifting which sets of constituents dominate. Demographics are not destiny, but, as we shall see next, Democrats are much more likely to win certain of these districts, and Republicans are much more likely to win others. As social change occurs, it affects who wins, and it also affects the kinds of concerns members of Congress have. These diverse districts create House members who are likely to have different policy concerns and who will vote differently. The diverging party voting in the House is in many ways the product of the changing composition of American society and its reflection in House election outcomes. It is those outcomes that we examine next.

Notes

1. A provision in which you could vote or not vote, depending on whether your grandfather had the right.

2. Certainly the findings produced by Timpone have some merit. As Campbell and Feagin note, the Voting Rights Act only provided the legal framework through which Southern blacks could register and vote. Blacks still had to organize and mobilize to register and vote under their own initiative (Campbell and Feagin 1975, 135). The efforts of organizations such as the Voter Education Project clearly facilitated these actions on the part of Southern blacks, as the U.S. Commission on Civil Rights emphasized in its 1975 report (USCCR 1975, 69-71). However, there can be no denial of the fact that the largest and most rapid gains in black registration and turnout came immediately following the enactment of the Voting Rights Act (Alt 1994, 366-367; Campbell and Feagin 1975, 133). Perhaps it is the case that the Voting Rights Act both removed legal barriers to black electoral participation in the South and created a more favorable climate for the organization and mobilization of the black electorate on the part of civil rights groups and other private organizations.

3. A few researchers, most notably Douglas Massey, have argued that the importance of the 1965 amendments for the recent increases in immigration has been overstated. Massey correctly points out that the 1965 legislation put the first cap on immigration from the Western Hemisphere (120,000 of the overall 290,000 limit), thereby making it more difficult for residents of those countries to legally get into the United States. Since a large percentage of the "new" immigrants come from Latin America, Massey claims that the increase in immigration from this region has occurred in spite of the 1965 amendments, not because of them (Massey 1995, 638). Although Massey's point is well-taken, it must not be carried too far. The 1965 overhaul of U.S. immigration policy has certainly been an important cause of increased immigration since the 1960s. The 1965 amendments removed the barriers to immigration from Asian nations. The result, as Massey and others point out, has been an explosion in immigration from this region (King 2000, 251; Massey 1995, 638; Keely 1971, 161–165). Massey also notes the importance of labor migration from less economically developed nations to more highly developed nations in recent years (Massey 1981, 60). In opening up U.S. borders to those from less-developed nations, the 1965 amendments significantly contributed to the resurgence of immigration that the United States has experienced since the 1960s. Regardless of what

caused the increase, it is clear that immigration to the United States has risen significantly since 1968, when the 1965 Amendments went into effect.

4. These figures are taken from U.S. Bureau of the Census, Current Population Reports, P6—203, *Measuring 50 Years of Economic Change Using the March Current Population Survey*, U.S. Government Printing Office, Washington, D.C, 1998. Table C–10, page C–19; 1999 and 2000 income data come from: "Historical Income Tables–Families," http://www.census.gov/hhes/income/histinc/f23.html; and, the CPI is taken from: Income 2000" http://www.census.gov/hhes/income/income00/cpiurs.html.

5. These data represent the aggregation of all districts with their demographic information within each decade of apportionment. For example, following the apportionment of 1972 the demographic profiles of these districts are published. Within each decade there are also changes in districts due to challenges to the initial set of districts established. We changed the data for districts drawn within each decade. The appendix on Congressional District Data discusses these changes. We then aggregated all districts within a decade. For the 1970s, for example, this means aggregating all districts for 1972, 1974, 1976, 1978, and 1980. The last year of each decade is included in the prior year because the census of the prior decade is used to profile the district.

6. To put family incomes in constant dollar amounts (adjusting for, or eliminating, inflation), the standard approach is to divide dollar figures by the Consumer Price Index for that year. The CPI index is first adjusted by multiplying it by .01, so an index of, say 200, is expressed in terms of the ratio of prices to a base of 1. If the ratio is 2 then prices are twice as high. If the median family income is $30,000 in one year and a decade later is $60,000, and the index goes from 100 (1.0) to 200 (2.0), then the real value of the tax base is $30,000 in each year. One further adjustment is made in this case. To make sure all figures are expressed in contemporary values, the index is set to have the current year or most recent year of 1990 equal 100. This is done by dividing the index for each year by the value for the most current year. If the index were 200 now, then division by 200 will give the current year a value of 1.0. If the index were 100 twenty years ago, then dividing by 200 will give an index for twenty years ago of 0.5. Dividing values from twenty years ago by 0.5 will double their real value. This should occur, since inflation has lowered the real value of incomes, and incomes before inflation were really worth more twenty years ago.

7. Two indicators of dispersion are used here, depending on the scale of the variable involved. The standard deviation is generally used as an indicator of dispersion. The standard deviation takes each deviation from the mean, squares it, and sums them. The measure is then an indication of the sum of deviations from the mean. The greater the sum of these deviations, the greater the diversity among districts. The difficulty in using this measure is that if the general scale of the variable increases over time (such as has occurred with income), then this results in higher deviation scores, and even if the deviations remain essentially the same, the deviations will be "larger" and the sum will be greater. The result will be a larger standard deviation, but the sum of deviations will not really be larger. The standard deviation, then, with variables such as median family income, appears to increase, but it may only be a result of the general increase in the scale.

If the scale is constant, then this is not a problem. In the case of these two variables, the scale increases for median family income, but not for the percentage of non-whites, since the scale is capped at 100. Since our goal is to measure dispersion–how much do districts vary, such that there are different constituent situations to be represented?–we use the standard deviation for percentage of non-whites and the coefficient of variation for median family income.

An example may help illustrate how the coefficient of variation captures changing diversity even as mean scores are changing. In this example, one set of numbers will have changing means over time, but constant real diversity. In the second set of cases the degree of diversity increases as mean values increase over time. Assume, in the first case, that in three different years there are three municipalities. In each year there is a mean score, a score 25 percent above the mean and another 25 percent below the mean. The mean changes over time, but the relative dispersion of cases around the mean (25 percent plus or minus) does not change. The scores are: Year 1: 7.5, 10, 12.5; Year 2: 15, 20, 25; Year 3: 22.5, 30, 37.5. The standard deviation for the three years is 2.5, 5.0, and 7.5, but the coefficient of variation for the three years is 25, 25, and 25. For the second set of numbers, the numbers are, Year 1: 7.5, 10, 12.5; Year 2: 13, 20, 27.5; Year 3: 18, 30, 42. In both sets of cases the mean values increase by the same amount over time, but there is greater dispersion around the mean in the second set of numbers. The coefficient of variation increases from 25 to 35 to 40 over the three years. This increasing coefficient of variation indicates a real increase in the degree of dispersion around the mean value.

8. Data for percent non-white and median family income for many districts are available at the web page: http://factfinder.census.gov/servlet/BasicFactsServlet. As of December 2001, median family income was not available for all districts. We were able to find non-white information for all 435 districts and income data for 210 districts. There is, of course, a potential problem that these 210 districts are not representative of all districts. The data for 2000 have a correlation with data from 1990 of 0.92.

Mean and Coefficient of Variation for House District, Real Median Family Income, by Decade, for the Nation and Regions, 1962 - 1992 (1990 dollars)

| | First Year Following Census Reapportionment | | | |
	1962	1972	1982	1992
North				
Mean	$ 42,351	$ 45,456	$ 43,123	$ 49,930
c. v.	17.5	17.8	18.6	24.1
South				
Mean	$ 28,905	$ 34,384	$ 36,264	$ 40,447
c. v.	24.2	21.1	19.7	25.3
Remainder				
Mean	$ 40,780	$ 42,216	$ 41,849	$46,943
c. v.	19.6	17.8	16.9	24.3

Table 4.12   Mean and Coefficient of Variation for House District

9. The regional patterns are shown in the accompanying table.

10. The approach to measuring the presence of minorities in American society understates change to some extent. The important issue is how Hispanics are counted. The Census Bureau allows respondents to classify themselves as Hispanic or non-Hispanic, and as "white" or "non-white." A proportion of Hispanics classify themselves as white. To the extent that an Hispanic heritage creates a sense of being different and of being a minority within American society, then a focus on non-whites neglects those Hispanics who also regard themselves as white. It is possible, using the 1990 census, to determine the number of respondents who check Hispanic but white. If this additional group is included, and the focus is on minorities (non-whites, plus Hispanics regarding themselves as white) then the percentage of House districts with 20 percent or more of minorities increases to 42 percent for the 1990s.

11. The correlation between district median family income, using the 210 districts that the Bureau of Census released income data on by December 2001 and the percentage non-white from the 2000 census, is -.55. This is an increase from prior decades. The correlations by decade have been: 1960s, -.38; 1970s, -.33; 1980s, -.36; 1990s, -.26. Whether this correlation level will occur for districts drawn for the 2002 elections, of course, remains to be seen.

5

Social Change, Realignment, and Party Polarization

The changes leading up to the 1970s left the parties in flux. The Democrats had long dominated the South and derived many of their seats from that region, but their dominance there was eroding. Republicans were losing their decades-long dominance in the Northeast, and there was no certainty that their success in the South would continue and provide a new geographical base. These trends coincided with changes in the parties' constituencies. Beginning in the 1930s the Democrats acquired more of an urban base. They were deriving more seats from the North, where the population was more liberal. By the 1950s and 1960s the party was a patchwork of Southern Democrats, with blacks in that area largely precluded from having any effect through voting, and a Northern, urban, ethnic, working class constituency. But while its reliance on an urban population was increasing, the Democratic Party still had a substantial reliance on the more conservative South. Republicans had lost seats in the North in the 1950s and 1960s and were making inroads in the South, but their future prospects in that region were not certain.

The consequence was two parties with diverse and internally conflicting electoral bases. Each party had a less than clear image of its policy concerns during the 1970s. Democrats were regularly accused of being too liberal (Edsall and Edsall 1991), but Southern Democrats dominated many House committees and their consistent conservative and negative reactions to legislation responding to social problems muddied the party's image. Blacks in the South were registered at much higher levels than in the 1950s, and their presence in campaigns appeared to reduce outright appeals to racism and put more emphasis on economic issues (Black 1976), but their overall electoral impact was not yet clear. Republicans, without Richard Nixon and his Southern strategy, did not seem sure of what direction to take and the future of the party was unclear.

The Argument

With the electoral bases and policy concerns of the parties somewhat un-settled as the 1970s began, social changes were developing in ways with the potential to shift the electoral bases of the parties. The three major changes reviewed in the prior chapter either had taken effect during the 1970s, or began to develop in that decade. Each social change contributed to further evolutions in the electoral bases and policy concerns of the con-gressional parties.

First, black registration, which had increased somewhat in the 1950s, rose dramatically in the 1960s, transforming the effective electorate in many House districts by the early 1970s. Northern Democrats espoused the concerns of Southern blacks in the early and mid–1960s, and with greater registration of this constituency, Democrats could count on elec-toral support in the South from this electoral base. Second, Latinos were steadily becoming a larger proportion of the U.S. population. They rep-resented a sizable new electoral base that could be mobilized. Third, in-equality steadily increased from the early 1970s through the 1990s. The combination of parties in flux and a changing American electorate even-tually culminated in the divisive electoral alignments that are driving the conflict we now see in the U.S. House.

By the 1980s, a clear process of realignment, to be discussed shortly, was under way. Ronald Reagan, elected president in 1980, articulated a distinct conservative vision and a clear argument against a significant role for the national government. He received considerable support in the South, and Republicans made further gains in House races in the South. The party was attracting more conservatives within the electorate and ac-quiring more of a conservative image. At the same time, the Democrats were finding their conservative base in the South declining as a part of the party. As economic inequality increased, the party was attracting less affluent voters and making more of an argument about the need to ad-dress issues of equity. Further, immigration was creating a new electoral base that needed government assistance and was prone to vote Democratic. The combination of a more conservative Republican Party and a Democratic Party with more constituents in need of government as-sistance pushed the parties further apart, and the electorate recognized this divergence. Finally, and most important for this analysis, these differing populations–conservatives and the affluent on one hand, and blacks, Latinos, and the less affluent on the other–spread across districts in an uneven fashion. A more diverse set of districts resulted, with the parties having very different rates of success in these divergent districts. The consequence was increasing polarization of party voting in the House of Representatives. These changes are complicated. Each will be explained in the following pages.

Notions of Realignment

The concept of realignment is widely used for thinking about American elections. It is often, however, used with different meanings (Petrocik 1981, 15–20). Some use the term to refer to a fundamental and enduring shift in the overall level of support for a party, without regard to who shifts. A major national event (a crisis such as the Depression or a party stand on an issue such as civil rights) may occur, and the electorate, reacting to the event, shifts its level of support for the two parties (Key 1955). Or, the shift can come about gradually because of erosion of support for one party (Key 1959). The issue of who shifts is sometimes of less interest than how overall levels of partisan support rise or fall after some event. A second use of the term refers to enduring shifts in support for a party within a group. Blacks may shift from supporting the Republican Party to the Democratic Party. Women may move to consistently support the Democrats more, as appears to have happened in the early 1980s. This shift in support by a group can occur abruptly or over a short period of time.

These two types of partisan changes can occur separately from each other. A general decline in support for one party could occur without any change in the relative support for the party across groups. Or a decline in support by one group (blacks) could be offset by greater support among another group (whites), but without a change in general levels of support for the two parties. Both can, of course, also occur at the same time.

While there is often considerable dispute about what kinds of change are more central to American politics–abrupt or gradual shifts in general levels of support, or shifts among groups, either abruptly or gradually–it appears that in this case both kinds of change are relevant for understanding House elections beginning in the 1980s. Within regions of the country there have been general and enduring shifts in levels of support for the parties. At the same time, there have been significant shifts in who supports each party. This has played out at the individual level, but most

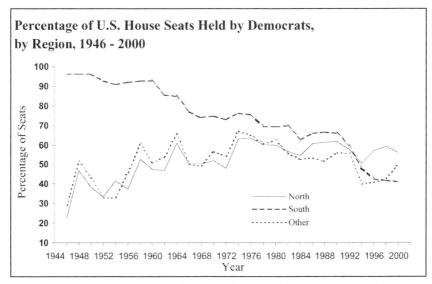

Percentage of U.S. House Seats Held by Democrats,
by Region, 1946 - 2000

FIGURE 5.1   Percentage of U.S. House Seats Held by Democrats, by
Region, 1946-2000

importantly for this analysis, at the district level. Further, while relationships between constituents and parties have evolved, the composition of
the nation, as discussed in the previous chapter, has changed. That has
created a new electoral base that simply was not present thirty years ago.
In part the parties have sorted out existing constituencies, but in part
there are now new constituencies. The cumulative result of all these
changes is a significant shift in the electoral bases of the two parties,
which has created the current party polarization.

The Broad Shifts in Partisan Support

The regional changes in loyalties under way during the 1950s and 1960s
did not slow down in subsequent decades. Figure 5.1 presents party success by region for 1946 through 2000. Democratic success in the South continued to decline after 1970, and following the 1994 elections, which gave
Republicans control of the House for the first time in fifty years, Democrats
experienced their greatest success in the North, while Republicans were
most successful in the South (Berkman 1993, 57–79). Each party, to be sure,
still wins seats in the regions largely dominated by the other party, but the
relative success of each party by region has shifted steadily and dramatically over time. This embodies the first notion of realignment, a fundamental shift in support for a party. In the South the shift was a remarkable

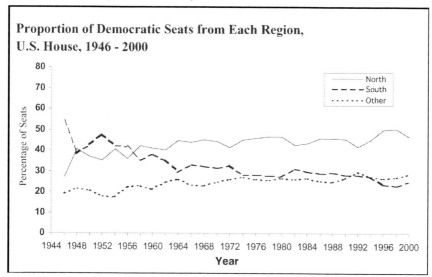

FIGURE 5.2 Proportion of Democratic Seats from Each Region, United
States House, 1946-2000

increase in support for the Republican Party, while in the North, across the
time period of 1946–2000, the Democratic Party made major gains.

The result has been a pronounced shift in the regional sources of party
support. Figures 5.2 and 5.3 indicate the percentage of Democratic and

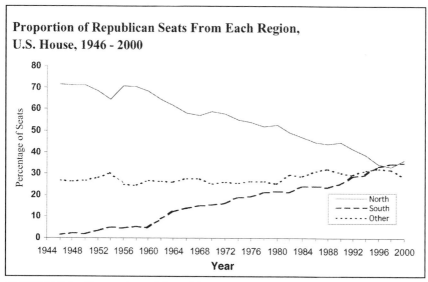

FIGURE 5.3 Proportion of Republican Seats from Each Region, United
States House, 1946-2000

Republican seats, respectively, derived from each region. The crucial matters are that over the last fifty years the Democratic Party has lost its heavy reliance on the South and become a party based more outside the South. The Republican Party, once heavily reliant on the North, now relies on the South as much as any other region. These trends began some time ago, as discussed in Chapter 3, but the last three decades have made the long-term shifts very clear.

While these changes in net levels of support are significant, the most important question is which constituents have shifted their party support as these regional shifts unfolded. The explanation of why the parties differ so much lies in who they represent and how that has changed in the last three decades.

Shifts in Group Support

The process of change is creating realignment at the individual and district level and is the basis for the party polarization occurring in the House. These changes have not come about quickly. The changes in economic situations and in the composition of the population have been gradual. The parties have taken some time to sense and react to the changes, and the electorate has surely reacted to changing party concerns with some delay. But with the advantage of perspective from the passage of time, the cumulative impact of changes is clear.

The important matter is how differences in party policy concerns have evolved over time such that groups of voters would see more reason to vote Republican or Democratic. For much of the 1940s and 1950s Democrats and Republicans in Congress did not differ dramatically in many of their policy positions. As noted earlier, the Democratic Party was a coalition of southern conservatives, and non-Southern moderates and liberals. Republicans in the North were relatively liberal and were not significantly different from Democrats (Sundquist 1983, 250–262). The 1950s witnessed the beginnings of change in the North. Within the Democratic Party, more liberally inclined Democrats began to replace older, more conservative Democrats. Liberal Republicans in Congress were replaced by liberal Democrats (Sundquist 1983, 262–268). While Democrats were gaining seats in the North, Republicans were winning more seats in conservative areas in the South and West. The party was developing a more conservative set of members (Rae 1989) and developing more of anti-government theme (Kazin 1995, 245–266).

Democratic officeholders and activists in the last several decades have begun to take contrasting and more liberal positions than Republicans on using government to support welfare spending, raising the minimum wage, providing tax credits for the working poor, and supporting job training programs (Pomper 1972; Wilson 1985, 300–307; Aldrich 1995, 169–173). Democrats in Congress increasingly voted for liberal positions, and Republicans voted for more conservative positions (Taylor 1996, 279–281). Democratic candidates for Congress are now more likely to support public spending on public education, health care, jobs retraining, and increased taxes on higher incomes (Erikson and Wright 1997, 137–138; 2001, 74–76).

One of the first and most significant issues to reflect the emerging differences between the parties involved race. The civil rights confrontations of the 1960s played a very significant role in initiating a redefinition of the parties. President Lyndon Johnson led the effort to enact legislation to establish rights for blacks, and Barry Goldwater, the Republican presidential candidate in 1964, firmly opposed these federal actions. After that Democrats became much more supportive of civil rights laws than Republicans, and black support for the Democratic Party increased significantly (Carmines, Renten, and Stimson 1984; Carmines and Stimson 1989). Beginning in the late 1960s many Republicans reinforced this party difference by appealing to the resentment felt by whites about government efforts to push for integration and later affirmative action. They portrayed government efforts to redress racial inequalities as treading on people's rights and government policymakers as elites forming policies that affected the masses more than elites (Kazin 1995, 245–266). The result has been a systematic and sustained shift of black support from Republicans to Democrats.

While race issues were dividing the parties, differences on economic issues also became greater in the 1980s and 1990s. As the 1980s unfolded Democrats regularly called attention to the shifting distribution of income and to the distributional effects of tax cuts. The party used the House Ways and Means Committee to regularly publish studies documenting the extent of inequality and arguing the need to address issues of equality of opportunity (DeParle 1991, A12). During the 1990s Republicans regularly proposed tax cuts with the bulk of benefits going to the more affluent. Democrats in turn sought to prevent large cuts for these voters and stressed the inequity in benefits by income level (Brinkley 1999; Stevenson 1999; Stonecash and Milstein 2001).

During the 1980s and 1990s the parties also have continually presented different positions on the role government should play in society. Republicans emphasized the importance of reducing the role of government and allowing free markets to determine outcomes, while Democrats consistently emphasized the importance of trying to respond to economic change by helping displaced workers make transitions to new jobs (Dionne 1997, 151–230). After Republicans gained control of Congress following the 1994 elections they continually sought to reduce government regulations on business and to reduce many benefits for the less affluent (Stonecash 2000, 82–84).

These positions did not go unnoticed by voters. As these differences in party policy positions developed, the proportion of the electorate seeing a difference between the parties increased from approximately 50 percent in the 1960s to 71 percent in 2000.[1] The proportion seeing the Republican Party as conservative has also increased, rising from 60 percent in the 1960s to 80 percent by the late 1990s (Sundquist 1983, 418–424, 444–446; Aldrich 1995, 174; Jacobson 2000a).

Electoral Alignments at the Individual Level

The concern here is with how changes involving House districts might explain increased partisan voting in the House. Changes at the district level are of primary concern, but how individuals have responded to the parties over the last several decades is also important. There are limits to focusing on individuals, which will be discussed, but the combination of individual and district-level changes tells us much about the sources of current polarization.

The simple principle of how electoral alignments emerge is that "realignment theory comes down to the notion that something happens and the public responds" (Carmines, Renten, and Stimson 1984, 545). If racial, economic, and ideological divisions have become more salient, we should see greater voting divisions by race, class, and ideology in the electorate. With regard to the first, the sharp difference in partisan voting between blacks and whites since the 1960s has been widely documented and need only be noted here (Carmines and Stimson 1989). Currently about 85–90 percent of blacks vote for Democratic candidates, while, as will be shown later, Latino/Hispanics in 2000 supported Democrats 64 percent to 35 percent, and about 45 percent of whites vote Democratic. The race divisions are fairly clear.

If economic inequality is increasing and the parties are diverging in their responses, we should also see greater partisan divisions by income over time. Table 5.1 summarizes the pattern of changes for the last five decades. The results are from the National Election Study, a national survey taken every two years. Only whites are included since most of the debate about class has focused on the behavior of whites (Stonecash 2000, 93–94). The table presents by income groups the percentage voting Democratic for presidential and House candidates, and the percentage identifying with the party. The results presented are the average of the yearly results within each decade. In addition, the table presents the difference between the averages for the bottom and top third of income groups by decade. In the 1950s differences in voting by income were limited. Beginning in the 1980s differences in voting for and identifying with the parties by income started to increase, and during the 1990s it was at the highest level recorded in the fifty years of NES results. The evidence suggests that realignment by income has developed since the 1970s (Stonecash and Mariani 2000; Stonecash et al. 2000; Brewer and Stonecash 2001).

Differences in ideology have also become more important as a source of partisan divisions since the 1970s (Abramowitz 1994, 12–16). The NES surveys ask respondents, since the 1970s, where they place themselves on a seven-point scale of liberal to conservative. In the 1970s differences in self-location were associated with which party people voted for, but in recent years this association has steadily increased (Abramowitz 1995, 878; Abramowitz and Saunders 1998; Jacobson 2000a, 2000b). Conservatives have steadily moved to identify with the Republican Party, and now constitute a larger proportion of the party (Stonecash 2000, 65; Jacobson 2000b; Abramowitz and Saunders 2000).

Finally, as party positions and electoral attachments have sorted out, the commitment of voters to their party has increased.[2] The percentage of those who identify with a party and also vote for candidates of the party was about 85 percent in the 1950s and 1960s, and then dipped into the mid–70 percent range in the 1970s. After that it rose steadily to the upper 80s (Bartells 2000). At the individual level, the evidence indicates increased divisions revolving around race and economic and ideological positions. The commitment to party has also increased.

This evidence of the polarization of the electorate is based on national surveys. We may assume that the pattern is occurring within most districts, though we cannot underestimate the ability of individual candidates to create unique appeals that dampen these divisions within their

Income and Ideological Divisions: Percent Voting and Identifying with Democrats, By Income and Ideological Groups, by Decade, 1950s-1990s Whites Only

Decade	Presidential Voting			House Election Voting			Party Identification		
Income	Low	High	Diff	Low	High	Diff	Low	High	Diff
1950s	42	38	4	56	48	8	55	51	4
1960s	49	47	2	56	52	4	54	51	3
1970s	42	33	9	61	49	12	53	45	8
1980s	46	30	16	62	48	14	53	40	13
1990s	56	38	18	61	41	20	54	39	15
Change	14	0	14	5	-7	12	-1	-12	11
Ideology	Lib	Cons	Diff	Lib	Cons	Diff	Lib	Cons	Diff
1970s	72	18	55	75	43	32	73	32	41
1980s	70	21	49	78	39	38	75	30	45
1990s	81	23	58	79	31	48	81	26	55
Change	9	5	3	4	-12	16	8	-6	14

Numbers are the percent indicating they either voted for Democrats in the presidential (vcf0705) and House elections (vcf0707), or identified with the Democratic Party (vcf0303). The percentages for each year within a decade are averaged. The data are taken from the National Election Studies files for 1952 - 1998. Source: Warren Miller and the National Election Studies, American National Election Studies Cumulative Data File, 1948 — 1998[Computer file]. 10[th]ICPSR version. Ann Arbor, MI: University of Michigan, Center for Political Studies [producer], 1999. Ann Arbor, MI: Inter-university Consortium for Political and Social Research [distributor], 1999. To derive the groupings of low and high (bottom and top third) of income groupings, the groupings of family income for each year were re-coded so that those in the 0 - 33 percentile were in the bottom third, and those in the 66 - 100 percentile were coded as top third. Whites only are included because for the last several decades this has been the conventional approach. To derive the ideology response groupings, scores of 1-3 were grouped as liberal, while those 5-7 were grouped as conservative. Those with a score of 4 are coded as moderate.

TABLE 5.1   Income and Ideological Divisions: Percent Voting and Identifying with Democrats, by Income and Ideological Groups, by Decade, 1950s to 1990s, Whites Only

own party. Unfortunately, the task of gathering sufficient-sized samples across 435 House districts is huge, we have no such samples now, and it is unlikely that we will have such samples in the near future.

The Crucial Issue of Population Composition Across Districts

While individual level analyses provide very useful information about broad electoral patterns in American politics, they do not accurately capture the connection between district constituencies and parties in congressional elections. National surveys involve a sample aggregated to the national level, and ignore the spatial distribution of differing groups across districts.[3] Members of Congress are elected in districts that differ in their composition. When candidates for the House conduct campaigns, they react to and seek to appeal to the population in their district (Rohde 1991; Herrnson 1998, 8–9; Jacobson 1997, 11–16). Democrats in liberal districts, measured as higher election support for Democratic presidential candidates, advocate liberal policy positions. Republicans in conservative districts (high support for Republican presidential candidates) advocate conservative positions (Snyder and Groseclose 2000; Ansolabehere et al. 2001).

Likewise, when parties assess their chances of winning seats, they decide which districts are most amenable to a victory for their candidates and focus their efforts there (Stonecash 1988; Stonecash and Keith 1996; Herrnson 1998, 76–80). If our concern is on the relationship between constituencies and member voting, then we need to focus on variations in district composition and how that composition affects which party wins elections (Stonecash 1989, 1992).

The importance of how populations are distributed is illustrated in Table 5.2. The top part of the table presents individual distributions and partisan inclinations for a single district. If all national results are aggregated, the results are treated as if one national district is involved. The first column on the left indicates the composition of the electorate in this district by income. The winner receives approximately 150 of the 300 votes and might be a Democrat or a Republican.

Assume that for this single district there is then a shift in support by groups, or in this example, a realignment by income. The right side of the table indicates the partisan inclinations of this more divided electorate. Even though there is a greater class division, it is still assumed to occur within one district. Since the distribution of the population across the district remains the same, an electorate divided more by income is just more divided, and either a Democrat or Republican could win. The impact on the district outcome is unknown.

The bottom part of the table introduces multiple districts and an uneven distribution of the population across districts. In the left side of the table, the three districts have the same electoral alignment. Because each district has a different population composition, the partisan outcomes differ. In District 1 a Democrat wins narrowly, in District 3 a Democrat loses narrowly, and in District 2 the outcome is unknown. If a realignment of the electorate by income occurs, as shown in the columns to the right, this combined with the distribution of the population results in larger margins of victory in the districts dominated by one income group or the other. Realignment matters for electoral outcomes, but in combination with how the population is distributed. Results of aggregated national

Alternative Distributions of a National Sample of Voters Across Districts

District & Income Groups	Number of Voters	Initial Alignment		After Realignment	
		% Voting Democratic	Democratic Votes	% Voting Democratic	Democratic Votes
Example one: one single district or all districts the same					
Low	100	55	55	70	70
Medium	100	50	50	50	50
High	100	45	45	30	30
Total Democratic Votes			150		150
Example two: districts diverse in population composition					
# 1					
Low	150	55	83	70	105
Medium	100	50	50	50	50
High	50	45	23	30	15
Total Democratic Votes			156		170
# 2					
Low	100	55	55	70	70
Medium	100	50	50	50	50
High	100	45	45	30	30
Total Democratic Votes			150		150
# 3					
Low	50	55	28	70	35
Medium	100	50	50	50	50
High	150	45	68	30	45
Total Democratic Votes			146		130

TABLE 5.2 Alternative Distributions of a National Sample of Voters Across Districts

surveys, while helpful for understanding broad national changes in alignments by income, race, and ideology, do not tell us anything about the distribution of the population across districts (Stonecash and Lindstrom 1999).[4] To understand the behavior of members, we need to focus on districts and their variations.

We also need to take into account the significant regional changes that have occurred. A national analysis conceals the regional changes occurring, and it also conceals the shifts in what kinds of districts vote Democrat and Republican. To understand these regional changes, we will first conduct separate regional analysis, with a focus on what changes have occurred that might explain the growing polarization of the parties in the House. We will then consider the entire nation.

In each region of the nation one or both of two crucial changes involving districts have occurred, and these changes have in turn shaped the constituency basis of conflict within the House. First, realignments have occurred, with the emergence of differences in partisan outcomes by the nature of the district that did not exist before. Second, the distribution of districts within regions has shifted. The explanation of the basis of the current situation lies in how these two changes have combined.

The North

Change has occurred in the North in the alignment of districts and in the composition of districts. As Table 5.3 indicates, the extent of urbanization and the racial composition of the district have affected partisan outcomes since the 1960s. Urban districts consistently elect Democrats at a much higher rate, as do districts that have more than 20 percent non-whites. The major change has involved income. In the 1960s there was virtually no relationship between the income of districts and partisan outcomes. Over time the relationship of income to partisan outcomes increased, with the correlation between income and the presence of a Democrat winner changing from -.07 to -.24. This negative association means that as income increases, the chances of a Democrat winning decrease. By the 1990s Democrats were less likely to win as income increases than in prior decades.

In regard to the diversity of districts over time, the most significant change is the increase in the percentage of districts that contain 20 percent or more of non-whites. This percentage is crucial because at about that level of non-whites the probability of a Democrat winning increases significantly. In the 1960s 11 percent of Northern House districts had 20 percent or more of non-whites. By the 1990 census 20 percent of Northern districts were in this category. As the predominance of these districts increases, it increases the probability that Democrats will win more northern seats in the House.

The South

The pattern of change in the South has been somewhat different. Over the last several decades the South has experienced dramatic economic change. There has been a steady migration to the South and a significant growth in the industrial and service sectors in the region (Black and Black 1987, 23–72). The diversity of income among districts has

Alignments and the Nature of Northern House Districts, 1960s to 1990s
District Distributions and the Percentage of Seats Won by Democrats,
All Elections Within a Decade Grouped

	1960s			1970s			1980s			1990s		
Income ($)	#	%	% D	#	%	% D	#	%	% D	#	%	% D
0-37,999	290	27	55	185	18	66	219	22	67	115	13	85
38-47,999	585	54	50	525	50	58	520	53	62	345	38	54
48,000 +	215	20	40	345	33	52	240	25	48	450	49	49
correlation			-.07			-.10			-.20			-.24
% Urban												
0-69	476	44	31	405	38	39	412	42	43	345	38	38
70-79	84	8	32	130	12	38	95	10	45	110	12	49
80-89	115	11	48	80	8	74	90	9	69	100	11	51
90 +	415	38	75	440	42	77	382	39	80	355	39	75
correlation			.38			.35			.32			.25
% Non-white												
0-9	850	78	41	780	74	49	624	64	48	510	56	42
10-19	125	11	69	150	14	67	190	19	72	220	24	59
20 +	115	11	95	125	12	94	165	17	93	180	20	90
correlation			.34			.29			.32			.34
Total	1090			1055			979			910		

The # is the number of elections held in that category of districts within the decade. The % is the distribution of districts across the grouped categories within a decade, and they sum down to 100. The % Dem is the percentage of districts within each category that were won by Democrats.

For the above results, all elections within a decade, following reapportionment, are grouped together. Since reapportionment does not take effect until two years following a census, this means that each decade's results begin in 1972, 1982, and 1992. The five elections for the 1970s are 1972, 1974, 1976, 1978, and 1980. The same pattern prevails for the 1980s and 1990s. The results are the number of elections (the number of seats * 5 elections) that occurred within the decade followed by the percentage of those elections won by Democrats. All income data have been corrected for inflation, and dollar values are expressed in 2000 dollar values. For sources, see the Appendix on Congressional District Data.

TABLE 5.3   Alignments and the Nature of Northern House Districts,
1960s to 1990s

increased. While the North is experiencing an increase in the number of House districts with a substantial percentage of non-whites, and no change in urbanization, the South is going in the opposite direction. Economic development is bringing about an increase in urbanization (Fenno 2000, 94–104) and an influx of whites. As Table 5.4 indicates, in the 1960s 57 percent of districts had 20 percent or more non-whites, and by the 1990s this had dropped to 51 percent. In the 1960s 9 percent of districts were 90 percent or more urban, and by the 1990s 24 percent of districts were in that category.

Alignments and the Nature of Southern House Districts, 1960s to 1990s
District Distributions and the Percentage of Seats Won by Democrats,
All Elections Within a Decade Grouped

Income ($)	1960s #	%	% D	1970s #	%	% D	1980s #	%	% D	1990s #	%	% D
0-37,999	520	92	81	429	75	72	445	72	72	300	46	64
38-47,999	35	6	69	120	21	73	125	20	58	255	39	35
48,000 +	10	2	50	25	3	44	45	7	22	100	15	23
correlation			-.14			-.18			-.33			-.31
% urban												
0-69	445	79	80	375	65	70	350	57	72	345	53	44
70-79	25	4	88	35	6	91	60	10	37	80	12	33
80-89	45	8	73	45	8	56	60	10	40	75	11	36
90 +	50	9	84	120	21	75	145	24	75	155	24	65
correlation			.01			-.04			-.13			.09
% non-white												
0-9	120	21	70	145	25	61	115	19	51	160	25	25
10-19	125	22	79	175	30	69	180	29	56	155	24	23
20 +	320	57	84	254	44	78	320	52	77	340	51	69
correlation			.18			.15			.25			.49
Total	565			572			615			655		

The # is the number of elections held in that category of districts within the decade. The % is the distribution of districts across the grouped categories within a decade, and they sum down to 100. The % Dem is the percentage of districts within each category that were won by Democrats.

For the above results, all elections within a decade, following reapportionment, are grouped together. Since reapportionment does not take effect until two years following a census, this means that each decade's results begin in 1972, 1982, and 1992. The five elections for the 1970s are 1972, 1974, 1976, 1978, and 1980. The same pattern prevails for the 1980s and 1990s. The results are the number of elections (the number of seats * 5 elections) that occurred within the decade followed by the percentage of those elections won by Democrats. All income data have been corrected for inflation, and dollar values are expressed in 2000 dollar values. For sources, see the Appendix on Congressional District Data.

TABLE 5.4   Alignments and the Nature of Southern House Districts, 1960s to 1990s

There have also been changes in the relationship of district composition to partisan success. Demography had a limited relationship to partisan success in the 1960s, but now the South looks more like the North. Districts that are heavily urban are prone to elect Democrats and there are now more of these districts. Rural districts are likely to elect Republicans, creating a relationship between urbanization and party. Districts that have 20 percent more of non-whites are prone to elect Democrats and in the South 50 percent of all districts are in this category. Black registration in these districts also is much higher than it was in the 1960s, giving blacks greater impact. Districts that are primarily white are electing

Republicans at high rates, creating a stronger relationship between racial composition and partisan outcomes.

Finally, the economic change in the South has created many more affluent districts, and these districts strongly support Republicans. An income-based alignment has emerged because of the greater income diversity of House districts and because of the emergence of a stronger association between income and partisan outcomes across the districts. The result of all these changes is that the South now has political alignments between income, urbanization, and racial composition much like those in the North.

The Remainder of the Nation

Changes in the remainder of the nation, all states excluding the North and South, are different from the other two regions. While income realignments now play a role in the North and South, there has been no such development in the remainder of the nation. For the last forty years, as shown in Table 5.5, at the district level within this region, there has not been a relationship between income and which party wins seats. However, there also has been a steady growth in the role of urbanization and percentage of non-whites. For both, the correlation between these conditions and partisan outcomes has increased over time.

While those changes are significant, the more significant changes have been in the prevalence of districts with high levels of urbanization and percentages of non-white. In the 1960s 30 percent of House districts in this region were 90 percent urban. By the 1990s the percentage of urban districts here had increased to 44. Perhaps the greatest change was in the percentage of districts that are 20 percent non-white. In the 1960s only 8 percent of House districts in this region fell into that category. By the 1990s 40 percent of districts were in that category, and the 2000 census shows an even greater increase. The immigration discussed earlier had a remarkable impact in this region in altering the types of districts.

The remainder of the nation, then, has experienced growing alignment around the urbanization and racial composition of House districts. At the same time the prevalence of districts with a substantial proportion of non-whites has increased dramatically. While there was a time when it was presumed that the Sunbelt states, particularly in the West, would drift Republican (Phillips 1969), the composition of the region is shifting toward a constituency base that is currently more favorable to the Democratic Party.

Alignments in Other House Districts, 1960s to 1990s
District Traits and Percentage of Seats Won by Democrats,
All Elections Within a Decade Grouped

	1960s			1970s			1980s			1990s		
Income ($)	#	%	% D	#	%	% D	#	%	% D	#	%	% D
0-37,999	171	33	53	160	29	52	185	32	58	125	20	49
38-47,999	255	49	61	255	47	65	290	50	58	270	44	47
48,000 +	95	18	43	130	24	59	105	18	34	215	35	45
correlation			-.08			.03			-.16			-.02
% urban												
0-69	276	53	52	210	39	52	196	34	46	175	29	32
70-79	45	9	43	70	13	70	89	15	42	65	11	37
80-89	45	9	56	50	9	52	65	11	38	100	16	31
90 +	155	30	64	215	39	66	230	40	69	270	44	64
correlation			.11			.15			.18			.23
% non-white												
0-9	440	84	49	420	77	54	235	41	39	205	34	32
10-19	36	7	89	75	14	76	170	29	42	160	26	36
20 +	45	9	88	50	9	82	175	30	85	245	40	65
correlation			.29			.18			.37			.43
Total	515			545			581			610		

The # is the number of elections held in that category of districts within the decade. The % is the distribution of districts across the grouped categories within a decade, and they sum down to 100. The % Dem is the percentage of districts within each category that were won by Democrats.

For the above results, all elections within a decade, following reapportionment, are grouped together. Since reapportionment does not take effect until two years following a census, this means that each decade's results begin in 1972, 1982, and 1992. The five elections for the 1970s are 1972, 1974, 1976, 1978, and 1980. The same pattern prevails for the 1980s and 1990s. The results are the number of elections (the number of seats * 5 elections) that occurred within the decade followed by the percentage of those elections won by Democrats. All income data have been corrected for inflation, and dollar values are expressed in 2000 dollar values. For sources, see the Appendix on Congressional District Data.

TABLE 5.5   Alignments in "Other" House Districts, 1960s to 1990s

The Nation

Regional changes have altered the national partisan alignment in ways obvious and subtle. In the 1960s, as shown in Table 5.6, there was a national relationship between income, levels of urbanization, and the percentage of non-whites. The income relationship was, however, largely a product of the regional distribution of income. The South was poor and overwhelmingly Democratic. The North was much more affluent and 50 percent Republican. The two regions occupied the opposite ends of the income distribution, and their partisan tendencies created an apparent national relationship between income and partisan outcomes in the 1960s.

Alignments in All House Districts, 1960s to 1990s
District Traits and Percentage of Seats Won by Democrats,
All Elections Within a Decade Grouped

	1960s			1970s			1980s			1990s		
Income ($)	#	%	% D	#	%	% D	#	%	% D	#	%	% D
0-37,999	981	45	69	774	29	52	849	39	68	540	25	65
38-47,999	875	40	54	900	47	65	935	43	60	870	40	46
48,000 +	320	15	41	500	24	59	390	18	42	765	35	44
correlation			-.22			-.13			-.23			-.16
% urban												
0-69	1197	55	54	990	46	53	958	44	54	865	39	40
70-79	154	7	46	235	11	55	244	11	41	255	12	41
80-89	205	9	55	175	8	63	215	10	52	275	13	40
90 +	620	28	73	775	36	74	757	35	76	780	36	69
correlation			.12			.16			.14			.19
% non-white												
0-9	1410	65	46	1345	62	52	974	45	46	875	40	36
10-19	286	13	76	400	18	69	540	25	57	535	25	41
20 +	480	22	87	429	20	83	660	30	83	765	35	73
correlation			.36			.25			.32			.38
Total	2175			2175			2175			2175		

The # is the number of elections held in that category of districts within the decade. The % is the distribution of districts across the grouped categories within a decade, and they sum down to 100. The % Dem is the percentage of districts within each category that were won by Democrats.

For the above results, all elections within a decade, following reapportionment, are grouped together. Since reapportionment does not take effect until two years following a census, this means that each decade's results begin in 1972, 1982, and 1992. The five elections for the 1970s are 1972, 1974, 1976, 1978, and 1980. The same pattern prevails for the 1980s and 1990s. The results are the number of elections (the number of seats * 5 elections) that occurred within the decade followed by the percentage of those elections won by Democrats. All income data have been corrected for inflation, and dollar values are expressed in 2000 dollar values. For sources, see the Appendix on Congressional District Data.

TABLE 5.6   Alignments in All House Districts, 1960s to 1990s

Beginning in the 1970s the diversity of districts by income began to increase in all regions, with the more affluent districts electing Republicans. In the North the less affluent districts began to elect Democrats, such that by the 1990s the relationship between income and partisan outcomes had increased. Little change occurred in the remainder of the nation in this regard. While the national table appears largely stable over time in this relationship, underlying it is the emergence of stronger relationships between income and party in two of the three regions of the nation.

In regard to the percentage of districts that are non-white, two significant changes emerged. The prevalence of districts with a substantial

proportion of non-whites increased, and the differences in partisan outcomes as the impact of increases in the presence of non-whites increased
became greater. With regard to the prevalence of non-whites, in the
South the percentage of districts in this category remained unchanged,
but in those districts blacks now have a direct effect on who wins elections. In the North and the remainder of the nation, there was a significant increase in the presence of districts with 20 percent or more non-
whites. In the 1960s 22 percent of all House districts had 20 percent or
more of non-whites. By the 1990s it was at 35 percent, and the 2000 census indicates that 50 percent of House districts are now in that category.

Further, the relationship between the presence of non-whites and
partisan outcomes, which declined in the 1970s, has increased–not nationally, and not in the North, but in the South and the remainder of
the nation. Much of this is because districts that are primarily white
have moved more Republican. In the 1960s there was a relationship between presence of non-whites and party choice, but it was largely due
to regional distributions of non-whites and partisan loyalties. There
were 480 cases where an election took place and a district had 20 percent or more non-whites. The 320 of these that were in the South overwhelmingly elected Democrats (84 percent). This regional concentration of non-whites and the heavy dominance of Democrats in that
region created a national relationship. By the 1990s there were 765 elections in such districts, and only 340 (44 percent of all) were in the
South. In all regions the presence of non-whites was strongly associated with the election of Democrats. Just as with income, the national
relationship now meant something about the differences in party success by district type, and the developing differences in the electoral
bases of the parties.

The Polarization of Party Support

The shifts shown here, while significant, are bivariate in nature. That is,
they present differences in electoral support by variation in just one district condition. The reality of American society is that districts are a combination of multiple traits. To capture some of the effects of these multiple traits, Table 5.7 classifies districts within each decade by relative
affluence (median family income, corrected for inflation, and expressed
in 1990 dollars) *and* the percentage non-white. Only two traits, rather
than all three, are used for each decade. To represent the relative support
for the parties, the partisan inclinations of districts are expressed as the

percentage advantage for Democratic candidates in the district. The vote percentage for the Republican candidate is subtracted from the percentage for the Democratic candidate. The result for each cell in the table is the average Democratic advantage or disadvantage for the district type. A negative number means that Democrats were losing to Republicans, on average. The important matter is what has happened to the average party advantage in recent decades by type of district.

In the 1960s Democrats had an advantage in most categories, but this advantage varied greatly by the constituency within a district. Their advantage was greatest in less affluent districts with a relatively high percentage of non-whites and least in primarily white, more affluent districts. Those districts along the diagonal from the upper left to the lower right fall between the two extreme types of districts, and their voting results are also in between the two. The Democratic advantage declined moving from the upper righthand corner (lower income–higher percentage of non-white) to the lower left hand corner (higher income–few non-whites), but Republicans did not have a significant advantage in the latter type of district.

By the 1990s the situation had clearly shifted in two ways. The average Democratic advantage had declined across all district types. The crucial change, however, was that Republicans moved from marginal success in the primarily white, more affluent districts to a distinct advantage in these districts. Polarization in party support has emerged by district type, with Republicans having much safer margins in the primarily white, more affluent districts and Democrats having much safer margins in more non-white, less affluent districts. This polarization of party support by district conditions has changed the electoral bases of the parties. Republicans now find themselves more secure in the former type of district, while Democrats still find themselves relatively secure in the latter type district. There are still, to be sure, districts where the "type" does not clearly favor one party or the other, and margins are close in those districts, but polarization of outcome has emerged at the edges of the tables in 5.7.

The Dynamics of Change

The shifts in the electoral bases of House party candidates did not happen in isolation. They were part of a larger shift in the connection, at the district level, between constituencies and partisan outcomes. The same district factors came to have a greater effect on presidential

The Polarization of Party Support:
Democratic Advantage in the Nation, 1960s - 1990s

District Median	Percentage Non-White		
Family Income ($)	0 - 9	10 - 19	20 plus
1960s			
0 - 37,999	5.7	38.3	52.8
38 - 47,999	.7	22.9	38.4
48,000 +	-8.6	7.6	16.0
1970s			
0 - 37,999	7.7	22.8	50.7
38 - 47,999	5.7	24.7	36.2
48,000 +	.8	5.1	41.5
1980s			
0 - 37,999	-4.7	19.9	46.3
38 - 47,999	4.8	7.3	27.3
48,000 +	-13.6	-9.6	18.5
1990s			
0 - 37,999	-6.1	-7.1	31.8
38 - 47,999	-18.7	-11.0	23.8
48,000 +	-10.4	-7.5	14.2

TABLE 5.7 The Polarization of Party Support: Democratic Advantage in the Nation, 1960s to 1990s

elections, with the result that the association between House and presidential results also increased. Table 5.8 presents the average Democratic presidential result by the demographics of House districts across decades. There has been a remarkable shift for two of the three demographic categories. Urbanization has had a consistent and positive impact on Democratic voting. For the other two traits, however, there has been a significant change. In the 1960s the correlation between district income and presidential voting was *positive*. That is, more affluent districts had higher percentages of support for Democratic candidates. In the 1970s the association became negative, and it has remained so since then.

Average Democratic Presidential Vote
by House District Demographics, 1960s - 1990s

Decade

Income ($)	60s	70s	80s	90s
0-29,999	42	49	58	62
30-34,999	51	45	44	51
35-39,999	55	44	42	47
40-44,999	56	45	43	45
45-49,999	56	41	45	46
50-54,999	51	41	41	49
55-59,999	51	41	38	48
60-64,999	54	40	35	48
65,000 +	44	37	40	47
correlation	.25	-.13	-.24	-.10
% urban				
0-69	47	41	41	42
70-79	51	41	37	43
80-89	55	42	40	45
90 +	61	49	51	57
correlation	.39	.23	.30	.45
% non-white				
0-9	53	41	41	42
10-19	55	44	40	45
20 +	48	53	52	56
correlation	-.02	.46	.61	.70

TABLE 5.8   Average Democratic Presidential Vote by House
District Demographics, 1960s to 1990s

Perhaps the most remarkable change has involved the relationship of
the racial composition of districts to presidential votes. In the 1960s this
relationship was slightly negative. Those districts with high percentages
of non-whites supported Democratic presidential candidates at rates
lower than primarily white districts. This was probably because in many

Southern districts with higher percentages of non-whites, blacks were prevented from voting. Nonetheless, the relationship was negative. Since then the relationship has become steadily more positive. Just as with House district results, the racial composition of districts has become more important in affecting partisan voting patterns.

These are again bivariate relationships, and since all these district traits are related, it is valuable to assess the independent effects of each of these traits. Table 5.9 presents the regression of the Democratic vote for House and presidential candidates by House district on the three demographic traits. A dummy variable for the South is also included to control for the enormous advantage Democrats had in this region for decades, and to assess whether the significance of region has declined over time. In the 1960s the relationships to party support for the two offices were very different. The presence of the South and higher levels of non-whites had a negative association with voting for Democratic presidential candidates, but in House elections they had a positive effect. From the 1970s to the 1990s both coefficients gravitated to the same levels in both types of elections. The South now has a negative coefficient in both elections.

For the demographic conditions, the most significant change is the emergence of the percentage non-white as a primary factor affecting voting for Democratic House and presidential candidates. District income and urbanization remain negative, but they have declined in impact, after controlling for other factors.

The result is that House and presidential voting patterns are now affected in similar ways by district conditions. The overall explanatory impact of district demographics is less for House elections, as might be expected. In those elections there are 435 candidates, as opposed to one presidential candidate, and individual candidates can create some diminished impact of district conditions, relative to presidential voting patterns. Nonetheless, the relationships for presidential and House elections are now more similar than was the case several decades ago.

The consequence of this similarity of the impact of demographic factors on House and presidential voting is that the correlation between House and presidential results has increased in the last several decades. This association in the 1960s was .60, and grew from the 1970s through the 1990s to the mid .80s (Jacobson 2000a, 21). As of the 1990s, it was at its highest levels in fifty years. These elections are now shaped by the same social conditions, regionalism plays less of a role, and a greater association between the two is to be expected.

	1960s	1970s	1980s	1990s
Effects of District Demographics on House and Presidential Democratic Vote, 1960s - 1990s (standardized regression coefficients)				
House elections				
Income	-.50	-.32	.25	-.18
Percent urban	.43	.27	.13	.13
Percent non-white	.21	.18	.22	.42
South	.17	.05	-.01	-.21
R^2	.37	.18	.16	.30
Presidential elections				
Income	-.37	-.26	-.25	-.08
Percent urban	.50	.26	.16	.16
Percent non-white	-.03	.39	.55	.64
South	-.46	-.21	-.37	-.24
R^2	.28	.28	.52	.57

Note: the coefficients are standardized regression coefficients, which indicate how a change in the dependent variable (in standard deviation units) is associated with a one standard deviation change in the independent variable.

TABLE 5.9   Effects of District Demographics on Hosue and Presidential Democratic Vote, 1960s to 1990s

An Unfinished Realignment?

The patterns just reviewed indicate that a realignment revolving around class, race, and urbanization has evolved over the thirty years beginning in the 1970s. To return to the discussion of Chapter 3, this change developed over one hundred years. In the early 1900s the Democratic Party was confined largely to its base in the rural and conservative South, where only whites voted. The Republican Party was based primarily in the North, where it won in urban and ethnic districts. Through a long process, the parties in many ways reversed constituencies, even as new constituencies have been added.

While realignment trends are clear, it is important to note that they are by no means complete. Demographics do not "determine" partisan outcomes. Republicans still win some seats in urban districts with substantial percentages of non-whites. Democrats still win seats in largely rural districts that are primarily white and have relatively low incomes. While a clear alignment has emerged, it is by no means complete and it has not lead to a complete polarization of electoral bases. Indeed, we have much to understand as to how such victories occur. We will also have to wait and see whether these patterns persist, or whether change continues and the electoral bases of the parties become more polarized. The possible responses of the parties to these trends and the future of party polarization will be discussed at the conclusion of the next chapter.

Regardless of whether realignment is finished, it is clear that social change and realignment have combined over the last several decades to create two parties with diverging electoral bases. In the next chapter, the connection of this polarization of electoral bases to voting in the House will be addressed.

Notes

1. The 71 percent figure is taken from the 2000 NES data released in spring 2001. Earlier years are from Aldrich (1995, 172).

2. In this case, leaners are added to those who identify or weakly identify.

3. Reliance on the NES data set is flawed because it is an aggregated sample of the entire nation. It is also flawed because the NES samples in only about one-fourth to one-third of the House districts in most years (Mann and Wolfinger 1980, 619). This is appropriate because the goal is to obtain a random sample of the U.S. population. That goal, however, results in most House districts not being included in the sample. The table below indicates the number of House districts in the sample for each year since 1952.

The consequence of this is that if the NES data set is used to discuss how members are viewed by their constituents and what kinds of connections exist with their constituents, roughly two-thirds to three-fourths of constituencies are not included and cannot really be commented upon. The only basis for making such inferences would be to assume that these connections are essentially the same across the nation, and they are the same for those included in the sample and those not included. That uniformity of relationships cannot be ascertained if the larger portion of House districts is not included in the sample.

4. The problem with the individual-level analyses is that they ignore the issues of the composition of districts and changes in this composition over time. Aldrich and Rohde, for example, argue that polarization has increased because: 1) party activists differ; 2) these differences have increased in recent decades, and 3) non-ideologues vote less (Aldrich and Rohde 2001, 275–278). While the evidence supports this assessment of change, this apparently assumes that the distribution of districts by demographic traits remains essentially the same over time, and the main source of change is the polarization within relatively stable districts. We agree that the electorate has polarized and cite many studies to that effect. But their explanation is limited to the first case in Table 5.1 and misses the remarkable

changes in the composition of American society in the last three decades. We accept their argument, but regard it as an accentuating condition, and probably not the primary source of change.

Number of House Districts Included in NES Samples, by Year			
Year	Number districts	Year	Number districts
1952	not coded	1976	163
1954	not coded	1978	108
1956	109	1980	113
1958	242	1982	169
1960	142	1984	134
1962	not coded	1986	181
1964	125	1988	131
1966	132	1990	120
1968	145	1992	185
1970	153	1994	191
1972	165	1996	248
1974	146	1998	129

TABLE 5.10   Number of House Districts Included in NES Samples, by Year

6

Constituencies and
Party Conflict

The Issue (Again)

The voting records of parties in the House of Representatives are steadily diverging. Using ratings of the Americans for Democratic Action ratings as an indicator, Figure 6.1 indicates that the average voting scores of Democrats and Republicans are moving further apart. During the 1970s the average Democratic ADA score was 54, while the Republican average was 20, a difference of 34 percentage points. By the 1990s Democrats had an average of 74 (a 20-point increase), while Republicans declined to an average of 14 (a 6-point decline). The average difference between the parties for the 1990s was 60, with the difference for 1998 reaching 71 percentage points. Party polarization in the House is increasing. The question is what changes are creating this divergence?

While much of this growing polarization has been attributed to changes in the South (Rohde 1991, 40–81; Bullock 2000, 39–64), the patterns for the two parties since the 1970s are fairly uniform across regions. Figures 6.2 and 6.3 present trends in ADA scores by region for each party. Democratic scores have increased in all regions since the 1970s, while Republicans had fairly constant ADA ratings in all regions until the 1990s, when their ratings dropped somewhat.

The South has, to be sure, experienced the greatest change. In the 1970s Southern Democrats were much more conservative than the remainder of the party. Since then their voting records have become much more liberal. The voting records of Democrats in the other regions have also become more liberal over time, but have not increased as much. The increases are national in scope.

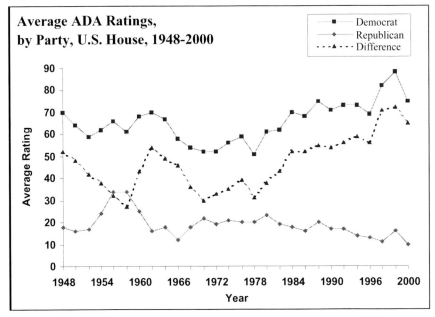

FIGURE 6.1   Average ADA Ratings, by Party, U.S. House, 1948-2000

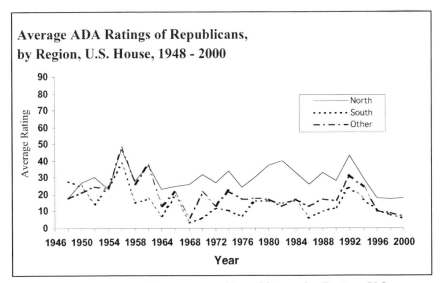

FIGURE 6.2   Average ADA Ratings of Republicans, by Region, U.S. House, 1948-2000

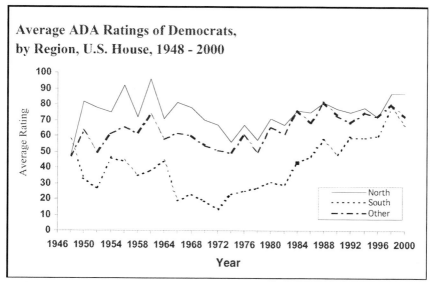

FIGURE 6.3   Average ADA Ratings of Democrats, by Region, U.S. House, 1948-2000

The Sources of Polarization: An Overview

The argument of this analysis is that party voting records are diverging because social change and realignment are creating parties with differing constituencies. The crucial basis of the analysis to follow is that the voting records of House members reflect, with some variation, the constituencies that elect them. Members from districts that are more rural and primarily white have more conservative voting records, reflected in lower ADA scores. Members from districts that are more urban and with a greater percentage of non-whites have more liberal voting records, and thus higher ADA scores.

Over the last several decades the changes discussed in Chapters 4 (social change) and 5 (realignment) have interacted to affect average party voting records. To simplify, realignment has brought the Democrats more districts with liberal inclinations while Republicans now win more districts that yield conservative inclinations. The demographic shifts within the nation are not, however, affecting each party equally. The major change to be explained is the increased liberal voting records of Democrats, since that party's voting records have experienced the greatest change. Social change has vastly increased the percentage of districts that tend to result in liberal voting records.

These broad changes have played out in different ways within regions. Within the South both social change and realignment have been significant. The registration of blacks in the South created Southern districts with substantial proportions of voting blacks. With the composition of the participating electorate altered, Southern districts with substantial percentages of minorities now elect liberal rather than conservative Democrats. The simultaneous emergence of relatively affluent suburban districts in the South created an electoral base more amenable to Republicans. Southern Republicans now win most of these more affluent districts and vote conservatively. The South has been transformed from a Democratic, but relatively conservative, region to a socially and economically diverse region with partisan divisions revolving around class and race. The relatively conservative wing of the Democratic Party has been replaced with a more liberal set of party members. At the same time, the Republican Party now derives more of its seats from the South, and these members come from districts that incline members to have conservative voting records.

In the North realignment resulted in the Democratic Party winning more of its seats in districts that are urban, lower-income, and more nonwhite. Members from these districts tend to have more liberal voting records. In the remainder of the nation, while realignment has played a minor role, the remarkable increase in the percentage of districts with significant proportions of non-whites has created more districts that result in members with liberal voting records.

The net effect has been a national increase in the number of districts that tend to produce more liberal voting records. To a considerable, but not complete, extent, the explanation of change is that the demographic profile of seats has shifted, such that there is now a greater base for liberal votes by Democratic Party members. While the changes are complicated, the goal here will be to simplify the changes so the larger concern of the source of diverging voting patterns becomes clear.

Constituency Divergence and
the Dynamics of Party Voting

All the changes just discussed lead to even greater party divisions. With realignment and social change, the parties acquire different constituencies and they advocate different policies. As they persist in presenting differing policies, the electorate increasingly sees a difference between the parties. As noted earlier, in the 2000 NES survey of the electorate, 71 percent indicated that they see an important difference between the two parties. This is the highest level recorded since the question was first asked in 1952. These perceived differences lead to the polarization of the electorate reviewed in Chapter 5. Conservatives support Republicans and liberals support Democrats.

⎮These diverging constituencies and policy positions lead to a greater sense of difference between party members. Members in turn are more inclined to give the leadership more power to pressure party members, and particularly moderates, to vote with the party against the other party⎮ (Rohde 1991). Much of this pressure to conform is directed at moderates. While systematically detecting this leadership pressure is difficult (Krehbiel 1993, 2000),[2] there are reasons to presume that moderate members may well be inclined to respond and vote with the party. The national polarization previously discussed is presumably playing out within most districts. This means that even Democrats and Republicans in districts with diverse populations are more likely to derive their votes from polarized constituents. Moderate Democrats and Republicans, relying on divergent constituencies, may not find it that difficult to respond to party pressures to vote with the party, resulting in even greater polarization on House votes. For all these reasons, then, party voting records are diverging.

District Traits and the Sources of Varying ADA Scores

The starting point for understanding voting patterns, and changes in them, is the effect of district composition on voting patterns. Districts that are central to, or typical of, party concerns produce members who vote with the party more often. Those from atypical districts are less loyal (Fiorina 1974, 9–11). ADA voting records reflect these patterns. Member voting, on average, reflects district constituencies. It is not that members are simply following the dictates of their constituents. Rather, there is an interaction between district composition and the political persuasions of those who run for office in the district. Liberals are far more likely to run and win in districts dominated by liberal Democrats. These districts are likely to be heavily urban or dominated by minorities. Conservatives are far more likely to run and win in districts dominated by Republicans. These districts are likely to be rural or suburban and largely white. Further, even if a district is diverse internally, party winners draw their electoral base from different constituents, and Democrats and Republicans from seemingly diverse and moderate districts will have different electoral bases.

Average ADA Scores by District Traits, 1970s - 1990s								
			Percentage of Non-Whites in District					
	0 - 9 %			10 - 19 %			20 or more %	
Urbanization	All	Rep	Dem	All	Rep	Dem	All	Rep	Dem
0 - 69	37	16	67	28	10	42	30	6	40
70 - 89	45	20	70	33	12	62	44	12	71
90 plus	50	18	75	56	20	76	76	20	83

TABLE 6.1   Average ADA Scores by District Traits, 1970s-1990s

Ultimately, these constituency differences create different voting patterns, and particularly different party voting patterns. Table 6.1 indicates average ADA scores by levels of urbanization and the presence of nonwhites, with all votes from 1970–2000 considered. Overall, the highest scores occur in districts that are more urban and have higher percentages of non-whites. For Democrats, scores increase as the district becomes more urban and has a higher percentage of non-whites. For Republicans, the lowest ADA scores occur in the least urban districts. The lowest Republican scores come in the least urban districts that have 20 percent or more non-whites. This may be because they draw on a polarized constituency within those districts, which leads to very conservative voting.

With this general association between district constituencies and voting records established, understanding the change of the last several decades involves the interaction of two crucial matters. How has realignment changed which constituencies each party represents? How has this interacted with the changing social composition of districts?

The Impact of Realignment and Social Change: Democrats

There have been changes revolving around income, urbanization, and the percentage of non-whites in districts. As shown in the previous chapter, the district condition that has had the greatest impact on electoral outcomes is the presence of non-whites. To simplify the analysis to follow, much of the focus will be on the impact of that district trait. As reviewed in Chapter 4, America is changing. In the 1970s 20 percent of House districts contained at least 20 percent non-whites. By the 1990s 35 percent of districts had this percentage, and if the definition is broadened to non-whites plus those Hispanics who define themselves as white, the percentage of districts with this composition rises to 42. As indicated in

Chapter 4, the 2000 census data indicate that the percentage of districts with more than 20 percent of non-whites is now 51.

Table 6.2 presents information on the impact of social change and re-alignment by region since the 1970s for Democrats. In the table, the first column within each decade first presents the percentage of seats won by district type. Then the percentage of party seats derived *from* each category, within the region, is presented. Then the average ADA score by category is presented. The final two columns to the right present the change in percentage points from the 1970s to the 1990s in party reliance on district types and then the change in ADA score averages within a category.

The Democratic Party has experienced significant changes since the 1970s in each region. In the North, the party's success by the percentage non-white has remained roughly the same. The most significant change is the increase in the percentage of their seats from districts with 20 percent or more of non-whites. In the 1970s 20 percent of Democratic seats came from those districts. By the 1990s it increased to 31 percent, and these districts have the most liberal voting records.

In the South three changes have occurred. The success of Democrats has become sharply defined by the racial composition of districts. In the 1970s the difference in the party's success from the low to the high category was 15 percentage points (from 62 to 77). By the 1990s the difference was 44 percentage points (from 25 to 69). The districts with high percentages of non-whites became more important to the party, increasing from 49 percent of the party's seats in the South to 75. With the emergence of black voting, the retirement of older conservative Democrats, and their replacement by a new generation of House members (Glaser 1996, 103–129), the average ADA score became much more liberal for Democrats from all types of districts. In summary, the party became more reliant on Southern districts that tend to produce more liberal voting records and lost much of its base among districts that produce lower ADA scores. Through realignment and replacement the South became much less of a conservative contributor to the party average and much more of a source of liberal voting within the party. As Figure 6.3 indicates, Democrats within the South now have ADA scores much like the remainder of the party.

The remainder of the nation has had its own dramatic change, at least with regard to the Democratic Party. As in the South, a greater partisan division revolving around racial composition has developed. In the 1970s the difference from the lowest to highest category in party success was 26 percentage points (from 54 to 80), and by the 1990s it was 31 points. The

The Shifting Base of the Democratic Party:
The Presence of Non-Whites, Democratic Success, and ADA Averages

Percent Non-white	1970s Percentage: within	from	ADA avg	1980s Percentage: within	from	ADA Avg	1990s Percentage: within	from	ADA avg	Changes in: Pct from	ADA avg
North											
0 - 9	50	64	69	48	51	79	43	43	81	-21	12
10 - 19	67	17	74	72	23	80	59	26	86	9	12
20 plus	94	20	80	93	26	87	90	31	89	11	9
South											
0 - 9	62	22	27	51	15	57	25	13	65	-9	38
10 - 19	68	29	34	55	25	43	23	12	49	-17	15
20 plus	77	49	29	77	61	50	69	75	70	26	41
Remainder											
0 - 9	54	70	66	39	30	72	34	24	73	-46	7
10 - 19	77	18	60	42	23	65	35	19	73	1	13
20 plus	80	12	79	85	48	87	65	56	86	44	7
Nation											
0 - 9	52	53	63	46	35	75	37	30	77	-23	14
10 - 19	69	21	54	57	24	65	41	20	76	-1	22
20 plus	83	27	52	83	42	71	72	50	80	23	28

Notes: The percentage within is the percentage of seats won by Democrats within each decade within the indicated category of districts. For example, in the North in the 1970s within districts with 0 - 9 percentage non-whites, Democrats won 50 percent of all elections. The percentage from is the percentage of Democratic seats in that region derived from districts in that category. For example, in the North in the 1970s, Democrats derived 64 percent of their seats from districts with 0 - 9 percent non-whites. The ADA average is the average ADA score for all Democrats who held seats in that category. For example, in the North in the 1970s, Democrats had an average ADA score of 69 in districts with 0 - 9 percent non-whites

TABLE 6.2   The Shifting Base of the Democratic Party: The Presence of
Non-Whites, Democratic Success, and ADA Averages

most important change, however, is in the increase in districts with 20 percent or more non-whites and the greater reliance of the Democratic Party on these districts. In the 1970s they derived 12 percent of their seats within this region from these districts, and by the 1990s it was 56 percent, or an increase of 44 percentage points. These districts have the highest ADA scores, so this increase raises the regional average to a much higher level. The net result of these changes is that the Democratic Party on a national basis now draws a higher percentage of its seats from the districts that have the highest ADA scores. As the bottom part of the table indicates, the percentage of all party seats from these districts has increased from 27 to 50 percent between the 1970s and the 1990s.

Further, on average, the ADA scores within each category of districts have increased. This again may be a result of electoral polarization within districts. Democrats from districts with substantial minority populations are likely to be very concerned with minority interests. With the ideological polarization of voters increasing nationally (Abramowitz 2000; Jacobson 2000a, 2000b), Democratic members are, on average, more likely to have a liberal electoral base within their district. This greater clarity of their electoral base results in Democrats having more liberal voting records. Pressures from the party leadership and attacks by Republicans on social programs should increase these tendencies. Regardless, the electoral base of the Democratic Party is shifting to greater reliance on substantially non-white districts, resulting in more members with more liberal voting records.

Republicans

The Republican Party has also experienced change, but to a lesser extent. Table 6.3 presents data for Republican winners by the same categories as those just reviewed for the Democrats. The table again presents, by decade, the percentage of seats won in each category, the percentage of party seats from each category, and the average ADA score for those within each category. To the far right is the change in the percentage of districts from a category from the 1970s to the 1990s, and the change in the average ADA score by category.

While the Republican Party is generally seen as having become more conservative over the last two decades, the data in Table 6.3 present a much more ambiguous picture. On one hand, in districts that are 90 percent or more white, there has been a decline in average ADA scores. To the extent that the party draws members from such districts, it does appear that the party has become more conservative. On the other hand, the largely white districts are declining as a source of party seats. Only in the South was there a net gain in such districts as a source of party seats. Overall, the party experienced a decline of 34 percentage points in the percentage of party seats from primarily white districts. Much as with Democrats, there has been an increase in the percentage of seats from districts with higher percentages of non-whites.

The interesting matter is that members in these districts moved only slightly more liberal. The average ADA score of Republicans in districts

The Shifting Base of the Republican Party:
The Presence of Non-Whites, Republican Success, and ADA Averages

	1970s			1980s			1990s			Changes in:	
Percent	Percentage:		ADA	Percentage:		ADA	Percentage:		ADA	Pct	ADA
Non-white	within	from	avg	within	from	avg	within	from	avg	from	avg
North											
0 - 9	50	87	26	52	83	21	56	73	16	-14	-10
10 - 19	33	11	28	28	14	32	41	23	30	12	2
20 plus	6	6	25	7	7	46	10	5	28	-1	3
South											
0 - 9	38	32	8	49	27	9	75	35	8	3	-
10 - 19	32	33	8	45	39	7	77	35	8	2	-
20 plus	23	35	9	23	35	6	31	30	7	-5	-2
Remainder											
0 - 9	46	87	14	61	54	12	66	42	9	-45	-5
10 - 19	23	8	7	58	39	9	65	31	9	23	2
20 plus	20	4	8	15	10	12	35	27	16	23	8
The Nation											
0 - 9	48	76	21	54	60	17	62	51	13	-25	-8
10 - 19	31	15	15	43	27	13	59	29	15	14	-
20 plus	17	9	10	17	13	12	27	19	13	10	3

Notes: The percentage within is the percentage of seats won by Republicans each decade within the indicated category of districts. For example, in the North in the 1970s within districts with 0 - 9 percentage non-whites, Republicans won 50 percent of all elections. The percentage from is the percentage of Republican seats in that region derived from districts in that category. For example, in the North in the 1970s, Republicans derived 64 percent of their seats from districts with 0 - 9 percent non-whites. The ADA average is the average ADA score for all Republicans who held seats in that category. For example, in the North in the 1970s, Republicans had an average ADA score of 69 in districts with 0 - 9 percent non-whites

TABLE 6.3　The Shifting Base of the Republican Party: The Presence of Non-Whites, Republican Success, and ADA Averages

with 20 percent non-whites increased only 3 percentage points. The party, while winning more seats in the 1990s, is also winning more seats in districts that traditionally produce more liberal voting records. The limited movement in ADA scores may be because winning members are drawing support from a more polarized electorate within their districts, such that they are drawing their support from the conservative portion of each district. Whether the party can continue to have conservative voting records in these districts and continue to win remains to be seen. The party faces pressures to cope with the shifting demographics of the nation. As the nation becomes more non-white and as income inequality affects large portions of the electorate, maintaining conservative voting records may result in the appearance of insensitivity to the problems of minorities and the less affluent, and the loss of seats for Republicans.

The Combined Effects of Urbanization and Non-Whites

The prior analyses examine just the relationship of the presence of non-whites to party success and ADA scores. This condition is correlated with urbanization, and together they are likely to have a reinforcing effect. To assess this joint impact on partisan success and voting, districts are first grouped into three categories. Category 1 consists of those districts that are less than 70 percent urban *and* less than 10 percent non-whites. Category 3 consists of those districts that are more than 80 percent urban *and* more than 15 percent non-white. All others go into the middle category. These groupings are arbitrary, but they allow for contrasts of different types of districts. Table 6.4 presents how many seats each party won within each category and each party's relative reliance on seats from each category. Then the average ADA score by category is indicated. To the right is the change in reliance on district categories and changes in the average ADA score.

Each party has experienced two kinds of change. There have been shifts in the relative sources of each party's seats, reflecting the changing

Table 6.4: Changes in Party Composition and Average ADA Scores By Combinations of Urbanization and Percent Non-White, 1970s – 1990s

Republicans	1970s			1980s			1990s			Change in	
Category	#	%	ADA	#	%	ADA	#	%	ADA	%	ADA
1	367	44	19	350	40	18	345	32	11	-12	-8
2	432	52	20	430	50	13	559	52	11	0	-9
3	38	4	19	89	10	19	171	16	18	12	-1

Democrats	1970s			1980s			1990s			Change in	
Category	#	%	ADA	#	%	ADA	#	%	ADA	%	ADA
1	294	22	58	249	19	73	194	18	73	-4	15
2	772	58	53	615	47	63	414	38	72	-20	19
3	272	20	72	439	34	81	484	44	85	24	13

Notes: Category 1 consists of those districts less than 70 % urban and less than 10 % non-white. Category 2 consists of those districts greater than 80 % urban and more than 15 % non-white. Category 3 is all those districts not falling into the first two categories. # is the number of districts held by each party within the decade. % is the percentage of all party seats from group 1, 2, and 3. ADA is the average ADA score for party members in that category. The change scores are the change in percentage points from the 1970s to the 1970s within each category.

TABLE 6.4   Changes in Party Composition and Average ADA Scores by Combination of Urbanization and Percent Non-White, 1970s-1990s

social composition of the nation, with the magnitude of the shifts greater for Democrats than for Republicans. In the 1970s 20 percent of Democratic seats were in Category 3. By the 1990s it was 44 percent, and reapportionments following the 2000 census may increase this reliance even more. These districts are the ones that result in the highest ADA scores and contribute to polarization. The effects of shifting social composition—a general increase in the predominance of Category 3 districts and greater Democratic reliance on them–is of considerable magnitude and may explain much of the greater polarization. Republican reliance on Category 1 districts declined by 12 percentage points and their reliance on Category 3 districts increased by 12 percentage points.

The evidence suggests, again, that House party members are increasingly finding themselves with distinct constituencies that differ from those of their partisan opponents. These differing electoral bases will pull members of each party more toward opposite ends of the political spectrum. This may explain changes in party ADA scores by category. Republican scores decreased in every category, but the biggest declines are in the districts with modest urbanization and with less than 10 percent of whites. These are core Republican districts and realignment and party pressures are prompting more conservative voting records in these districts.

The Democrats are somewhat different, with the average ADA scores increasing in all categories. If Democrats in Categories 1 and 2 were trying to move to more moderate positions, they would be unlikely to behave this way. If, however, their district electorate is polarizing, and they are being pressured by the more liberal members to go along with liberal positions, then we would expect to see the greatest changes in these districts. Again, there is much we need to learn about what is occurring within districts. Regardless, it is clear that for Democrats their primary source of seats is becoming the districts that are more urban and more non-white, and members from these districts have the most liberal voting records. Further, the rest of the party is moving to more liberal voting records.

The Congruence of Presidential and House Results

While the primary concern here is with the House of Representatives, the evidence suggests that a broader realignment is occurring. A greater congruence has developed among House elections, House members' votes, and presidential election results. As noted in the previous chapter, the association between partisan voting for presidential and House candidates has been increasing since the 1970s. Districts that vote strongly for

Democratic presidential candidates increasingly vote strongly for Democratic House candidates. These results are also more closely associated with district demographics than they were thirty years ago (See Table 5.9 and discussion).

There is also a greater connection between the ideological voting of House members and presidential voting results. Table 6.5 summarizes how this voting connection has developed and its relationship to voting. Using presidential voting results as a basis (Schwarz and Fenmore 1977; Nice 1983; Lucas 1999; Erikson and Wright 2000, 168–177; Brady, Canes-Wrone, and Cogan 2000, 178–192),[3] we can classify House districts within each decade as liberal, moderate, or conservative. This is done by ranking districts from most supportive of Democratic presidential candidates (liberal) to least supportive (conservative), and then grouping them into thirds. Those in the top third are defined as liberal, and those in the bottom third as conservative. We then calculate the percentage of the liberal, moderate, and conservative districts that Democratic House candidates win and the percentage of Democratic Party House members (winners) that come from each category of district. Finally, we examine the average ADA score of Democratic and Republican House members by these district groupings.

There have been several important changes in recent decades. To repeat, the association between presidential and House partisan voting patterns has increased. For example, for Democrats in the 1970s the difference in the success of their House candidates between the liberal and conservative districts was 32 percentage points. Democrats won 79 percent of contests in liberal districts and 47 percent in conservative districts. During the 1990s this difference in success by district type increased to 71 percentage points, with Democrats winning 86 percent of contests in liberal districts and only 15 percent in conservative districts. This growing difference in party success reinforces the evidence of polarization of party support that was reviewed in Chapter 5.

As part of this realignment, the sources of party seats have changed over time. House Democrats derived 40 percent of their seats from liberal districts in the 1970s, and by the 1990s 60 percent of its seats came from these districts. While Democrats were increasing their reliance on liberal districts, Republicans were increasing their reliance on conservative districts. During the 1970s the party received 46 percent of its seats from conservative districts, and during the 1990s it received 55 percent of its seats from these districts. Each party is deriving a larger part of its electoral base from districts that are at opposite ends of the ideological spectrum. Liberal and conservative districts do not embody extremism,

The Congruence of Presidential and House Votes,
And Party Reliance on Liberal - Conservative Districts, 1970s-1990s

	1970s			1980s			1990s			Change in Percent		
	Percentage		Avg	Percentage		Avg	Percentage		Avg	From 1970s to 1990s		
Democrats	Won	From	ADA	Won	From	ADA	Won	From	ADA	Won	From	ADA
Liberal	79	40	60	91	54	80	86	60	85	7	20	25
Moderate	53	31	58	58	34	62	51	31	69	-2	-	11
Conservative	47	29	47	23	12	44	15	8	49	-32	-21	2
Republicans												
Liberal	21	15	32	9	8	37	13	11	26	-8	-4	-6
Moderate	47	38	20	42	36	20	48	35	16	1	-3	-4
Conservative	53	46	14	77	56	10	85	55	9	32	9	-5

Difference in party success between liberal and conservative districts (both parties)

32   67   71

TABLE 6.5   The Congruence of Presidential and House Votes and Party Reliance on Liberal-Conservative Districts, 1970s-1990s

but they are at opposing ends of the ideological spectrum within American politics.

The patterns of change in the ADA ratings coincide with the earlier analyses. Republicans have in general become more conservative, though the changes are modest. Among Democrats the major change has been in the liberal districts. In those districts the average ADA score increased by 25 percentage points in two decades. As noted before, the combination of an increase in reliance on liberal districts (measured by presidential results) plus the increase in liberal voting records in these districts, has produced a significant increase in the average Democratic ADA score.

Social Change and Party Responsiveness

The emergence of a significant presence of non-whites in many House districts is one of the major changes of recent decades. That change may have significant effects on the future prospects and behavior of each party. For Democrats, it would appear that this trend is beneficial. As a party they have benefited from two types of change. In the 1950s and early 1960s blacks in Southern districts were not registered and were not electorally relevant. By the 1970s they registered and became politically relevant, which required greater sensitivity to black interests. Over the same time, immigration resulted in more districts with a significant non-white presence. These two constituencies strongly support the

**Vote by Race for President and House Candidates,
2000 Elections, Based on Exit Polls**

	President		House Elections	
	Gore	Bush	Democrat	Republican
White	42	54	43	55
African-American	90	9	88	11
Hispanic	62	35	64	35
Asian	55	41	58	40

Source: *http://www.cnn.com/ELECTION/2000/results/index.epolls.html.*
These results were posted immediately after the election.

TABLE 6.6   Vote by Race for President and House Candidates, 2000
Elections, Based on Exit Polls

Democratic Party. Table 6.6 presents exit poll results from the 2000 presidential and House elections. Republicans won a majority of white voters, but lost Hispanic voters by large margins in both the presidential and House elections. Given the steady growth in non-whites, and their strong support for the Democratic Party, it would seem that fortunes of the Democratic Party should be improving, while those of the Republican Party should be deteriorating.

Quite to the contrary, in recent years the situation of Republicans has improved in several ways. In 1994 Republicans won a majority of seats in the House for the first time since 1952. They held that majority in 1996, 1998, and 2000, even though the size of their majority slipped in each election. Further, as Figure 6.4 indicates, Republicans are now winning by larger margins (Abramowitz 2000). During the 1950s Democratic winners received much larger percentages of the vote than Republican winners. That is, Republicans in the House were less secure than Democrats. During the 1970s Republicans came closer to Democrats in their winning percentages, and by the 1980s and 1990s, Republicans were doing as well as Democrats. Over the 1990s Republicans were less likely to be in the "marginal," or close election category (Stonecash 2002b). In contrast, over time the vote proportion of Democratic winners has been gradually declining. Within the electorate, identification with the Democratic Party is also decreasing nationally (Meffert et al. 2001, 955). It would appear that the Republican Party, with its improved electoral fortunes, is in a very good situation.

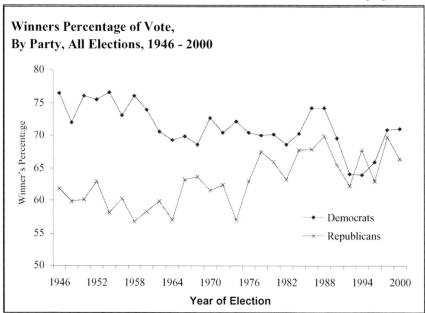

**Winners Percentage of Vote,
By Party, All Elections, 1946 - 2000**

FIGURE 6.4   Winners' Percentage of Vote, by Party, All Elections, 1946-2000

Despite the electoral trends of the late 1990s, the future of each party is far from clear. The increase in non-whites in American society presents serious dilemmas for both Democrats and Republicans (Stonecash 2002a). The crucial matter for each party is how to handle responsiveness to a growing segment of the population. Democrats have to be responsive to non-whites, but not so much that they become too closely identified with non-whites and receive a lower percentage of the white vote. Non-whites do not vote as much as whites, so greater reliance on non-whites could harm Democratic prospects.[4]

Republicans have a different, but equally difficult task. They need to recognize the growing importance of non-whites in American society and not alienate them as an electoral base. The problems and possibilities for them are evident in how they have responded to change in California and Texas. As noted earlier, California has undergone a significant growth in the presence of non-whites, with almost all the growth coming from the increase in Hispanics (Gimpel 1999, 32–79). The Republican Party has experienced difficulties with this increase in diverse ways. Individual members have struggled with this change. Robert Dornan, the Republican in the Forty-Sixth District in southern California, had developed a very conservative voting record by the 1990s. He did not respond to his changing

district composition and maintained adamant and aggressive conservative positions even as his district experienced an increase in Latinos
(Barone and Ujifusa 1993, 196–198). He was eventually challenged in 1996
by the Latino candidate Linda Sanchez, who narrowly beat him. The important matter was that Dornan as a conservative did not change his behavior to try to survive in a changing district. The result was the loss of
a Republican seat.

The party also stumbled at the state level. Pete Wilson, a Republican,
was governor of the state from 1991 until 1999. As noted earlier, during
that time the state experienced a tremendous increase in legal and illegal
immigrants, and most of the illegal immigrants were Hispanic. In 1994,
through the initiative process, Proposition 187 was placed on the ballot to
deny government services to illegal immigrants and their children.
Wilson took a strong stand in favor of the proposition (Nieves 1999). He
also moved to take advantage of a provision in the 1996 congressional
welfare reform bill that allowed him to issue an executive order to cut off
state services to illegal immigrants (Golden 1996). Whatever the legal
merits of Wilson's moves, with whites a minority of the state's population (Maharidge 1999), Wilson's actions alienated Latinos, and the
Republican Party suffered severe damage in its support among Hispanics
(Purdum 1997; Greenhouse 2000). During the 2000 elections the state was
widely regarded as one that Republicans could not win because of their
poor standing among minorities. The party is still struggling to recover
from the image created of a lack of concern for Hispanics.

It is possible for Republicans to avoid this situation. Texas has also experienced a significant increase in Latinos. George W. Bush, while governor of Texas, sought to respond to change by emphasizing his concern for
Latinos. He regularly stressed his concern for their problems and sought
to present the Republican conservative message of individualism in terms
of his concern for opportunity, rather than the traditional individualistic
statement that everyone in American society *should* make it on his or her
own. While liberals criticized him as making symbolic gestures, he
sought to convey a message of recognizing the aspirations of minorities,
rather than criticizing them for not succeeding. While the Republican
Party has generally not made great progress in making connections to
Hispanics, such gains have occurred to some degree in places like Texas.
Again, it is a problem the party will address as long as social change continues.

These are only anecdotes, and the important matter is how responsive
party members are to non-whites. If Democratic members are responsive

**The Relationship of ADA Voting Records
and District Demographic Conditions, by Decade, 1960s - 1990s**

| | *Republicans by Decade* | | | | *Democrats by Decade* | | | |
	60s	70s	80s	90s	60s	70s	80s	90s
Income	.00	.00	.00	.00	.01	.01	.00	.00
Non-white %	-.39	-.35	-.20	.08	-.32	.10	.14	.19
Urban %	.25	.04	-.06	-.02	.37	.31	.27	.29
R^2	.13	.07	.03	.10	.41	.31	.27	.29
N								

Note: The coefficients are standardized regression coefficients. As such, they express the impact of change in district conditions on changes in ADA scores.

TABLE 6.7   The Relationship of ADA Voting Records and District Demographic Conditions, by Decade, 1960s-1990s

to their growing electoral base of non-whites, then we would expect that members with high percentages of non-whites will have more liberal voting records. If the party is becoming responsive over time, this relationship should increase over time. If Republicans are to avoid alienating non-whites, then members with higher percentages of non-whites should also have somewhat more liberal voting records. Given the growing presence of non-whites, this relationship might also increase if members are going to avoid alienating this constituency.

Table 6.7 presents evidence of how this sensitivity has progressed. It presents the regression of ADA scores on the percentage of non-whites, controlling for urbanization and income, by decade. The coefficients indicate the relationship between ADA scores and percentages of non-whites within each decade. For Democrats, the major change is that the relationship between the percentage of non-whites and ADA scores has changed from strongly negative to a fairly strong positive relationship. Much of this is probably a result of the changes in the South, where blacks began to register and Southern Democrats began to respond to them. But given the national pervasiveness of districts with substantial percentages of non-whites across the nation, the change is clearly national in nature.

For Republicans, there has also been significant change associated with non-whites. During the 1960s and 1970s, members with higher percentages of non-whites had lower ADA scores. By the 1980s the strength of this relationship declined, and by the 1990s a positive relationship developed. Republicans with more non-whites now have relatively liberal voting records within the party. This evidence suggests that the presence of non-whites is being acknowledged by both parties. Members within each party who have more of such constituents are more responsive to their presence.

The Future of Party Polarization

The changes shown in Table 6.5 represent the current state of the process of change first discussed in Chapter 3. In the early 1900s the Democratic Party derived many of its seats from more rural and conservative Southern districts. The Republican Party drew many of its seats from more liberal urban Northern districts. The 1930s began a process of shifts in the electoral bases of the parties. Democrats won many seats in Northern urban districts as a part of Roosevelt's success. The party was not able to hold many of those seats during the 1940s, but beginning in the 1950s the party began to steadily increase the percentage of seats from urban districts (Turner and Schneier 1970, 119). At the same time, the Republican Party began to pick up seats in white conservative Southern districts.

These trends followed shifts that were already under way in presidential elections. Republican presidential candidates had started to do relatively well in the South in the 1950s and 1960s, and Democratic candidates were doing well outside the South. House party candidates had not yet caught up to the success of their presidential candidates, such that by the 1970s the association between presidential and House partisan results in districts was not strong, as shown in Table 6.5. House results began to follow presidential results and the alignment of party success with district demographic and ideological leanings (as shown by presidential results) steadily increased during the 1980s and by the 1990s the association between the two was stronger.

The important question is what trends are likely in the future. Social change and party polarization could well increase. Continued increases in inequality could exacerbate tensions over inequality in American society and increase party conflict and polarization. While there is evidence of stronger associations among demographics, presidential and House election results, and ADA scores, it is also clear that electoral divisions are by no means complete. Republicans, as Table 6.4 indicates, still win seats in highly urban districts with higher percentages of non-whites. Democrats still win seats in less urban, primarily white districts. The party bases, while more distinct than they have been in some time, are not completely divergent. The differences in party success (for presidential and House candidates) by demographics of districts could increase, as could the association between presidential and House partisan voting. The result could be a further separation in party bases and a greater divide in the House in voting.

While that is possible, it is unlikely. If Republicans are to remain a majority party, they need to continue to win seats in highly urban districts with at least moderate percentages of non-whites. If the party leaders and conservatives push the party to more conservative positions, they run the risk of losing those seats. Moderates within the party are likely to make the case for moderation within the party. Further, the 2000 census confirms that the nation is changing in ways not politically favorable to Republicans. The party will have to respond to demographic changes or return to minority status within the House. The Democratic Party also has reasons to moderate itself. While the demographics may be changing in ways favorable to the party, the party still wins seats in districts that are primarily white and less urban. It is now the minority party and losing these seats will make it harder for the party to become a majority. The result is that the members in the primarily white and less urban districts will make the case for moderating party positions and image if they are to survive.

The early 2000s, then, will hold considerable tension within each party. The constituency bases of each party are diverging because of realignment and social change. The result is parties that differ in their concerns and policy positions. This has led to battles over tax cuts, how much to fund social programs, and how much to fund unemployment, among other things. Those differences are not short term and will persist. The party differences are reflections of differing constituencies, needs, and philosophies about the role of government. Yet, at the same time there are strong pressures within each party—the desire not to be relegated to the minority—that will drive each party to try to moderate polarization. The challenge will be in the skill with which each party can manage these internal tensions.

Notes

1. The argument here is that certain district conditions *tend* to produce particular outcomes, but not that they *determine* voting patterns. The behaviors that create this association may vary from district to district. We presume that candidates differ in their preoccupation with creating secure election outcomes and that they vary in their calculation about whom they must please. Some will find voting in accord with their district easy because the district is homogeneous and the member shares the views of district constituents. Others will encounter a diverse

district and will vary in how they react to this because they have diverse political values and make differing calculations as to how to respond to that situation. Some members will want to reduce reelection risks and will try to anticipate constituency opinions as they vote. Others will tolerate more risk and rely more on their own values as they vote. Fiorina (1974, 29-42) provides a valuable theoretical overview of these possibilities. Regardless, our presumption is that, on average, members end up reflecting the composition of their district.

2. Krehbiel makes a valuable point about the problems of detecting the effects of party pressures on voting records. His argument is that votes are the record of the final decision of a legislator. They could be the result of the legislator's own preferences and/or the result of party pressures. It is not possible to take this final act and make any simple assertion about what created this. This criticism has led some to try to find measures of candidate policy positions during campaigns and compare them with recorded votes once in office to assess how much the two diverge (Ansolabehere et al. 2001a). To the extent campaign-announced positions differ from voting records, it is possible that party pressures created the divergence, but it is still not possible to verify that party pressures created the difference between a legislator's initial and final position.

While Krehbiel makes a valid argument about the difficulties of separating the role of legislator preferences from party pressure, his larger argument about parties has gotten some attention and deserves a comment because of its implications for the analysis presented here. Krehbiel argues that if members vote together because they share preferences, then their behavior could also be defined as nonpartisan and there would then be little party behavior occurring.

The issue is what it means to say there is no party if members vote together because of their shared preferences. On one hand, the issue could be semantic. It could be that Krehbiel means to say that party leadership pressures are of limited significance if members are voting with the party because their constituencies and their own preferences incline them to do so. This confines his observations about the nature of party to just the specific aspect of party involving leader-member interactions and the extent to which leaders and members pressure other members within the party. Such a statement would not be about the absence or presence of parties but about an aspect of within-party interactions. If this is his argument, then the magnitude of the effect of party pressures on members could be the subject of logical and empirical analyses (Rohde 1994; Ansolabehere 2001b).

On the other hand, Krehbiel appears to be arguing (1991, 237–241) that he is commenting about the existence of parties per se. He argues that partisanship is not a relevant factor if the activity of some members voting together and against another set of members is a product of the distribution of initial preferences. In making this argument he creates a false distinction between all the partisan processes that lead to the association, for House members, between constituencies, party affiliation, and preferences for party members. The distribution of partisan preferences of Democrats and Republicans—in the electorate and for House members—is a result of a long process. Issues emerge and are reacted to differently by party candidates and the electorate. Liberal voters and candidates select the Democratic party as sympathetic to their concerns. Conservative voters and candidates select the Republican Party. The distribution of preferences for Democratic and Republican House members differs because of electorate and candidates sorting into differing party groups. Krehbiel takes all the process that lead to the creation of groups of party members with differing policy preferences and essentially redefines these groups as just groups of differing people, with an involved partisan process apparently playing no role. He treats party as reflected only in situations in which "individual legislators vote with fellow party members *in spite of their disagreement* about the policy in question" (1991, 238). He defines party as involving just those situations in which party pressure is applied. Thus party does not exist if all members agree on preferences and vote together. It exists only if there is within-group diversity and conflict. While many would treat this range of situations as simply reflecting the degree of unity within a party, he singles out the situation of internal divisions and defines party as occurring only in the situation of high internal diversity that results in pressures to forge within-party unity. One case of party interaction becomes the definition of party.

This is a *very* limited notion of party. It is also built around a serious fallacy. In asserting a conceptual distinction between member preferences and party he excludes from "party" the entire process and its outcomes of sorting people and politicians into differing groups. The differing sets of members are treated as individuals with preferences. It is after those grouped preferences are set that he begins his search for party. If realignment occurs and creates party groups with clearly differing constituencies, party apparently does not exist in his definition. Why he proposes this definitional twist and what it is to contribute to our understanding of parties is never clear. His approach could easily lead to the suggestion that party has come to mean less in the U.S. House in recent decades, while we argue that the cumulative effect of the processes of partisan realignment and increasing social diversity have created the differing groups that vote differently. We argue that party, as a collection of individuals with similar preferences, is now more prevalent in the House. In other words, the condition of party homogeneity is greater. Krehbiel's logic leads to analysis in which preferences are treated as control variables and then a party dummy is added as variable to pick up additional variance, representing the extent to which party exists (Snyder and Groseclose 2000; Krehbiel 2000; Ansolabehere et al. 2001b). Such analyses *may* be picking up the effects of party pressures on members, but we argue that they do not capture our sense of party. Indeed, they ignore most of what constitutes party.

3. We are heavily indebted to DeWayne Lucas for an approach to this analysis that he presented in his 1999 SPSA paper. In that paper he provides a table that captures these various changes. While we group House districts somewhat differently than he does, and we used unadjusted rather than adjusted ADA scores, we draw on his way of organizing the data. Prior analyses have found that the presidential elections that created the greatest ideological voting across House districts were those in 1964, 1972, and 1988. In those years the differences across House districts were strongly associated with other attributes of states (taxes, welfare liberalism) that reflect liberal–conservative differences (Leogrande and Jeydel 1997; Erikson and Wright 2001). In other years the association between presidential voting and liberal-conservative variations declines significantly. The presumption is, therefore, that how a district voted in 1964 is a good indicator of the ideological inclinations of voters in that district and that characterization can be

applied across all elections in the 1960s. The same is true for the 1972 election for the 1970s and the 1988 election for the 1980s and for the 1990s.

4. For the last decade or so, blacks have had turnout rates that range from 5–10 points lower than that for whites. Hispanics have been 20–25 percentage points lower than whites. Data for 1970 through 1996 are from an October 17, 1997, release from the Bureau of the Census. The web site is: http://www.census.gov/.

7

Interpreting Congressional Elections: The Limits of the Candidate-Centered Framework

This analysis is concerned with how district composition affects electoral outcomes and the voting patterns of members. While those concerns are primary, this analysis also has implications for the broader issue of interpreting contemporary House elections. Two very different interpretations of post-World War II U.S. House elections coexist in the academic literature. The candidate-centered view portrays House members as largely autonomous actors seeking to shape their electoral fortunes independent of broad partisan electoral forces. A second view portrays representatives as members of polarized party entities that have increasingly homogeneous constituencies and divergent voting patterns. Party affiliation is something party members downplay in the former view, while it is central to the latter. Each has its own body of supporting research. But the two contradict each other.

Articulating these different views, understanding their consequences, and attempting to resolve which is most relevant for interpreting congressional elections is crucial for understanding what shapes elections and how representation is connected to elections. We will first summarize the two differing interpretations, assess the evidence for each, and then reconsider the fundamental question of how election outcomes are connected to electoral constituencies.

Candidate-Centered Elections

The first, and dominant, interpretation of House elections argues that campaigns are increasingly organized by candidates and the focus is on candidates. Mayhew provided a summary of this view (1974a). He argued that candidates are relatively autonomous from parties because primaries free candidates from party control of their fortunes (1974a, 25). The establishment of primaries during the early 1900s started the reduction of a party role in influencing nominations (Schlesinger 1985). This freedom has prompted House candidates to organize their own campaigns, raise their own resources, and, if they are incumbents, exploit the resources that accompany being a member of the House to gain reelection (Mayhew 1974a, 26).

This ability of candidates, rather than parties, to become the focus of campaigns is facilitated by an electoral context in which there is greater electoral detachment from parties. Beginning in the 1950s voter identification with parties started to decline and split-ticket voting began to increase (Flanigan and Zingale 1998: 61–64). Candidates faced with an electorate less inclined to vote a straight party ticket and declining party organizations have responded by raising their own campaign funds and relying more on pollsters, consultants, political ad specialists, and direct mail operations. Once in office, the goal of incumbents is to raise their name recognition and discourage challengers. Incumbents use the resources of office (the ability to obtain funding for local special projects, government funding of travel to the district, newsletters, and help for constituents with specific problems) to create a favorable image. They raise large sums of campaign funding to run ads that further increase their visibility and shape election outcomes. Incumbents, using all these resources, have increased their average margin of victory in House elections, and incumbents have become more successful at surviving (Jacobson 2001, 21–100). The primary causes of electoral outcomes are candidate quality, campaign resources, and strategic actions.

Candidate-centered politics is more than just the emergence of independent campaign organizations, however. Fiorina summarizes the conclusion that this leads to a reduction in the role of issues.

> The result [of changes in party organizations and new issues] was the growth of candidate-centered politics, wherein candidates personalized campaigns and elections, running not as members of long-lived teams, but as individuals who would behave independently in office. Members of Congress were particularly adept at developing electoral techniques that

enabled them to personalize their electoral coalitions. Increasingly, they were able to avoid association with their party's larger issues of national policy. Instead, they were able to win on the basis of their personal characteristics, their personal policy positions, their record of service to the district, and the great resource advantages that enabled them to discourage strong challengers and beat those whom they could not discourage. (2001, 145)

With this kind of behavior occurring, the role of parties as vehicles to create policy options and pressure party members to accept them, so that cohesive, differing parties occur, is limited. As Mayhew put it:

"No theoretical treatment of the United States Congress that posits parties as analytic units will go very far (1974a, 27). . . . The best service a party can supply to its congressmen is a negative one; it can leave them alone. And this in general is what the congressional parties do. Party 'pressure' to vote one way or another is minimal. (1974a, 99–100)

Diverging Constituencies and Parties

Recently a very different view of parties and American politics has begun to emerge. This alternative view focuses on how the relationship between district constituencies and House members is changing over time and the implications for party voting. Central to this view is alignment, or which social and economic constituencies votes for which party candidates. The candidate-centered view focuses on the ability of candidates to create a district electoral alignment independent of national alignments, while the latter implies the spread of national alignments to all districts. National issues do not affect local voting in the former view but are central to the latter. While the candidate-centered view was prompted in large part by evidence of trends in electoral behavior, this reconsideration of the role of constituencies has been prompted by evidence of the increasing party polarization in Congress.

The focus on the effect of district composition on which party wins elections and how House members vote was once very common in congressional studies (Turner 1951; Froman 1963; Mayhew 1966; Cummings 1966; Turner and Schneier 1970). It is an approach that has virtually disappeared from the literature (for exceptions, see Stonecash and Lindstrom 1999; Lucas 1999; Stonecash, Brewer, and Mariani 2002; Stonecash 2000).

The inclination to return to a focus on the constituency composition of districts was prompted by emerging evidence that the Republican and Democratic parties are acquiring clearly defined constituency bases. Who is in a district matters for the likely partisan outcome. At the individual level, the electorate is polarizing along ideological and class lines. Voters who identify with Republicans are increasingly conservative and affluent, while those who identify with Democrats are increasingly liberal and less affluent (Abramowitz and Saunders 1998, 2000; Jacobson 2000b). Class political cleavages are increasing (Stonecash 2000).

At the district level, parties in Congress increasingly derive their seats from districts with differing populations. Democrats are more likely to win in districts that are populated by the less affluent (Stonecash and Lindstrom 1999) and non-whites. The parties are steadily diverging in their constituency bases, policy concerns, and willingness to vote together (Rohde 1991). They regularly engage in fierce ideological battles over policy proposals. Republicans want large tax cuts while Democrats oppose them. Republicans propose welfare "reform" and Democrats oppose change. Legislators within each party increasingly vote together and against the opposing party, and party polarization is steadily increasing (Groseclose 1999; Fleischer and Bond 2000a, 2000b; Jacobson 2000a).

The Implications of the Alternative Views

Resolving these different interpretations is important. The candidate-centered framework suggests that electoral outcomes are largely driven by the resources available to candidates. Since incumbents generally have more of these resources, and particularly more campaign funds, they are more likely to win (Abramowitz 1991; Gaddie and Bullock 2000, 35–36). The important matter is what this view implies about representative democracy. This framework implies, generally without a precise accompanying statement, that candidates are able to reduce the tendency of specific constituency groups to vote Democratic or Republican. The composition of the district fades in importance in this framework.

An electorate that is less attached to parties and engages in more ticket-splitting is amenable to being influenced by experienced incumbents with high name recognition, extensive campaign funds, and a staff that respectfully responds to all constituent inquiries (Mayhew 1974a; Fiorina 1977; Gaddie and Bullock 2000, 13–51; Jacobson 2001, 21–100). If these resources are exploited successfully, constituency traits, "party affiliation, national tides, and presidential coattails" have less influence over district electoral outcomes (Jacobson 1997, 77). Candidates increase their personal visibility and their favorable ratings within the district, create some insulation from electoral pressures and vulnerability, and create more of a "personal vote." The implication is that parties just need to recruit experienced candidates and raise substantial campaign funds, and some disconnection from national issues can occur.[1] In contrast, the other view suggests that the composition of districts matters because groups generally follow national voting patterns. Who lives in a district shapes electoral outcomes and the voting behavior of members.

Both interpretations are unlikely to be true. If candidates are concerned primarily with enhancing their electoral margins, they will seek to increase their visibility and image to insulate themselves from broad electoral trends. If campaigns are candidate-centered and politicians are concerned about surviving and building a career in Congress (Polsby 1968), their goal is to reduce the connection of their electoral results to broad national partisan reactions and shifts (Burnham 1982, 208–210). This involves creating independence from electoral swings by reducing the extent to which the electorate sees the national party and the local candidate as inseparable. Candidates cannot achieve this independence of image and voting patterns by lining up and voting with their party each time. A legislator who votes consistently with his or her party is much more likely to be seen in partisan terms and risks being caught up in broad national partisan reactions. The candidate-centered view makes the emergence of party polarization somewhat puzzling, while the view that focuses on the constituency-party connection helps explain it. The essential questions are whether there is a clear constituency-party outcome connection and whether this affects the extent to which members of Congress work with their party.

Resolving the Conflicting Interpretations

The argument to be presented here is that the evidence for the candidate-centered view is not persuasive. It may apply to some districts, but only to a few. For most districts, it is fundamentally inaccurate. Over the last three decades electoral realignment has occurred at the individual and district level. Individual ideology and income now have a stronger effect on how people vote. At the district level, income, urbanization, and the presence of non-whites now have a stronger effect on partisan outcomes. At the same time, the diversity among House districts has increased, with the proportion of House districts that are lower-income and non-white increasing. Social change is increasing the percentage of American society that is black and Latino and that is changing the composition of House districts and creating an electoral base that leads to greater party polarization. In many House districts it matters little which candidate a party runs. A Democrat (any Democrat) or Republican (any Republican) is likely to win most district races because of the constituency composition in the district. Democrats are unlikely to lose districts that are urban, less affluent, and have a significant presence (20 percent or more) of blacks or Latinos. Republicans are unlikely to lose rural, white districts or relatively affluent, suburban, white districts. To portray the broad array of districts and their elections as if they are candidate-centered in nature fundamentally misrepresents the constraining effect of constituencies on partisan outcomes.[2]

There are, to be sure, in the midst of this broad continuum of district types, districts that are swing districts or ones that either party could win.[3] It is in these districts that candidate quality, campaign resources, and strategy matter a great deal. Candidate-centered politics defines many of these swing districts, but it defines only these districts. We will return to the issue of how many such districts exist later in this chapter.

The Empirical Underpinnings of the Candidate-Centered Interpretation

The argument that elections are candidate-centered developed from the study of elections in general. The conclusion was that party-centered voting was declining, and this was creating an environment in which candidates could have more impact on their own electoral margins. As early as the 1960s studies found a decline in partisan turnover in House seats and in the connection between presidential and House candidate results in House districts (Cummings 1966). At the same time, individual-level studies were finding that voter identification with parties was declining, that party voting (someone identifying with a party voting for candidates of that party) was declining, and that split-ticket voting was increasing (Flanigan and Zingale 1979).

Then in the mid–1970s Mayhew published a study that appears to have structured many of the studies that followed for the next several decades (1974b). He found that from 1958 to 1972 the proportion of competitive House races had declined. He speculated that the most plausible explanation of this change was the increased resources that House members had available to them. He also argued that House candidates should be seen as fairly autonomous actors (1974a). This framework quickly became dominant (Brady, Cogan, and Fiorina 2000, 5). These analyses were followed by a steady flow of studies examining the nature and extent of the incumbency effect (Cover 1977; Born 1979; Payne 1980; Alford and Hibbing 1981; Collie 1981; Campbell 1983), the role of legislator activity and resources in affecting reelection rates (Johannes 1979; Johannes and McAdams 1981; Fiorina 1981; Jacobson 2001, 21–100), the name recognition of incumbents (Ferejohn 1977; Mann and Wolfinger 1980), and analyses of changes in the vote proportion won by House members (Garand and Gross 1984; Gross and Garand 1984). At the same time, individual level studies continued to emerge documenting the decline in attachment to parties.

Empirical evidence has been crucial to the emergence of the candidate-centered view. Specifically, the argument has been that more House members are winning reelection and that margins of victory are higher than in the past (Jacobson 2001, 24–25), that voter identification with parties and party voting are declining, and that split-ticket voting is increasing. Given that these empirical trends served as a basis for the candidate-centered view, each deserves some review.

Reconsidering Reelection Rates

One of the most important indicators of change is the trend in reelection rates of incumbents। The rate of success has risen since World War II, and a common pattern has been to point out that this increase corresponds with the increase in legislative resources (Fiorina 1977; Jacobson 2000, 24–25). The argument is that incumbents use the resources of office to increase their visibility and margin of victory. The difficulty is that, as Figure 7.1 indicates, and as Garand and Gross argue (1984), the reelection rates in the House have been steadily rising since the mid-1800s.[4] It is hard to conclude that the steady rise in margins of victory is a product of greater resources when professionalism of Congress is a relatively recent development. The same discrepancy in timing has occurred for state legislatures (Stonecash 1993), suggesting something broader is shaping change. Instead of focusing on post–World War II election rates, Figure 7.1 suggests two other questions, one that has been largely unexamined and one that has not been answered satisfactorily. First, why did the desire to run for reelection start to rise in the mid-1800s and increase so steadily for so long? Second, why did the reelection rate of members begin to rise about the same time, and why did it also steadily rise? This longer time period makes the preoccupation of the last several decades with the presumed increase in reelection rates appear misplaced. The more interesting question is clearly the longer-term issue.

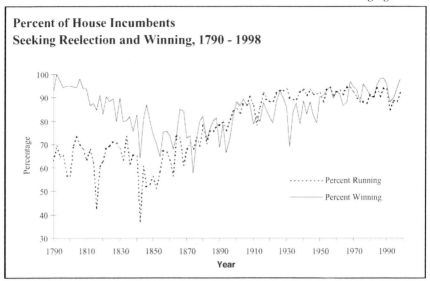

Percent of House Incumbents
Seeking Reelection and Winning, 1790 - 1998

FIGURE 7.1   Percent of House Incumbents Seeking Reelection and
Winning, 1790-1998

It seems questionable to presume that there has been some significant
increase in reelection rates in recent decades and that this provides evidence for some relatively recent candidate-centered politics. The late
1800s are generally regarded as the party-centered era, and reelection
rates were rising even during that time. If higher reelection rates are a
product of the recent emergence of candidate-centered campaigns, we
also would not expect them to rise during a time when party cohesion
and voting were at their peak.

Margins of Victory

Central to the candidate-centered view has been the presumed increase
over time in the proportion of the vote that incumbents receive. This increase has been presented as evidence that incumbents are using their resources to improve their electoral fortunes. This trend bears reexamining.[5]
There is first the issue of what time frame should be employed in examining these proportions. Garand and Gross (1984) argue that whatever increase there is began long ago, and it is implausible to attribute a trend of
approximately 150 years to post–1946 increases in candidate resources.

There is also the issue of how to calculate the percentage. Most studies
measure the incumbent's percentage of the vote as a percentage of the

two-party vote (Mayhew 1974a, 297; Born 1979, 812; Alford and Hibbing 1981, 1045; Gross and Garand 1984, 226; Jacobson 2001, 25). In many states third-party candidates run in the November elections. If their votes are excluded from the denominator, it reduces the vote total, and increases the apparent vote percentage of winners. As an example, assume a Republican wins 55 percent, a Democrat wins 35 percent, and third-party candidates win 10 percent of the total vote. If the third-party vote is excluded, the Republican winning percentage is now 55/90, or 61.1 percent. If our concern is the percentage of the vote that incumbents receive, and whether it is increasing, it seems highly inappropriate to measure and present percentages that are not the actual percentages that candidates attain.[6] The practice of using only the two party-vote total as the denominator has the effect of systematically increasing the apparent percentage of the vote received, relative to what was actually received. Given the focus on percentages, that may be misleading. It also has the effect of reporting incumbent percentages across districts and over time with a continually shifting denominator base, making the results less reliably comparable over time.[7]

The more serious issue, however, is whether the vote percentage of incumbents[8] has actually increased. The question revolves around which races to examine. Mayhew began the focus on this issue with an examination of percentages for incumbents as distinct from elections that were open seats, where no incumbent was present (Mayhew 1974b). The initial follow-up studies modified the group of incumbents to be considered and chose to focus only on contested races, sometimes excluding the South and sometimes including the South (Ferejohn 1977; Garand and Gross 1984; Gross and Garand 1984; Jacobson 1987, 1997). The argument for excluding the South was that the region had such a unique political history that its largely uncontested elections should be excluded (Alford and Hibbing 1981, 1046). More generally, elections uncontested by one of the major parties were excluded on the grounds that only "meaningful" races should be examined.

The crucial matter is the empirical effect of excluding uncontested seats. The difficulty is that the number of uncontested races has changed and varied dramatically over time, and the pattern of this variation affects the average incumbent vote percentage over time. If an uncontested race is excluded, but then the district changes to being contested, it generally involves adding into the calculation of the mean for the next year a district with a high percentage for the winner. The change from uncontested to contested is unlikely to produce an immediate, relatively

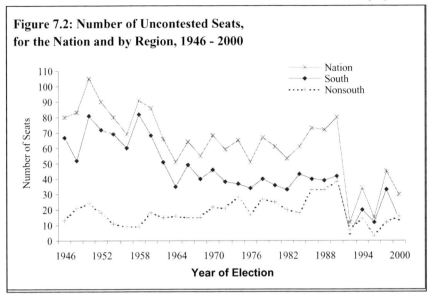

FIGURE 7.2   Number of Uncontested Seats, for the Nation and by Region,
1946-2000

competitive election as the transition occurs. The addition of the previously uncontested race means adding to the calculation a higher-than-average vote percentage, which contributes to the impression that the average incumbent percentage is increasing. If there is a declining number of uncontested races over time, it means continually adding to the calculation districts with relatively high winning percentages. This results in the impression of a rising percentage for incumbents, when the "real" source of change may be expanding the set of districts considered. The odd consequence is that even though the number of uncontested races is declining, and all races are in a sense becoming more competitive, the method will give the impression that races are becoming less competitive.

On the other hand, if there is an increase in uncontested races over time, it means consistently removing cases that winners previously won with relatively large proportions. The effect of removing will be declining winners' percentages. In this case, while races overall become less competitive, removing these districts will give the impression that elections are becoming more competitive. The issue, then, is whether the number of uncontested races has been declining or increasing.

Figure 7.2 indicates the number of uncontested races involving incumbents since 1946 by region and for the nation. During the 1950s and the

1960s most, but not all, uncontested elections were in the South, and almost all of those were Democratic seats. The number of such districts in the South began to decline in the early 1960s (precisely the time when Mayhew noticed a change in electoral outcomes). This means that if the focus is on the entire nation, beginning in the early 1960s there is the steady addition of districts in which winners receive relative high proportions. Since many of these races were in the South, Garand and Gross (1984) argue that this region should be excluded. If this is not done (Jacobson 1997), the trend of an increase might be simply a product of the changing pool of districts. The issue of what to do with uncontested races is still with us, however. From the 1960s through the 1990s the number of uncontested races is erratic and still relatively high in some years. Indeed, in 1998 there were ninety-three uncontested races. The issue of whether to exclude uncontested races is still very much with us.[9]

If the concern is tracking closeness of electoral outcomes for incumbents over time, there are several reasons why excluding these races is suspect. Perhaps the simplest and most important reason is that excluding them fundamentally misrepresents the average percentage of the vote for incumbents in U.S. House elections. Given that in the 1950s there were between ninety and 110 uncontested elections per year, 20 to 25 percent of House elections are excluded. It is a questionable practice to purport to assess how incumbents are faring, while excluding those who do particularly well. Excluding the South also presents significant problems. The analysis becomes a regional study, not a study of House elections. Further, not all elections in the South were uncontested, and, indeed, by the late 1950s and early 1960s many Democratic incumbents were encountering Republican opponents who were receiving substantial vote proportions. If the South is excluded for the 1950s and 1960s, there comes a point, given the rise of Republican successes in the region, when the South has to be added to the series. That point will inevitably be arbitrary, and it will alter the nature of the time series. Finally, uncontested races are not confined to the South, and we do not know what the effect of adding and removing cases does to results. If our concern is how incumbents are faring in House elections, and not among some shifting subset of elections, then it seems more appropriate to include all incumbents.

While there are conceptual reasons to debate whether to include or exclude some districts, the more interesting question is whether the decision matters empirically. Does it change the conclusion that incumbents are obtaining higher percentages of the vote? The trends in vote proportions for only incumbents in contested elections and then for all elections

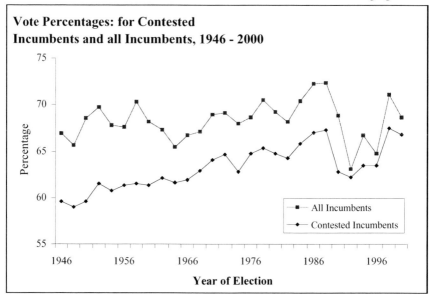

FIGURE 7.3   Vote Percentages, for Contested Incumbents and All Incumbents, 1946-2000

are shown in Figure 7.3. The important matter is what happens when all incumbent contests are included in the analysis. As might be expected, given the steady decline in uncontested races from the 1950s through the 1980s, the average vote proportion starts lower and rises for contested races and increases over time as these newly contested races are added in.

To precisely assess the two trends, the series shown in Figure 7.3 are regressed on time. This provides a precise estimation of the trend over time. The results, shown in Table 7.1, indicate that the choice of whether to include contested and uncontested elections matters a great deal. If the focus is on only incumbents involved in contested elections, the trend is fairly positive. "Time" explains a considerable proportion of the variance in the trend, indicating the trend is consistently upward. In contrast, the trend for all incumbent elections is virtually flat, and time explains very little of whatever variation exists. The difference in these trends, again, is that the former includes only incumbents in contested elections and is affected by the decline of uncontested seats and the addition of these higher vote proportions over time. This addition occurred, somewhat erratically, from the late 1950s through the 1980s and increased the average vote proportions for contested incumbents over that time. In contrast, if all elections are examined, there is virtually no upward trend.

Trends in Incumbent Vote Proportion, House Contested and All Elections, 1946 — 2000 (Regression of percentages on year)				
	n	b	R^2	probability
Contested	28	.106	.56	.00
All	28	.014	.01	.65

TABLE 7.1 Trends in Incumbent Vote Proportion, House Contested and All Elections, 1946-2000

This analysis indicates that the presumed increase in electoral margins has not occurred. For the last several decades analyses of House elections have presumed an increase in margins of victory and have made explaining this increase a central concern.[10] The trend has been taken as evidence that incumbents can use the resources of their office and campaign funds to alter their electoral margins and create a candidate-centered politics, rather than politics shaped by the relationship between specific constituencies and partisan connections. The reality is that an increase did not occur, unless we exclude some races and ignore the effects of gradually adding over time these previously uncontested races. If the focus is the general competitiveness of elections, this hardly seems appropriate.

The Individual Level Data on Partisan Decline

Another key part of the basis of the candidate-centered interpretation is the individual-level data documenting that voters have become less attached to parties, vote for their party candidates less often, and split their ticket more often. The evidence also does not support the expectation that there are long-term trends in the directions suggested. The data do indicate that the presumed trends developed from the 1960s through the 1970s, but those trends reversed as the 1980s evolved. The evidence clearly indicates that identification with parties is rising, that party voting is rising, and that split-ticket voting is declining (Aldrich 1999; Bartells 2000; Jacobson 2000a, 2000b). It is difficult to accept an interpretation of elections that portrays candidates as creating unique electoral connections ("the personal vote") when voters are more attached to parties and partisan voting is rising. Further, a review of these trends for the last fifty years indicates that even at their lowest points, levels of partisan attachment and voting were hardly low. At the lowest level, 85 percent of the electorate identified with or leaned to one of the two major parties, 80 percent of partisans were voting for their party candidates, and 70 percent of voters were voting for the presidential and House candidate of the same party. Again, it is difficult to see this as an electoral world in which partisanship does not matter and "personal votes" are shaping elections.

How, then, might we interpret the dip and then revival of partisanship over the last forty years? The data conform to the pattern we would expect if parties were significantly re-sorting their constituency bases over the last several decades. As reviewed in Chapter 5, in the last half of the twentieth century several significant shifts occurred. In the 1950s there was limited class division in American politics (Stonecash 2000, 44–48). The Democratic Party was a combination of conservative Southern and moderate–liberal members from outside the South. The Republican Party was a combination of Northern Republicans somewhat sympathetic to government playing a role, and Western Republicans less supportive of a role for government. Since then Democrats have emerged in the North and Republicans have emerged in the South. In the North Democrats have made gains since the 1940s, and they have steadily increased their electoral support among the less affluent (Stonecash et al. 2000). In the South Republicans have made steady gains with their greatest support now among the more affluent (Brewer and Stonecash 2001). These gradually evolving transitions resulted in less clarity of party images, reducing the strength of partisan behavior.

We now have parties with more distinct electoral bases and more divergent policies. That sorting out is culminating in a more "ordered" electoral alignment. Conservatives are more likely to identify with and vote for the Republican Party (Abramowitz and Saunders 2000). The ideological differences between party identifiers declined through the 1970s, then started increasing (Jacobson 2000a). As Jacobson so clearly documents, a wide array of data indicates that conservatives are more likely to identify as Republicans and liberals as Democrats. The parties have in turn adopted differing stances, and party identifiers are engaging in higher levels of partisan voting. After a drop in the 1970s, the percentage of partisan identifiers voting for their party candidates has increased in the 1980s and 1990s (Bartells 2000). At the individual level, split-ticket voting is declining (Aldrich 1999, 23; Jacobson 2000a, 20). At the congressional House district level the correlation between party voting for the president and the House candidate has increased (Jacobson 2000a, 21). It seems highly implausible to interpret elections are "candidate-centered" at a time when partisan attachments and divisions are steadily increasing.

In summary, the candidate-centered view of congressional elections has two fundamental problems. First, the evidence for the view that electoral outcomes were changed in the 1960s by legislative and campaign resources is very weak. Reelection rates have barely risen in post-World War II politics, and whatever major increases occurred began in the mid–1800s. Margins of victory for incumbents have not increased. Partisan voting in the electorate dipped somewhat in the mid–1970s, but then returned to earlier levels. Second, the framework provides no explanation for why more party members in the House would begin to vote together. House members seeking to separate themselves from broad partisan electoral reactions would not be inclined to line up and vote consistently as party members.

Party Probabilities

The analyses presented here indicate that the composition of districts plays a significant role in affecting partisan outcomes. Democrats are likely to win districts that are urban, heavily non-white, and less affluent. Republicans are likely to win districts that are less urban, primarily white, and more affluent. In most House districts, the possibilities of only one party winning the seat are very high (Abramowitz 1991, 36–37; Abramowitz and Saunders 2000, 1). The result is that most districts are essentially "party" districts, or so affected by who comprises the district that it is highly probable that only one party will win the seat (Erikson and Wright 2001, 78). In the early 1900s the percentage of districts electing the same party during a decade was in the 50–60 range (Schantz 1987, 374). In the 1970s (1972–80) 65 percent of districts did not change which party held the district across five elections. In the 1980s 79 percent of districts remained held by the same party across the five elections. As Table 7.2 indicates, 73.3 percent of House seats in the 1990s did not change from one party to another, and this was during an era that experienced one of the largest partisan shifts in the history of the House. Indeed, in the fifty-two years after 1946, despite continual turnover in the House, 73 percent of open seat contests were won by the party that held the seat in the prior election (Jacobson 2000a, 37).

In a political world where most districts are likely to remain Democratic and Republican, and where during the 1990s only 25 percent of seats actually changed from one party to another at least once, it seems questionable to classify House elections as candidate-centered. If so, they can be regarded as "candidate-centered" in only the most limited sense that a party candidate organizes a largely certain partisan outcome.

Partisan Seat Changes in the 1990s (Out of 5 Elections)						
	Number of Times Seat Won by Democrat					
	0	1	2	3	4	5
All Districts	35.3	9.2	6.2	5.3	6.0	38.0
Income						
0 - 37,999	17.8	10.3	12.2	0	4.7	55.1
38 - 47,999	37.4	11.7	5.9	5.9	7.0	32.2
48,000 plus	45.1	5.9	2.6	8.5	4.6	33.3
% Urban						
0 - 69	40.8	13.0	10.1	4.1	8.8	23.1
70 - 79	37.3	19.6	7.8	3.9	0	31.4
80 plus	30.3	3.8	2.8	6.6	4.3	52.1
% Non-white						
0 - 9	47.4	10.4	5.8	6.9	6.9	22.5
10 - 19	42.9	11.4	7.6	4.8	2.9	30.5
20 plus	16.6	6.6	5.3	3.3	6.0	62.3

TABLE 7.2   Partisan Seat Changes in the 1990s

Further, the extent to which one party holds onto a seat is not random but is clearly associated with the population composition of the district. As Table 7.2 indicates, districts that are less than 20 percent non-white, less urban, and more affluent are likely to be held continuously by Republicans. Districts that are more than 20 percent non-white, heavily urban, and less affluent are likely to be held continuously by Democrats. Much as it is in many state legislatures, the chances of one party taking a seat from another seat in some areas is very low (Stonecash 1999). Candidates of the minority party, no matter how strong they are, know that, and they are unlikely to come forth to challenge the candidate of the party that dominates the district. Even if "quality" minority party candidates emerge, their chances of winning are limited. Again, to discuss elections as if the qualities and resources of candidates shape electoral outcomes seems largely unconnected to the reality of elections.

This reality is widely recognized by those who handicap elections well in advance of November. Services such as *The Cook Report*, *Roll Call*, and *CQ* regularly classify districts as to the likely outcomes. *Cook* classifies districts into safe or likely for each party, leaning to either party, or as a tossup (Cook 2000). Table 7.3 summarizes the classifications for 2000 and indicates how those classifications are associated with demographic traits. Those districts that are safe or likely for one party are grouped together for each party. Cook classifies only 13.1 percent of all House districts as leaning to either party or tossups.

The important matter is that the likely outcome in districts is again associated with the demographics of districts. Less affluent districts are more likely to be Democratic districts, while more affluent districts are more likely to be Republican. Districts with a substantial non-white composition or that are heavily urban are more likely to be Democratic districts, while primarily white and less urban districts are likely to be Republican. To be sure, there are districts that do not fit the pattern. As noted earlier, Republicans are projected to win in some districts that have 20 percent or more of non-whites. Polarization by district traits is by no means complete, and we have much to understand about how these seemingly odd outcomes occur. Nonetheless, there are clear patterns as to where Republicans and Democrats are likely to win.

Respecifying the Relevance
of the Candidate-Centered Argument

This review suggests two matters. First, the evidence for the candidate-centered interpretation of House elections does not support a portrait of increasing electoral security for incumbents and declining electoral attachment to parties. Second, the evidence suggests that the composition of districts plays a significant role in partisan outcomes. Democrats are more likely to win in some districts and Republicans are more likely to win in many others. In only a distinct minority of districts is the winner uncertain.

These realities in turn affect the inclination of experienced candidates to run for office and their ability to raise money.[11] Experienced candidates are more likely to emerge when the district composition and past voting patterns favor their party (Gaddie and Bullock 2000: 76). Contributors and party leaders are aware of which races are likely to be close. If a race is likely to be one-sided, "the need for substantial money decreases as the core constituency becomes so large that the partisan outcome is preordained" (Gaddie and Bullock 2000, 104). Contributions are more likely to flow to elections that either party might win, if it has the resources. This results in more money flowing to close elections. As anyone involved in campaigns will indicate, the likely closeness of elections is the primary cause of how much money races attract (Jacobson and

**Likely Outcomes in 2000 House
Elections, and by Demographics**

	Rep	Toss-up	Dem
All Districts	47.8	13.1	39.1
Income			
0 - 24,999	38.8	8.6	52.6
25 - 34,999	52.5	9.3	38.1
35,000 plus	47.5	14.7	37.9
% Urban			
0 - 69	57.9	11.6	30.5
70 - 79	68.1	6.4	25.5
80 plus	32.0	12.5	55.5
% Non-white			
0 - 9	60.3	13.0	26.7
10 - 19	57.3	11.7	31.1
20 plus	23.8	9.5	66.7

Source: Cook Report (2000).

TABLE 7.3   Likely Outcomes in 2000 House Elections, and by
Demographics

Kernell 1983, 37; Stonecash, 1988, 1994; Stonecash and Keith 1996). Table
7.4 indicates for the 1998 elections the expenditure by Democratic and
Republican House candidates, and total spending. More money was
spent in close elections. The spending had some effect on the closeness,
but total spending was largely in response to the perception that a race
was going to be close.[12] In districts likely to go to one party, the candidates in the other party were less able to raise money. While many assume that the differential in spending causes the outcome, it is more
likely that candidates running in a district dominated by the other party
are unable to raise much money. Perhaps the most important matter is
that there were a relatively limited number of districts where there was
some uncertainty about the outcome. Three hundred thirty-two, or 76
percent of districts, were regarded as safe for one of the parties. Again,

Campaign Spending in 1998 by Projected Outcome						
Cook 98			Spending by:		Percent Spent by:	
Projection	n	Dem	Rep	Total	Dem	Rep
Safe Rep	180	60,728	678,633	678,633	8.0	92.1
Likely Rep	21	448,593	985,211	1,422,047	31.4	68.6
Lean Rep	17	1,009,633	1,295,490	2,305,123	40.1	59.9
Toss-up	23	1,153,778	1,183,949	2,337,727	49.9	50.1
Lean Dem	17	1,153,778	900,961	2,058,729	59.2	40.8
Likely Dem	32	779,866	356,447	1,136,314	69.0	31.0
Safe Dem	144	407,585	69,985	476,762	86.5	13.5

TABLE 7.4   Campaign Spending in 1998 by Projected Outcome

to characterize House elections as candidate-centered seems a highly inaccurate portrait of election realities.

Does this mean that the candidate-centered argument is invalid? Does it mean that money does not matter? The answer to both questions is, of course, no. For most House elections, it is difficult to accept a view that the crucial matters are the quality of the candidates, their visibility, and their access to legislative resources and campaign finance funds. Winners in most districts may have more of these than losers, and these advantages are more likely to be held by incumbents than challengers. But the likely success of most winners and their greater resources did not emerge just because a better candidate works harder or is more connected to influential donors. Some candidates have these advantages because a specific party is likely to win most districts because of the composition of the district. That in turn leads to that party's having a greater ability to raise more of the resources necessary to win the election. Those candidates end up with greater visibility.

This scenario, however, does not cover all districts. Some districts have a relatively evenly divided partisan mix. These are the districts in which an attractive candidate, with a well-organized campaign, who skillfully presents issues, identifies and contacts persuadable voters, and mobilizes his supporters well has an excellent chance of winning elections relative to a candidate who does not do these things well. It is in these districts that the candidate-centered framework has relevance. These districts also draw the greatest party efforts. These districts are, however, at least in recent years, no more than about 25 percent of all House districts, and that may be overstating the case. There are races that are candidate-centered, but it hardly seems appropriate to define House elections as candidate-centered when a maximum of one-fourth of House districts fall into this category.

Instead, it seems that the more fruitful approach is to focus on understanding how the dynamics of social conditions and partisan responses have created a situation in which roughly 75 percent of districts have fairly predictable partisan outcomes. That focus might lead us to understand the sources of the growing party polarization in the House and the ability of party leaders to get members to vote together (Rohde 1991; Sinclair 1995, 1998). Our first hope is that such research will receive more attention.

A focus on the constituency-party connection will also direct us back to the central issue of a democratic political process: Do elections and the representation process contribute to constituent views getting heard and considered? We think that the spatial distribution of social, economic, and racial concerns, the connection of partisan outcomes to these concerns, and the workings of the parties create more democratic representation than many critics of Congress presume exists. The portrait of candidate-centered elections conveys a sense that personality, campaign funds, and the exploitation of office resources drive election outcomes and that somehow issues and representation of the public get lost. The evidence shows, to the contrary, that who populates a district affects partisan outcomes and how that elected member of Congress votes. The result is conflict, largely because of the tremendous diversity of American society and how it is distributed across districts. While the conflict is often disturbing, it is a result of a democratic process by which constituencies get represented. Our second hope is that the extent of democratic representation gets more consideration in the future.

Notes

1. It is not quite clear exactly what is meant by the statement that candidate-centered politics and incumbency buffer or insulate candidates from normal electoral forces. Despite the widespread use of the term "candidate-centered" politics, there is a remarkable dearth of specific statements of just what this means for voting patterns within districts, which is where elections actually happen. We know of no studies that explore or test precisely what candidate-centered politics means for what happens to electoral alignments within districts. Regardless, two possibilities, among many, are reviewed here. The concern is first with what happens within districts, and then what this means for patterns of division across districts. The basic presumption, it would seem, is that a candidate can somehow increase electoral support from what it would be without candidate-centered politics in effect.

First, this means that successful candidates can reduce normal partisan cleavages by making themselves and their personality central to the campaign, rather than allowing social cleavages to operate. In the table below, assume that a Republican is running in a district where the income composition is 50 percent lower, 30 percent middle, and 20 percent higher. These groups differ in their support for social programs, and for their general level of support for any Republican candidate. If these factors play out, then we can calculate the likely support from each group. Lower income voters are 50 percent of the district, and 35 percent support a Republican. That results in 17.6 percent of district voters, from this group, voting Republican (.50 * .35). If this pattern plays out among middle and higher income groups, the Republican candidate receives a total of 45.6 percent of district votes, and the Republican loses.

Alternative Impacts of Candidate-Centered Politics on Voting Patterns: Republican Situation

Alternative Fates of a Moderate-conservative Republican

Income Group	% of district	% favoring soc prog	% in support of Rep	District vote For Rep	Partisan Outcome
Without candidate-centered politics					
Lower	50	65	35	17.6	
Middle	30	50	50	15.0	
Higher	20	35	65	13.0	
				45.6	R loses
With candidate-centered politics — division by income reduced					
Lower	50	65	50	25.0	
Middle	30	50	60	18.0	
Higher	20	35	65	13.0	
				56.0	R wins
With candidate-centered politics — general favorability improves					
Lower	50	65	50	25.0	
Middle	30	50	65	19.5	
Higher	20	35	80	16.0	
				60.5	R wins

A Republican candidate, faced with losing, may try to alter within-district patterns. One solution is to downplay issue positions and present the candidate as a good and affable person, and thereby reduce the opposition among less affluent voters. The result might be that issue divisions, while they might still exist, would have less impact on voting. The Republican candidate could then increase her support among the lower- and middle-income groups and, with this greater support, win the district. The incumbent's goal in subsequent elections would then be to maintain a focus on being a good person who responds to everybody, attends many local events, and has high visibility, while avoiding issue positions that would activate "natural" opposition from lower- and middle-income groups.

In contrast, a Republican candidate might accept the income divisions of opinion that exist in the district, but focus on a general improvement in visibility and imagery that would raise support among all groups. The result would be higher levels of support among all groups, and a Republican victory.

Alternative Impacts of Candidate-Centered Politics on Voting Patterns:
Democratic Situation

Alternative Fates of a moderate-liberal Democratic

Income Group	% of district	% favoring soc prog	% in support of Dem	District vote For Dem	Partisan Outcome
Without candidate-centered politics					
Lower	50	65	65	13.0	
Middle	30	50	50	15.0	
Higher	20	35	35	17.5	
				45.5	D loses
With candidate-centered politics — division by income reduced					
Lower	50	65	65	13.0	
Middle	30	50	60	18.0	
Higher	20	35	50	25.0	
				56.0	D wins
With candidate-centered politics — general favorability improves					
Lower	50	65	80	16.0	
Middle	30	50	65	19.5	
Higher	20	35	50	25.0	
				60.5	D wins

Either of these approaches would transform a "normally" Democratic district into a Republican district. There are other possibilities, of course. A Republican might seek to rely on lower turnout among lower-income groups, and win by small margin, or he might try to polarize the electorate around class issues, and increase support among the middle- and higher-income groups. The latter approach, however, might not qualify as candidate-centered politics, because the focus would be on issues and not the candidate. If this approach, and the first one, in which class divisions are downplayed, are central, it seems they are less candidate-centered than they are attempts to use issues to change voting patterns. If issues are not central, then presumably this is a variant on candidate-centered politics.

Notwithstanding ambiguities about when candidate-centered politics is evident or not, there are approaches that a Republican candidate might employ to alter a "normal" outcome and win a district.

A Democrat, running in a more affluent district, might pursue similar strategies. He or she could seek to soften partisan divisions by income, or generally increase his visibility, and win in a district that is 50 percent higher, 30 percent middle, and 20 percent lower. The second table in this note indicates a pattern similar to that shown for the Republican.

The crucial matter is what these examples of the impacts of candidate-centered politics might mean for national relationships. If the first situation, a moderate-conservative Republican running and winning in a district dominated by the less affluent, occurs in some modest number of districts, it reduces Democratic success in such districts. If a few Democrats win in more affluent districts, then it reduces Republican success in such districts. The result will be less of a relationship between district income and partisan success. The role of district composition will be less, and presumably Republican and Democratic members of Congress will be less inclined to let district composition affect how they vote on class issues. For example, a Democrat may have a unique personal appeal that attracts all constituents and makes him or her less inclined to vote with other Democrats on class issues.

2. If referring to "candidate-centered" elections is meant to imply only that candidates establish their own campaign organizations, raise their own funds, and make their own strategic decisions, then there is probably considerable truth to that. If the argument is made that this is what the phrase implies, however, it avoids all the implications about what shapes electoral outcomes and voting behavior.

3. Districts are also, of course, affected by broad electoral forces, and swing districts are affected by these forces more than others. A large body of research indicates that changes in the popularity of the president and changes in the economy affect aggregate party success (Kramer 1971; Tufte 1975; Jacobson and Kernell 1983; Abramowitz 1986). While these aggregate effects exist, the concern of this analysis is variations in party success across types of districts. These national forces may shift results toward one party across all types of districts for specific elections, but the focus of this analysis is the variation in party success *across* districts.

4. The data are taken from Benjamin and Malbin, *Term Limits* (1992, 291–295), plus additions of more recent results.

5. The data for this were originally taken from the ICPSR file on House election results including the years 1790–1990, with subsequent results added by the authors. Subsequent inspections of the data indicated that there were significant errors in that file. See the Appendix on congressional election data for an explanation of the steps taken to correct these errors.

6. The same problem applies to calculating the percentage of candidates who win by more than 60 percent, used as an indicator of relative safeness (Gross and Garand 1984, 226–27; Jacobson 2000a, 27). If the percentage of the two-party vote is used, it increases the apparent electoral success of winners and makes it appear that a greater proportion won by safe margins. If the goal is to track the actual percentage winning by more than some level, using a percentage derived from a calculation with a shifting denominator of an unknown magnitude is very questionable.

7. Whether using the two-party denominator affects the apparent increase over time will depend, of course, on whether third-party vote totals increase or decrease over time. If they increase, it will lower the actual denominator used in calculations, and, while winners are receiving lower percentages, it will appear that they are winning with higher percentages. If the third-party vote increased over time, and winning candidates continue to receive 55 percent, the winning percentage would appear to be higher, while it will actually be unchanged. The magnitude of the impact of third-party votes over time could be assessed by tracking the third-party vote and its percentage of the total vote, but studies do not even begin to explore this. While that could be done, the fundamental point is that if the goal is to represent the proportion of the vote that winners are receiving, it is that proportion that should be reported. There are few candidates in American politics with 40 percent of the vote (out of 70 percent of the vote going to the two-party candidates) who would regard their vote proportion as 57. It certainly seems odd that studies have been done using this measure. It seems far more appropriate to just use the actual percentage of the vote of winners.

8. A second issue is whether to examine incumbents or open-seat candidates. If the concern is primarily with whether incumbents are increasing their vote percentages (as Mayhew focused upon), then separating these two is appropriate. While that is a legitimate focus, several studies have found that the vote percentages for winning incumbents and winning open-seat candidates are essentially the same (Garand and Gross 1984; Gross and Garand 1984). If the concern is the trend in the percentage of the vote winners receive, then excluding open-seat races removes cases that are just as important to explain as those of incumbents. Further, the number of open seats varies considerably over time, so an irregular number of cases is removed over time, and the number of cases being examined is also varying. Since the concern here is the more general one of the percentage of votes winners receive, the focus will be on races involving both incumbents and open-seat winners.

9. Uncontested races are also less and less confined to Democratic winners. During the 1950s and 1960s most beneficiaries of uncontested elections were Democrats. The number of Republican candidates without a Democratic opponent has steadily increased, and by the 1990s Republicans had more uncontested elections than the Democrats. This trend also has implications for representing House election results. Excluding uncontested elections understates Democratic percentages during the 1950s–1980s, and it then understates Republican percentages during the 1990s as they enjoyed more uncontested seats.

10. As expressed by Jacobson, "From the 1950s through the 1980s, the electoral importance of individual candidates and campaigns expanded, while that of party labels and national issues diminished. The emergence of a more candidate-centered electoral process helped one class of congressional candidates to prosper: the incumbent office-holders. Indeed, the electoral advantage enjoyed by incumbents, at least as measured by electoral margins, increased so notably after the mid–1960s that it became the main focus of congressional electoral research for the next quarter century." (2000, 21).

11. Each candidate, of course, calculates the probability of winning, and he or she is more likely to run when the possibilities of winning are greater. These probabilities are, of course, affected by the aggregate fortunes of parties, affected by scandal, recessions, and so forth (Jacobson and Kernell 1983, 19–34), but the differences across districts in the possibility of winning are still, on average, a product of the district composition.

12. While it is widely recognized that it is more accurate to say that closeness draws money, rather than that money creates outcomes, the standard practice in campaign analyses continues to be treating expenditures as the independent variable and margin of victory or proportion of the vote won as the dependent variable. The result is the continuing, standard, and odd conclusion that the more a challenger spends, the greater the vote proportion, and that for incumbents, the more they spend, the worse they do (Jacobson 1978, 2001, 40–46). The way out of this clearly implausible language is to recognize the interaction between probable outcomes and money raised and spent, but that would mean abandoning the use of campaign finance as an independent variable, which most scholars appear very reluctant to do.

Congressional District Data: 1920–2000

Demographic Data on House Districts

Data on House Districts: 1920s–1930s

There have been analyses of House districts for the 1920s and the 1930s using the demographic traits of districts. Julius Turner, in *Party and Constituency* (1951), assessed whether the presence of a metropolitan and rural district affected party voting and cohesion. He indicated in footnote 5, page 74, that "The term 'metropolitan' as used hereafter describes an area in which 50.1 per cent or more of the population lives in a metropolitan area as defined by the United States Census of 1930 or 1940. All districts not metropolitan are termed 'rural,' although they may contain a large number of persons from towns or small villages." He did not, however, explain how districts were classified. Since no published data existed on these indicators, it must be presumed that he used maps, and since many districts represented whole counties, he must have added together multiple county data to arrive at a way to classify districts.

We obtained his dissertation, entitled *Voting Behavior in the House of Representatives: A Study of Representative Government and Political Pressure*, submitted in 1949 to Johns Hopkins University, to see if it contains a listing of districts. The dissertation does not. On page 147, in footnote 6, he explained that he did not use urban, because urban areas involve areas with only 2,500 or more people, and such a criterion would result in most districts being urban.

Data on House Districts: 1940s

The only Bureau of Census document that provides any information about House districts is the Special Report, *Population of the United States by Congressional Districts*, issued in 1945. It reports only the population per House district and does not allow characterizing districts by population composition, income status, or percentage urban.

Data on House Districts: 1950s

The primary source of data for districts from the 1950s is from the *County and City Data Book 1956*, "Appendix G: Selected Data for Congressional Districts." This book presents data for voting for 1952, 1954, and 1956. It also presents 1950 census data for the total population, the number living in urban areas, the farming population, limited data on the age distribution of the population, the percent foreign born, and the percent non-white.

Limits of the 1950 Data Source. Of the data in the 1956 report, the information on the urban population is useful for characterizing districts in the 1950s. As noted, these data are from the 1950 census, and following the pattern that we use for the other decades, they provide an indication of the population composition at the beginning of the decade. These data, however, are presented only for districts that consist of whole counties (either one whole county or multiple whole counties). The Census Bureau was able to provide district data in such cases. If a district is part of a county, but does not comprise the entire county, no data are reported. The result is that urban districts, which generally include multiple districts, have no 1950 census data for the percentage of the district that is urban.

Percent Non-White. The same problem that occurs for urban data occurs for the percentage non-white. Districts that are part of a county have no data on the percentage non-white. Since many of these districts may have a high percentage of non-whites, the presence of non-whites may be underreported across districts because of the missing data.

Median Family Income. A final limitation of the 1956 report is that it contains no information on the economic situation of individuals or families in districts. There are no data for per capita or median family income in the 1956 report.

Data on House Districts: 1960s–1990s

Beginning in 1961 the Bureau of the Census began to publish a series of documents entitled *Congressional District Data Book*. This appears after states have redistricted following the most recent census. These books provide relatively detailed information on districts, and form the basis for almost all the data used in our analysis. There are also periodic challenges in particular states to the districts drawn after a census. If the lawsuit is successful, and districts are redrawn within a state, the Census Bureau issues new demographic profiles of the new districts, drawing on the data from the prior census. We were able to find most of these reissued reports in various libraries, and we changed the data for those districts that were redrawn in the middle of a decade.

Data on House Districts: 2000 Census for Districts Created in the Early 1990s

Data for percent non-white and median family income for many districts are available at the web page: http://factfinder.census.gov/servlet/BasicFacts Servlet. As of December 2001, median family income was not available for all districts. We were able to find non-white information for all 435 districts, and income data for 210 districts.

Election Results

The matter of the accuracy of election results is not discussed in most studies, but it may be relevant here. To the extent that analyses are based on ICPSR study 7757, accuracy issues are very important. We began with the data from this ICPSR study, compared it to the election results printed in the *Congressional Quarterly's Guide to U.S. Elections*, Third Edition (1994), and discovered numerous errors. We then consulted the *CQ Guide* to try to determine what the results were for a particular district. In addition, when this source did not seem adequate, as was true for Louisiana results, we consulted Michael J. Dubin, *United States Congressional Elections, 1788–1997* (1998), to find further results. Assuming these two sources are accurate, which we cannot verify, the following kinds of errors were detected. In some cases, the percentage for the Democratic or Republican candidate was missing. In other cases a single-digit percentage was recorded for a Democrat or Republican, but that candidate actually received no votes. In all these cases, we corrected the results using the two volumes cited. In general, we relied on the Dubin book, because it appears to be more complete in reporting results. That is, this book consistently reports results for more minor party candidates. Because these other candidates are included, the percentage won by the major party winner is reflective of the actual percentage of all votes received by the winning candidate.

One kind of "error" is particularly noteworthy. In both California and New York, cross-endorsement of candidates has occurred. In California, a candidate might run with the endorsement of the Democratic and Republican Parties. In these cases, the *CQ* volume records the actual party affiliation of candidates. In the ICPSR data set many of these districts have no recorded votes, and these districts end up missing in analyses of vote percentages. In New York candidates can be cross-endorsed and then have their name listed on both lines. We checked these cases against the official results printed in the *Legislative Manual* for various years. While the votes on the separate lines should be added together and recorded as only a Democratic or Republican vote, the ICPSR data set records the vote on the Democratic line as the vote for the Democratic candidate and the vote on the Republican line as the vote for a Republican candidate. The result is that a district is recorded as contested and competitive to some degree, when it was uncontested by a major party candidate. Races were recorded as closer than they were. In both of these cases, we corrected the data. In California, I used the *CQ* designation of the candidate's actual party affiliation and recorded the total votes for the candidate on that party line. The other party line was given a 0. The logic of this is that the general concern is the partisan vote for major party candidates. In each district, almost all candidates will have an initial party affiliation, and that will be known in the district. If the candidate receives the endorsement of another party, the actual vote is still for a candidate of a specific party. In New York the same logic applies. While a name is listed on two (or more) lines, the party affiliation of each candidate is well-known, and the vote is for that candidate, regardless of on which line it is received.

A similar issue involves Wisconsin voting. For years the Democrat-Farmer-Labor Party served as the vehicle for representing the Democratic Party in the state. The ICPSR shows no vote for Democratic candidates in the years that the DFL was relevant. We recorded the DFL percentages as the Democratic vote. Again, the concern is not the vote percentage recorded on a party line, but the vote percentage that a candidate of a particular party received. The DFL, which operated as a fusion party, should not have no recorded vote because it is a merger of other concerns.

Finally, results in Louisiana present a difficult issue of how to record results. For some years Louisiana held an open primary which all party candidates could enter. If no candidate received a majority, a runoff would be held between the two candidates with the highest percentages, even if they were in the same party. If a candidate received enough votes to avoid a runoff, the apparent result in November is 0 (no votes) or 100 percent, for no opponent. Neither option may reflect the vote proportion the candidate won in the open primary. In a study of vote percentages of members of Congress, the options of 0 or 100 percent are not satisfactory indicators of the situation the candidate faced.

These races might simply be excluded, but that also is not very satisfactory. An option is to return to the results from the *United States Congressional Elections, 1788–1997*. This presents both the open primary and runoff results. In many of these districts, several Democrats ran along with several Republicans, and the winning percentage might be, for example, only 30 percent, compared to 13 percent for a Republican. Since in this particular study the concern is the vote proportion of candidates, and their relative security, the decision in this case is to record the percentages of the leading Democrat and that of the leading Republican. This is not completely satisfactory, since the leading Democrat might receive 30 percent, followed by a Democrat with 22 percent and then a Republican with 14 percent. Recording only the leading Democrat and Republican will underrepresent the closeness of the second highest vote recipient. That is, however, also a potential issue in a state like California where the second highest vote recipient could run on the Progressive Party ticket and not show up if only Democrats or Republicans are recorded. While this is a problem, it is minor because the focus in these vote records is on the proportion of winners, and the practice of recording 30 and 14 will reflect the percentage of the winner. The virtue of recording these percentages is that the winner actually received only 30 percent, which is not a secure position. Accurately recording and reflecting that low percentage seems appropriate in this case, and is what was done. If a candidate was unopposed in the open primary, the candidate is recorded as unopposed and receiving 100 percent.

The problems in California and Wisconsin may not affect results for members of Congress, if those doing data runs took care to record the vote of winners, regardless of the party lines involved. If, on the other hand, a district were recorded as having a Democratic or Republican winner, but no percentages were recorded on the Democratic or Republican line, then these districts may show up as missing in analyses. It is not possible to tell if this occurred because most studies contain no discussions of these specifics. In New York the problem could create clear errors of percentages. If a cross-endorsed Democrat in New York City has his vote across two lines, his vote proportion might be interpreted as 65, when the actual percentage is 95, and there is no major opponent. If only contested races are assessed, the New York situation would lead to this district being included, when it should have been excluded. Again, it is unknown whether this problem actually occurred in published studies because there is no discussion of such issues.

Bibliography

Congressional Quarterly Service, Inc. *Representation and Apportionment*. Washington, D.C.: 1966.

Congressional Quarterly. *Congressional Quarterly's Guide to U.S. Elections*, Third Edition. Washington, D.C: *Congressional Quarterly* Press, 1964.

Dubin, Michael J. *United States Congressional Elections, 1788–1997*. Jefferson: McFarland and Company, Inc., 1998.

Turner, Julius. *Voting Behavior in the House of Representatives: A Study of Representative Government and Political Pressure*. Dissertation, Johns Hopkins University, 1949.

_____. *Party and Constituency: Pressures on Congress*. The Johns Hopkins University Studies in Historical and Political Science, Series LXIX, No. 1. Baltimore: The Johns Hopkins Press, 1951.

U.S. Department of Commerce, U.S. Bureau of the Census. *Population of the United States by Congressional Districts*. Population—Special Reports. Series p–45, No. 6. July 3. Washington, D.C.: U.S. Government Printing Office, 1945. 1–2.

U.S. Department of Commerce, U.S. Bureau of the Census. *County and City Data Book 1956*. "Appendix G: Selected Data for Congressional Districts." Washington, D.C.: U.S. Government Printing Office, 1957. 495–512.

U.S. Bureau of the Census. *Congressional District Data Book (Districts of the Eighty-Seventh Congress)*—A Statistical Abstract Supplement. Washington, D.C.: U.S. Government Printing Office, 1961.

U.S. Bureau of the Census. *Congressional District Data Book (Districts of the Eighty-Eighth Congress)*—A Statistical Abstract Supplement. Washington, D.C.: U.S. Government Printing Office, 1963.

U.S. Department of Commerce, Bureau of the Census. *Congressional District Profiles, Ninety-Eighth Congress: Supplementary Report* PC80-S1–11, September. Washington, D.C.: U.S. Government Printing Office, 1983. 28 pp.

Figure, Map and Table Credits

Figure 1.1: Ornstein et al. 2000, 201, and data for 1999 and 2000 from end of the year CQ Weekly Reports

Figure 1.2: Derived from information in Ornstein et al. 2000, 201; data for 1999 and 2000 from end of the year CQ Weekly Reports.

Figure 1.3: Derived from information in Ornstein et al. 2000, 202-203; data for 1999 and 2000 from end of the year CQ Weekly Reports.

Figure 1.4: Source: ADA ratings for 1946 - 1994 are from Tim Groseclose's website: http://wesley.stanford.edu/groseclose We then acquired the ADA ratings for the years 1995 - 1999 at: http://www.adaction.org/

Figure 1.5: Compiled from data presented in Richard Fleisher and Jon R. Bond, 2000b, "Partisanship and the President's Quest for Votes," in *Polarized Politics*, ed., Jon R. Bond and Richard Fleisher. Washington, DC: Congressional Quarterly Press, p. 166.

Figure 1.6: Derived from information in Ornstein et al. 2000:, 201; data for 1999 and 2000 from end of the year CQ Weekly Reports.

Table 2.1: Data on urbanization compiled by author (See Appendix). Data on votes taken from *Congressional Quarterly Almanac,* (Washington, D.C: Congressional Quarterly Press, 1966), pp. 950-951.

Table 2.2: Hypothetical situation, created by authors.

Table 2.3: Hypothetical situation, created by authors

Figure 3.1: Data compiled by authors. See Appendix on Congressional District Data.

Figure 3.2: Data compiled by authors. See Appendix on Congressional District Data.

Figure 3.3: Data compiled by authors. See Appendix on Congressional District Data.

First map: provided by the Census Bureau.

Figure 4.1: Data from Immigration and Naturalization web page, which
presents data from the *2000 Statistical Yearbook of the
Immigration and Naturalization Service.*
http://www.ins.usdoj.gov/graphics/aboutins/statistics/IM
M00yrbk/IMM2000tables.pdf.

Figure 4.2: Data from Immigration and Naturalization web page, which
presents data from the *2000 Statistical Yearbook of the
Immigration and Naturalization Service.*
http://www.ins.usdoj.gov/graphics/aboutins/statistics/IM
M00yrbk/IMM2000tables.pdf.

Second map: provided by the Census Bureau.

Table 4.4: The 1990 data are taken from the *1994 City and County Data
Book* (Bureau of the Census, 1996), "Table A States—
Population Characteristics." P. 3. The 1999 data are from
their web page: http://www.census.gov/population/projec-
tions/state/stpjpop.txt. For more detailed information, see
Population Paper Listing #47, "Population Projections for
States, by Age, Sex, Race, and Hispanic Origin: 1995 to
2025." The totals for Hispanics and blacks are from their
website:
http://www.census.gov/population/projections/state/
stpjrace.txt. Series Projections. For more details, see PPL
#47," Population Projections for States, by Age, Sex, Race,
and Hispanic Origin: 1995 to 2025."

Figure 4.3: These figures are taken from U.S. Bureau of the Census,
Current Population Reports, P6-203, *Measuring 50 Years of
Economic Change Using the March Current Population Survey,*
U.S. Government Printing Office, Washington, D.C, 1998.
Table C-10, page C-19; 1999 and 200 income data come
from: "Historical Income Tables—Families" and the CPI is
taken from: "Income 2000."

Table 4.5: Danziger and Gottschalk 1995: 53.

Table 4.6: Shapiro, Greenstein, and Primus. Center on Budget and
Policy Priorities, Washington, D.C., May 31, 2001, p. 10.

Table 4.7: Data compiled by authors, and data from website:
http://factfinder.census.gov/servlet/BasicFactsServlet

Table 4.8: Data compiled by authors, and data from website:
http://factfinder.census.gov/servlet/BasicFactsServlet

Table 4.9: Data compiled by authors, and data for percent non-white
for all 435 districts are available at: http://factfinder.census.gov/servlet/BasicFactsServlet

Table 4.10: Data compiled by authors, and data from:
http://factfinder.census.gov/servlet/BasicFactsServlet

Table 4.11: Data compiled by authors.

Figure 5.1: Warren Miller and the National Election Studies, American
National Election Studies Cumulative Data File, 1948 - 1988
[computer file].

Figure 5.2: Data compiled by authors

Figure 5.3: Data compiled by authors

Table 5.2: Hypothetical situation, created by authors

Table 5.3: Data compiled by authors

Table 5.4: Data compiled by authors

Table 5.5: Data compiled by authors

Table 5.6: Data compiled by authors

Table 5.3: Data compiled by authors

Table 5.8: Data compiled by authors

Table 5.9: Data compiled by authors

Figure 6.1: Source: ADA ratings for 1946 - 1994 are from Tim
Groseclose's website: http://wesley.stanford.edu/groseclose
ADA ratings for the years 1995 - 1999 are from:
http://adaction.org/

Figure 6.2: Source: ADA ratings for 1946 - 1994 are from Tim
Groseclose's website: http://wesley.stanford.edu/groseclose
ADA ratings for the years 1995 - 1999 are from:
http://adaction.org/

Figure 6.3: Source: ADA ratings for 1946 - 1994 are from Tim
Groseclose's website: http://wesley.stanford.edu/groseclose
ADA ratings for the years 1995 - 1999 are from:
http://adaction.org/

Figure 6.4: Data compiled by authors

Table 6.1: Data compiled by authors

Table 6.2: Data compiled by authors

Table 6.3: Data compiled by authors

Table 6.4: Data compiled by authors

Table 6.5: Data compiled by authors
Table 6.6: Has tag line
Table 6.7: Data compiled by authors

Figure 7.1: Data from Benjamin and Malbin, *Term Limits*, (1992, 291-
            295), plus additions of more recent results from CQ Weekly.
Figure 7.2: Data compiled by authors.
Figure 7.3: Data compiled by authors.
  Table 7.1: Data compiled and analyzed by authors.
  Table 7.2: Data compiled and analyzed by authors.
  Table 7.3: Data compiled and analyzed by authors.
  Table 7.4: Cook Report (2000) and Federal Election Commission
            Reports, taken from their web page.

Bibliography

Abramowitz, Alan I. "Determinants of the Outcomes of U.S. Senate Elections." *Journal of Politics* 48, No. 2 (May 1986): 433–439.

_____. "Incumbency, Campaign Spending, and the Decline of Competition in U.S. House Elections." *Journal of Politics* 53, No. 1 (February 1991): 34–56.

_____. "Issue Evolution Reconsidered: Racial Attitudes and Partisanship in the U.S. Electorate." *American Journal of Political Science* 38, No. 1 (February 1994): 1–24.

_____. "The End of the Democratic Era? 1994 and the Future of Congressional Election Research." *Political Research Quarterly* 48, No. 4 (December 1995): 873–889.

Abramowitz, Alan I., and Kyle L. Saunders. "Ideological Realignments in the U.S. Electorate." *Journal of Politics* 60, No. 3 (August 1998): 634–652.

_____. "Ideological Realignment and U.S. Congressional Elections." Paper presented at the Annual Meeting of the American Political Science Association, Washington, D.C., September 2000.

Aldrich, John H. *Why Parties?* Chicago: University of Chicago Press, 1995.

_____. "Political Parties in a Critical Era." *American Politics Quarterly* 27, No. 1 (January 1999): 9–32.

Aldrich, John H., and David W. Rohde. "Measuring Conditional Party Government." Paper presented at the Annual Midwest Political Science Association Meeting, Chicago, Illinois, April 1998.

_____. "The Logic of Conditional Government: Revisiting the Electoral Connection." In *Congress Reconsidered*, seventh edition, edited by Lawrence C. Dodd and Bruce I. Oppenheimer, 269–292. Washington, DC: Congressional Quarterly Press, 2001.

Alford, John R., and John R. Hibbing. "Increased Incumbency Advantage in the House." *Journal of Politics* 43, No. 4 (November 1981): 1042–1061.

Allen, Jodie T. "Rich and Poor: Yachts Still Float Higher Than Dinghies." *U.S. News and World Report* (May 24, 1999): 57.

Allswang, John M. *A House for All Peoples: Ethnic Politics in Chicago, 1890–1936.* Lexington, Ky.: The University Press of Kentucky, 1971.

_____. *The New Deal and American Politics: A Study in Political Change.* New York: John Wiley & Sons, 1978.

Alt, James E. "The Impact of the Voting Rights Act on Black and White Voter Registration in the South." In *Quiet Revolution in the South: The Impact of the Voting Rights Act, 1965–1990*, edited by Chandler Davidson and Bernard Grofman, 351–377. Princeton: Princeton University Press, 1994.

Alvararez, Lizette, and Eric Schmitt. "Undignified and Screaming, Senate Seeks to Right Itself." *New York Times* (June 7, 2000): A26.

Andersen, Kristi. *The Creation of the Democratic Majority 1928–1936.* Chicago: University of Chicago Press, 1979.

Ansolabehere, Stephen, James M. Snyder Jr., and Charles Stewart III. "Candidate Positioning in U.S. House Elections." *American Journal of Political Science* 45, No. 1 (January 2001a): 136–159.

_____. "The Effects of Party and Preferences on Congressional Roll-Call Voting." *Legislative Studies Quarterly* 26, No. 4 (November 2001b): 533–573.

Bain, Richard C. *Convention Decisions and Voting Records.* Washington, D.C.: Brookings Institution Press, 1960.

Barone, Michael, and Grant Ujifusa. *The Almanac of American Politics 1994.* Washington, D.C.: National Journal, 1993.

Bartells, Larry M. "Partisanship and Voting Behavior, 1952–1996." *American Journal of Political Science* 44, No. 1 (January 2000): 35–49.

Bartley, Numan V. "The South and Sectionalism in American Politics." *Journal of Politics* 38, No. 3 (August 1976): 239–257.

Bass, Harold F., Jr. "Presidential Party Leadership and Party Reform: Franklin D. Roosevelt and the Abrogation of the Two-Thirds Rule." *Presidential Studies Quarterly* 18, No. 2 (spring 1988): 303–317.

Benjamin, Gerald, and Michael J. Malbin. *Limiting Legislative Terms.* Washington, D.C.: Congressional Quarterly Press, 1992.

Bensel, Richard Franklin. *Sectionalism and American Political Development 1880–1980.* Madison, Wis.: The University of Wisconsin Press, 1984.

Berke, Richard. "Partisanship Lapping at Senate, Too." *New York Times* (January 8, 1999): A15.

Berkman, Michael B. *The State Roots of National Politics.* Pittsburgh: University of Pittsburgh Press, 1993.

Bernstein, Irving. *The Lean Years.* Boston: Houghton Mifflin Company, 1960.

Bettelheim, Adriel. "Votes Belie Partisan Intensity." *Congressional Quarterly Weekly Report.* (January 6, 2001): 56.

Black, Earl. *Southern Governors and Civil Rights.* Cambridge, Mass.: Harvard University Press, 1976.

Black, Earl, and Merle Black. *Politics and Society in the South.* Cambridge, Mass.: Harvard University Press, 1987.

Blakely, Edward J., and Mary Gail Snyder. *Fortress America: Gated Communities in the United States.* Washington, D.C.: Brookings Institution Press, 1997.

Bond, Jon R., and Richard Fleisher. Editors. *Polarized Politics: Congress and the President in a Partisan Era.* Washington, D.C.: Congressional Quarterly Press, 2000.

_____. "The Disappearance of Moderate and Cross-Pressured Members of Congress: Conversion, Replacement and Electoral Change." Presented at the 297th Annual Meeting of the American Political Science Association, San Francisco, August-September 2001.

Born, Richard. "Generational Replacement and the Growth of Incumbent Reelection Margins in the U.S. House." *American Political Science Review* 73, No. 3 (September 1979): 811–817.

Brady, David W. *Critical Elections and Congressional Policymaking*. Stanford: Stanford University Press, 1988.

Brady, David W., Brandice Canes-Wrone, and John F. Cogan (Eds.). "Differences in Legislative Voting Behavior Between Winning and Losing House Incumbants." *Continuity and Change in House Elections*. Stanford: Stanford University Press, 2000: 178-192.

Brady, David W., Joseph Cooper, and Patricia A. Hurley. "The Decline of Party in the U.S. House of Representatives, 1887–1968." *Legislative Studies Quarterly* IV, No. 3 (August 1979): 381–407.

Brady, David W., John R. Cogan, and Morris P. Fiorina. "An Introduction to Continuity and Change in House Elections." In *Continuity and Change in House Elections*, edited by David W. Brady, John F. Cogan, and Morris P. Fiorina, 1-9. Stanford: Stanford University Press, 2000.

Brewer, Mark D., and Jeffrey M. Stonecash. "Class, Race Issues, Declining White Support for the Democratic Party in the South." *Political Behavior* Vol. 23, No. 2 (June 2001): 131–155.

Briggs, Vernon M., Jr. *Mass Immigration and the National Interest*. Armonk, N.Y.: M. E. Sharpe, 1992.

Brimelow, Peter. *Alien Nation: Common Sense About America's Immigration Disaster*. New York: Random House, 1995.

Brinkley, Joel. "Clinton Says No to Any Tax Cut of $500 Billion." *New York Times* (July 26, 1999): A1.

Bullock, Charles S., III. "Congressional Voting and the Mobilization of a Black Electorate in the South." *Journal of Politics* 43, No. 3 (August 1981): 662–682.

————. "Regional Realignment from an Officeholding Perspective." *Journal of Politics* 50, No. 3 (August 1988): 533–574.

Bullock, C. S. III. "Partisan Changes in the Southern Congressional Delegation." In *Continuity an Change in House Elections*, edited by David W. Brady, John F. Cogan, and Morris P. Fiorina, 39-64. Stanford: Stanford University Press, 2000.

Bullock, Charles S., and David W. Brady. "Party, Constituency, and Roll-Call Voting in the U.S. Senate." *Legislative Studies Quarterly* VIII, No. 1 (February 1983): 29–43.

Burden, Barry, Gregory A. Caldiera, and Tim Groseclose. "Measuring the Ideologies of U.S. Senators: The Song Remains the Same." *Legislative Studies Quarterly* XXV, No. 2 (May 2000): 237–258.

Burner, David. *The Politics of Provincialism: The Democratic Party in Transition, 1918–1932*. New York: Alfred A. Knopf, 1968.

Burnham, Walter Dean. "The Changing Shape of the American Political Universe." *American Political Science Review* 59, No. 1 (March 1965): 7–28.

————. "Insulation and Responsiveness in Congressional Elections." In *The Current Crisis in American Politics*, edited by Walter Dean Burnham, 207–228. New York: Oxford University Press, 1982.

Cain, Bruce E., D. Roderick Kiewiet, and Carole J. Uhlaner. "The Acquisition of Partisanship by Latinos and Asian Americans." *American Journal of Political Science* 35, No. 2 (May 1991): 390–422.

Campbell, David, and Joe R. Feagin. "Black Politics in the South: A Descriptive Analysis." *Journal of Politics* 37, No. 1 (February 1975): 129–162.

Campbell, James E. "The Return of the Incumbents: The Nature of the Incumbency Advantage." *Western Political Quarterly* 36, No. 3 (September 1983): 434–444.

Cantor, David M., and Paul S. Herrnson. "Party Campaign Activity and Party Unity in the U.S. House of Representatives." *Legislative Studies Quarterly* XXII, No. 3 (August 1997): 393–415.

Carlson, Alvar W. "America's New Immigration: Characteristics, Destinations and Impact, 1979–1989." *Social Science Journal* 31, No. 3 (1994): 213–236.

Carmines, Edward G., and Robert Huckfeldt. "Party Politics in the Wake of the Voting Rights Act." In *Controversies in Minority Voting: The Voting Rights Act in Perspective*, edited by Bernard Grofman and Chandler Davidson, 117–134. Washington, D.C.: Brookings Institution Press, 1992.

Carmines, Edward G., Steven H. Renten, and James A. Stimson. "Events and Alignments: The Party Image Link." In *Controversies in Voting Behavior*, second edition, edited by Richard G. Niemi and Herbert F. Weisberg, 545–560. Washington, D.C.: Congressional Quarterly Press, 1984.

Carmines, Edward G., and James A. Stimson. "The Politics and Policy of Race in Congress." In *Congress and Policy Change*, edited by Gerald C. Wright, Leroy N. Rieselbach, and Lawrence C. Dodd, 70–93. New York: Agathon Press, 1986.

_____. *Issue Evolution: Race and the Transformation of American Politics*. Princeton: Princeton University Press, 1989.

Carson, Richard T., and Joe A. Oppenheimer. "A Method of Estimating the Personal Ideology of Political Representatives." *American Political Science Review* 78, No. 1 (March 1984): 163–178.

Clausen, Aage. *How Congressmen Decide*. New York: St. Martin's Press, 1973.

Clausen, Aage, and Carl E. Van Horn. "The Congressional Response to a Decade of Change, 1963–1972." *Journal of Politics* 39, No. 3 (August 1977): 624–666.

Clines, Francis X. "Partisan Rancor: Not Always So Bad for the National Soul." *New York Times* (October 11, 1998): Week in Review, Section 4, Page 3, Column 1.

Clubb, Jerome M., and Howard W. Allen. "The Cities and the Election of 1928: Partisan Realignment?" *American Historical Review* 74, No. 4 (April 1969): 1205–1220.

Clubb, Jerome M., and Santa A. Tarugott. "Partisan Cleavage and Cohesion in the House of Representatives, 1861–1974." *Journal of Interdisciplinary History* VII, No. 3 (winter 1977): 375–401.

Clucas, Richard A. "Party Contributions and the Influence of Campaign Committee Chairs on Roll Call Voting." *Legislative Studies Quarterly* XXII, No. 2 (May 1997): 179–194.

Collie, Melissa P. "Incumbency, Electoral Safety, and Turnover in the U.S. House of Representatives, 1972–1976." *American Political Science Review* 75, No. 1 (March 1981): 119–131.

_____. "Universalism and the Parties in the U.S. House of Representatives, 1921–1980." *American Journal of Political Science* 2, No. 4 (November 1988): 865–883.

Congressional Digest. "Immigration Policy: Balancing National Interests." *Congressional Digest* 75, No. 5 (May 1996): 129–160.

Congressional Quarterly Almanac, 1993. "Fiscal 1993 Stimulus Bill Killed." Washington, D.C.: Congressional Quarterly Press, 1993: 706-709.

Congressional Quarterly Almanac, 1994. "Democratic Stronghold Ends Along with 103rd Congress." Washington, D.C.: Congressional Quarterly Press, 1994: 9-13.

_____. "Clinton's Legislative Strategy Falters." Washington, D.C.: Congressional Quarterly Press, 1994: 29-32.

Congressional Quarterly Almanac, 1998. Washington, D.C.: Congressional Quarterly Press, 1998.

_____. "Partisan Voting on the Rise: Ideology Impedes Bills; Some Welcome the Contrast." Washington, D.C.: Congressional Quarterly Press, 1998: B6.

_____, 1999. Washington, D.C.: Congressional Quarterly Press, 1999.

Converse, Philip E. "On the Possibility of Major Political Realignment in the South." In *Elections and the Political Order*, edited by Angus Campbell, Philip E. Converse, Warren E. Miller, and Donald E. Stokes, 212–242. New York: John Wiley & Sons, 1966a.

_____. "Religion and Politics: The 1960 Election." In *Elections and the Political Order*, edited by Angus Campbell, Philip E. Converse, Warren E. Miller, and Donald E. Stokes, 96–124. New York: John Wiley & Sons, 1966b.

Cook, Charles. "The GOP Just Might Keep the House." *The Cook Report*, March 18, 2000:897-899.

Cooper, Joseph, and Gary Young. "Partisanship, Bipartisanship and Crosspartisanship in Congress Since the New Deal." In *Congress Reconsidered*, sixth edition, edited by Lawrence C. Dodd and Bruce I. Oppenheimer, 246–274. Washington, D.C.: Congressional Quarterly Press, 1997.

Cosman, Bernard. "Republicanism in the South: Goldwater's Impact upon Voting Alignments in Congressional, Gubernatorial, and Senatorial Races." *Southwestern Social Science Quarterly* 48, No. 1 (June 1967): 13–23.

Cover, Albert. "One Good Term Deserves Another: The Advantage of Incumbency in Congressional Elections." *American Journal of Political Science* 21, No. 3 (August 1977): 523–541.

Cox, Gary W., and Mathew D. McCubbins. "On the Decline of Party Voting in Congress." *Legislative Studies Quarterly* XVI, No. 4 (November 1991): 547–570.

_____. *Legislative Leviathan: Party Government in the House.* Berkeley: University of California Press, 1993.

_____. "Toward a Theory of Legislative Rule Changes: Assessing Schickler and Rich's Evidence." *American Journal of Political Science* 41, No. 4 (October 1997): 1376–1386.

Cummings, Milton C. *Congressmen and the Electorate.* New York: Free Press, 1966.

Danzinger, Sheldon, and Peter Gottschalk. *America Unequal.* Cambridge, Mass.: Harvard University Press, 1995.

David, Paul T. *Party Strength in the United States, 1872–1970.* Charlottesville, Va.: University Press of Virginia, 1972.

David, Paul T., Ralph M. Goldman, and Richard C. Bain. *The Politics of National Party Conventions.* Washington, D.C.: The Brookings Institution Press, 1960.

Davidson, Chandler. "The Voting Rights Act: A Brief History." In *Controversies in Minority Voting; The Voting Rights Act in Perspective*, edited by Bernard Grofman and Chandler Davidson, 7–51. Washington, D.C.: The Brookings Institution, 1992.

Davidson, Roger H., and Walter J. Oleczek. *Congress and Its Members,* third edition. Washington, D.C.: Congressional Quarterly Press, 1990.

Degler, Carl N. "American Political Parties and the Rise of the City: An Interpretation." *Journal of American History* 51, No. 1 (June 1964): 41–59.

DeParle, Jason. "Democrat's Invisible Man Specializes in Making Inequity of the Poor Easy to See." *New York Times* (August 19, 1991): A–12.

DeSipio, Louis, and Rodolfo O. de la Garza. *Making Americans, Remaking America.* Boulder: Westview Press, 1998.

Dionne, E. J. *They Only Look Dead.* New York: Touchstone, 1997.

Dodd, Lawrence C., and Bruce I. Oppenheimer, editors *Congress Reconsidered,* fourth edition. Washington, D.C.: Congressional Quarterly Press, 1989.

_____. "Consolidating Power in the House: The Rise of a New Oligarchy." In *Congress Reconsidered,* fourth edition, edited by Lawrence C. Dodd and Bruce I. Oppenheimer, 39–64. Washington, D.C.: Congressional Quarterly Press, 1989.

Dolbeare, Kenneth M., and Linda J. Medcalf. *American Ideologies Today.* New York: McGraw-Hill, 1993.

Drew, Elizabeth. *Showdown: The Struggle between the Gingrich Congress and the Clinton White House.* New York: Simon & Schuster, 1996.

_____. *The Corruption of American Politics: What Went Wrong and Why.* New York: Overlook Press, 2000.

Drier, Peter, Todd Swanstrom, and John Mollenkopf. *Place Matters: Metropolitics for the Twenty-First Century.* Lawrence: University Press of Kansas, 2001.

Edsall, Thomas B., and Mary D. Edsall. *Chain Reaction: The Impact of Race, Rights, and Taxes on American Politics.* New York: W. W. Norton, 1991.

Endersveld, Samuel J. "The Influence of Metropolitan Party Pluralities in Presidential Elections Since 1920: A Study of Twelve Key Cities." *American Political Science Review* 43, No. 6 (December 1949): 1189–1206.

Erikson, Robert S., and Gerald C. Wright. "Policy Representation of Constituency Interests." *Political Behavior* 2, No. 1 (1980): 91–106.

_____. "Voters, Candidates, and Issues in Congressional Elections." In *Congress Reconsidered,* sixth edition, edited by Lawrence C. Dodd and Bruce I. Oppenheimer, 132–161. Washington, D.C.: Congressional Quarterly Press, 1997.

_____. "Representation and Constituency Ideology in Congress." In *Continuity and Change in House Elections,* edited by David W. Brady, John F. Cogan, and Morris P. Fiorina, 149-177. Stanford: Stanford University Press, 2000.

_____. "Voters, Candidates, and Issues in Congressional Elections." In *Congress Reconsidered,* seventh edition, edited by Lawrence C. Dodd and Bruce I. Oppenheimer, 67–95. Washington, D.C.: Congressional Quarterly Press, 2001.

Ewing, Cortez A. M. *Congressional Elections 1896–1944, The Sectional Basis of Political Democracy in the House of Representatives.* Norman, Okla.: University of Oklahoma Press, 1947.

Fallon, Joseph E. "The Impact of Immigration on U.S. Demographics." *Journal of Social, Political and Economic Studies* 21, No. 2 (summer 1996): 141–166.

Fenno, Richard F., Jr. *Congress at the Grassroots: Representational Change in the South, 1970-1998.* Chapel Hill, N.C.: University of North Carolina Press, 2000.

Ferejohn, John A. "On the Decline of Competition in Congressional Elections." *American Political Science Review* 71, No. 1 (March 1977): 166–176.

Fiorina, Morris P. *Representatives, Roll Calls, and Constituencies.* Lexington, Mass.: Lexington Books, 1974.

———. *Congress: Keystone to the Washington Establishment.* New Haven, Conn.: Yale University Press, 1977.

———. *Retrospective Voting in American National Elections.* New Haven: Yale University Press, 1981.

———. "Keystone Reconsidered." In *Congress Reconsidered*, seventh edition, edited by Lawrence C. Dodd and Bruce I. Oppenheimer, 141–162. Washington, D.C.: Congressional Quarterly Press, 2001.

Flanigan, William H., and Nancy H. Zingale. *Political Behavior of the American Electorate*, fourth edition. Boston: Allyn and Bacon, 1979.

———. *Political Behavior of the American Electorate.* ninth ed. Washington, DC: Congressional Quarterly Press, 1998.

Fleisher, Richard. "Explaining the Change in Roll-Call Behavior of Southern Democrats." *Journal of Politics* 55, No. 2 (May 1993): 327–341.

Fleisher, Richard, and Jon R. Bond. "Congress and the President in a Partisan Era." In *Polarized Politics: Congress and the President in a Partisan Era*, edited by Jon R. Bond and Richard Fleisher, 1–8. Washington, D.C.: Congressional Quarterly Press, 2000a.

———. "Partisanship and the President's Quest for Votes on the Floor of Congress." In *Polarized Politics: Congress and the President in a Partisan Era*, edited by Jon R. Bond and Richard Fleisher, 154–185. Washington, D.C.: Congressional Quarterly Press, 2000b.

———. "Where Have All the Moderates Gone, Long Time Passing? The Disappearance of Cross-Pressured Republicans in Congress." Presented at the 2000 American Political Science Association Meetings. Washington, D.C.: August-September 2000c.

Fowler, Linda L. "How Interest Groups Select Issues for Rating Voting Records of Members of the U.S. Congress." *Legislative Studies Quarterly* VII, No. 3 (August 1982): 401–413.

Frey, William H. "Immigration, Domestic Migration, and Demographic Balkanization in America: New Evidence for the 1990s." *Population and Development Review* 22, No. 4 (December 1996): 741–763.

———. "Regional Shifts in America's Voting-Aged Population: What Do They Mean for National Politics?" Report 00–459, Population Studies Center at the Institute for Social Research, University of Michigan, 2000.

Froman, Lewis A., Jr. *Congressmen and Their Constituencies.* Chicago: Rand McNally and Company, 1963.

Frymer, Paul. "Ideological Consensus within Divided Party Government." *Political Science Quarterly* 109, No. 2 (summer 1994): 287–311.

Gaddie, Ronald Keith, and Charles S. Bullock, III. *Elections to Open Seats in the U.S. House: Where the Action Is.* Lanham, Md.: Rowman and Littlefield, 2000.

Garand, James C., and Donald A. Gross. "Changes in the Vote Margins for Congressional Candidates: A Specification of Historical Trends." *American Political Science Review* 78, No. 1 (March 1984): 17–30.

Garrow, David J. *Protest at Selma: Martin Luther King, Jr. and the Voting Rights Act of 1965.* New Haven: Yale University Press, 1978.

Garson, Robert A. *The Democratic Party and the Politics of Sectionalism, 1941–1948.* Baton Rouge, La.: Louisiana State University Press, 1974.

Gimpel, James G. *Separate Destinations: Migration, Immigration and the Politics of Places.* Ann Arbor, Mich.: The University of Michigan Press, 1999.

Gimpel, James G., and James R. Edwards Jr. *The Congressional Politics of Immigration Reform.* Boston: Allyn and Bacon, 1999.

Glaser, James M. *Race, Campaign Politics and the Realignment in the South.* New Haven: Yale University Press, 1996.

Golden, Tim. "California Governor Cuts Off Aid for Illegal Immigrants." *New York Times* (August 28, 1996): A1.

Goldman, Ralph M. *Search for Consensus: The Story of the Democratic Party.* Philadelphia: Temple University Press, 1979.

Greenblatt, Alan. "History of Immigration Policy." *Congressional Quarterly Weekly Report* 53 (April 15, 1995): 1067.

Greenhouse, Steven. "About Face: Guess Who's Embracing Immigrants Now." *New York Times* (March 5, 2000): X1.

Grofman, Bernard, Lisa Handley, and Richard G. Niemi. *Representation and the Quest for Voting Equality.* New York: Cambridge University Press, 1992.

Groseclose, Tim, Steven D. Levitt, and James M. Snyder Jr. "Comparing Interest Group Scores across Time and Chambers: Adjusted ADA Scores for the U.S. Congress." *American Political Science Review* 93, No. 1 (March 1999): 33–50.

Gross, Donald A., and James C. Garand. "The Vanishing Marginals, 1824–1980." *Journal of Politics* 46, No. 1 (February 1984): 224–237.

Gulati, Jeff. "Constituency Diversity and the Puzzle of Electoral Competition." Paper presented at the Annual Meeting of the American Political Science Association, San Francisco, California, August-September 2001.

Hall, Richard L. and Bernard Grofman. "The Committee Assignment Process and the Conditional Nature of Committee Bias." *American Political Science Review,* Vol. 84, No. 4 (December 1990): 1149-1166.

Hayghe, Howard V. "Developments in Women's Labor Force Participation." *Monthly Labor Review* (September 1997): 41–46.

Heard, Alexander. *A Two Party South.* Chapel Hill, N.C.: University of North Carolina Press, 1952.

Herrera, Richard, Thomas Epperlein, and Eric R. A. N. Smith. "The Stability of Congressional Roll-Call Indices." *Political Research Quarterly* 48, No. 2 (June 1995): 403–416.

Herrnson, Paul S. *Party Campaigning in the 1980s.* Cambridge, Mass.: Harvard University Press, 1988.

_____. *Congressional Elections: Campaigning at Home and in Washington.* Washington, D.C.: Congressional Quarterly Press, 1998.

_____. *Congressional Elections: Campaigning at Home and in Washington,* third edition. Washington, D.C.: Congressional Quarterly Press, 2001.

Hetherington, Marc J. "Resurgent Mass Partisanship: The Role of Elite Polarization?" *American Political Science Review* 95, No. 3 (September 2001): 619–632.

Hicks, John D. *Republican Ascendancy, 1921–1933*. New York: Harper & Brothers, 1960.

Hill, Kim Quaile, Stephen Hanna, and Sahar Shafqat. "The Liberal-Conservative Ideology of U.S. Senators: A New Measure." *American Journal of Political Science* 41, No. 4 (October 1997): 1395–1413.

Hood, M. V., III, Quentin Kidd, and Irwin L. Morris. "The VRA and Beyond: The Political Mobilization of African Americans in the Modern South." Paper presented at the Annual Meeting of the Southern Political Science Association, Atlanta, Georgia, November 2000.

Huckfeldt, Robert, and Carol W. Kohfeld. *Race and the Decline of Class in American Politics*. Urbana, Ill.: University of Illinois Press, 1989.

Huthmacher, J. Joseph. *Massachusetts People and Politics 1919–1933*. Cambridge, Mass.: The Belknap Press of Harvard University Press, 1959.

Ingbarman, Daniel, and John Villani. "An Institutional Theory of Divided Government and Party Polarization." *American Journal of Political Science* 37, No. 2 (May 1983): 429–471.

Jackson, John E., and John W. Kingdon. "Ideology, Interest Group Scores, and Legislative Votes." *American Journal of Political Science* 36, No. 3 (August 1992): 805–832.

Jackson, Kenneth T. *Crabgrass Frontier: The Suburbanization of the United States*. New York: Oxford University Press, 1985.

Jackson, Robert A. "Latino Electoral Participation." Presented at the Seventy-Third Annual Meeting of the Southern Political Science Association, Atlanta, Georgia. November 2001.

Jacobson, Gary C. "The Effects of Campaign Spending in Congressional Elections." *American Political Science Review* 72, No. 2 (June 1978): 469–491.

_____. "Money and Votes Reconsidered: Congressional Elections, 1972–1982." *Public Choice* 47, No. 1 (1985a): 7–62.

_____. "The Republican Advantage in Campaign Finance." In *The New Direction in American Politics*, edited by John E. Chubb and Paul E. Peterson, 143–173. Washington, D.C.: The Brookings Institution Press, 1985b.

_____. "The Marginals Never Vanished: Incumbency and Competition in Elections to the U.S. House of Representatives, 1952–1982." *American Journal of Political Science* 31, No. 1 (February 1987): 126–141.

_____. *The Politics of Congressional Elections*, fourth edition. New York: Longman, 1997.

_____. "Party Polarization in National Politics: The Electoral Connection." In *Polarized Politics: Congress and the President in a Partisan Era*, edited by Jon R. Bond and Richard Fleisher, 9–30. Washington, D.C.: Congressional Quarterly Press, 2000a.

_____. "The Electoral Basis of Partisan Polarization in Congress." Paper presented at the Annual Meeting of the American Political Science Association, Washington, D.C., August 2000b.

_____. *The Politics of Congressional Elections*, fifth edition. New York: Addison Wesley Longman, 2001.

Jacobson, Gary C., and Samuel Kernell. *Strategy and Choice in Congressional Elections*, second edition. New Haven: Yale University Press, 1983.

Jamieson, Kathleen Hall, and Erika Falk. "Continuity and Change in Civility in the House." In *Polarized Politics: Congress and the President in a Partisan Era*, edited by Jon R. Bond and Richard Fleisher, 96–108. Washington, D.C.: Congressional Quarterly Press, 2000.

Jargowsky, Paul A. "Take the Money and Run: Economic Segregation in U.S. Metropolitan Areas." *American Sociological Review* 61, No. 6 (December 1996): 984–998.

Johannes, John R. "Casework as a Technique of U.S. Congressional Oversight of the Executive." *Legislative Studies Quarterly* IV, No. 3 (August 1979): 325 351.

Johannes, John R., and John C. McAdams. "The Congressional Incumbency Effect: Is it Casework, Policy Compatibility or Something Else?" *American Journal of Political Science* 25, No. 3 (August 1981): 512–542.

Johnston, David Cay. "Gap Between Rich and Poor Substantially Wider." *New York Times* (September 5, 1999): A16.

Judd, Dennis R., and Todd Swanstrom. *City Politics: Private Power and Public Policy*, second edition. New York: Longman, 1998.

_____. *City Politics: Private Power and Public Policy*, third edition. New York: Longman, 2002.

Katznelson, Ira, Kim Geiger, and Daniel Snyder. "Limiting Liberalism: The Southern Veto in Congress, 1933–1950." *Political Science Quarterly* 108, No. 2 (summer 1993): 283–306.

Kazin, Michael. *The Populist Persuasion*. New York: Basic Books, 1995.

Keely, Charles B. "Effects of the Immigration Act of 1965 on Selected Population Characteristics of Immigrants to the United States." *Demography* 8, No. 2 (May 1971): 157–169.

Key, V. O., Jr. *Southern Politics in State and Nation*. New York: Alfred A. Knopf, 1949.

_____. "A Theory of Critical Elections." *Journal of Politics* 17, No. 1 (February 1955): 3–18.

_____. "Secular Realignment and the Party System." *Journal of Politics* 21, No. 2 (May 1959): 198–210.

King, Desmond. *Making Americans: Immigration, Race, and the Origins of the Diverse Democracy*. Cambridge, Mass.: Harvard University Press, 2000.

Kleppner, Paul. *Continuity and Change in Electoral Politics, 1893–1928*. Westport, Conn.: Greenwood Press, 1987.

Koford, Kenneth. "Dimensions in Congressional Voting." *American Political Science Review* 83, No. 3 (September 1989): 949–962.

Kousser, J. Morgan. "The Voting Rights Act and the Two Reconstructions." In *Controversies in Minority Voting: The Voting Rights Act in Perspective*, edited by Bernard Grofman and Chandler Davidson, 135–176. Washington, D.C.: The Brookings Institution, 1992.

Kramer, Gerald H. "Short-Term Fluctuations in U.S. Voting Behavior, 1896–1964." *American Political Science Review* 65, No. 1 (March 1971): 131–143.

Krehbiel, Keith. "Where's the Party?" *British Journal of Political Science* 23, No. X (1993): 235–266.

_____. "Deference, Extremism and Interest Group Ratings." *Legislative Studies Quarterly* XIX, No. 1 (February 1994): 61–77.

_____. *Pivotal Politics: A Theory of U.S. Lawmaking.* Chicago: University of Chicago Press, 1998.

_____. "Party Discipline and Measures of Partisanship." *American Journal of Political Science* 44, No. 2 (April 2000): 212–227.

Kreps, Juanita M., and R. John Leaper. "Home Work, Market Work, and the Allocation of Time." In *Women and the American Economy: A Look to the 1980s,* edited by Juanita M. Kreps, 61–81. Englewood Cliffs, N.J.: Prentice-Hall, 1976.

Kyvig, David E. *Repealing National Prohibition.* Chicago: University of Chicago Press, 1979.

Lemann, Nicholas. *The Promised Land.* New York: Alfred A. Knopf, 1991.

Leogrande, William M., and Alana S. Jeydel. "Using Presidential Election Returns to Measure Constituency Ideology: A Research Note." *American Politics Quarterly* 25, No. 1 (January 1997): 3–18.

Levy, Frank. *Dollars and Dreams: The Changing American Income Distribution.* New York: W. W. Norton, 1988.

_____. *The New Dollars and Dreams: American Incomes and Economic Change.* New York: Russell Sage Foundation, 1998.

Leyden, Kevin M., and Stephen A. Borrelli. "Party Contributions and Party Unity: Can Loyalty be Bought?" *Western Political Quarterly* 43, No. 2 (June 1990): 343–365.

_____. "An Investment in Goodwill: Party Contributions and Party Unity among U.S. House Members in the 1980s." *American Politics Quarterly* 22, No. 4 (October 1994): 421–452.

Lubell, Samuel. *The Future of American Politics,* second edition. Revised. Garden City, N.Y.: Doubleday Anchor Books, 1956.

Lucas, DeWayne. "Partisan Polarization: A Change in the Election of Candidates." Paper presented at the Annual Meeting of the Southern Political Science Association, Savannah, Ga., November 1999.

MacRae, Duncan. "The Relationship Between Roll-Call Votes and Constituencies in the Massachusetts House of Representatives." *American Political Science Review* 46, No. 4 (December 1952): 1046–1055.

_____. *Dimensions of Congressional Voting.* Berkeley: University of California, Publications in Sociology and Social Institute, 1958.

Maharidge, Dale. "In California, the Numbers Tell the Story." *New York Times* (March 29, 1999): A1.

Mann, Thomas E., and Raymond E. Wolfinger. "Candidates and Parties in Congressional Elections." *American Political Science Review* 74, No. 3 (September 1980): 617–632.

Martinez, Gebe. "Democrats Hope to Win by Staying Unified in Defeat." *Congressional Quarterly Weekly Report* (July 24, 1999): 1777–1779.

Massey, Douglas S. "Dimensions of the New Immigration to the United States and the Prospects for Assimilation." *Annual Review of Sociology* 7 (1981): 57–85.

_____. "The New Immigration and Ethnicity in the United States." *Population and Development Review* 21, No. 3 (September 1995): 631–652.

Massey, Douglas S., and Nancy Denton. *American Apartheid: Segregation and the Making of the Underclass.* Cambridge, Mass.: Harvard University Press, 1993.

Matthews, Donald R., and James W. Prothro. "Social and Economic Factors and Negro Voter Registration in the South." *American Political Science Review* 57, No. 1 (March 1963): 24–44.

_____. "Southern Images of Political Parties: An Analysis of White and Negro Attitudes." *Journal of Politics* 26, No. 1 (February 1964): 82–111.

Mayhew, David R. *Party Loyalty Among Congressmen*. Cambridge, Mass.: Harvard University Press, 1966.

_____. *The Electoral Connection*. New Haven: Yale University Press, 1974a.

_____. "Congressional Elections: The Case of the Vanishing Marginals." *Polity* VI, No. 3 (Spring 1974b): 295–317.

McKinney, John C., and Linda Brookover Bourque. "The Changing South: National Incorporation of a Region." *American Sociological Review* 36, No. 3 (June 1971): 399–412.

Meffert, Michael F., Helmut Norpoth, and Anirudh V. S. Ruhl. "Realignment and Macropartisanship." *American Political Science Review* Vol. 95, No. 4 (December 2001): 953–962.

Menefee-Libey, David. *The Triumph of Candidate-Centered Politics*. New York: Chatham House, 2000.

Miringoff, Marc, and Marque-Luisa Miringoff. *The Social Health of the Nation: How America is Really Doing*. New York: Oxford University Press, 1999.

Mortenson, Thomas G. "Educational Attainment by Family Income 1970–1994." *Postsecondary Education Opportunity* 41 (November 1995): 1–8.

New York Times. "Getting Along in Congress." *The New York Times* (March 1, 1999): A20.

Nice, David C. "Representation in the States: Policymaking and Ideology." *Social Science Quarterly* 63, No. (1983): 404–411.

Nieves, Evelyn. "California Calls Off Effort to Carry Out Immigrant Measure." *New York Times* (July 30, 1999): A1.

Nokken, Timothy P. "Dynamics of Congressional Loyalty: Party Defection and Roll-Call Behavior, 1947–97." *Legislative Studies Quarterly* XXV, No. 3 (August 2000): 417–445.

Noogle, Burl. *Teapot Dome: Oil and Politics in the 1920's*. New York: W. W. Norton & Company, 1962.

Orfield, Gary, and John T. Yun. *Resegregation in American Schools*. Cambridge, Mass.: Civil Rights Project, Harvard University, June 1999.

Ornstein, Norman J., Thomas E. Mann, and Michael J. Malbin. *Vital Statistics on Congress, 1999–2000*. Washington, D.C.: American Enterprise Institute Press, 2000.

Patterson, Samuel C., and Gregrory A. Caldiera. "Party Voting in the United States Congress." *British Journal of Political Science* 18, No. 1 (January 1988): 111–131.

Payne, James L. "The Personal Electoral Advantage of House Incumbents, 1936–1976." *American Politics Quarterly* 8, No. 4 (October 1980): 465–482.

Petrocik, John R. *Party Coalitions: Realignments and the Decline of the New Deal Party System*. Chicago: University of Chicago Press, 1981.

_____. "Realignment: New Party Coalitions and the Nationalization of the South." *Journal of Politics* 49, No. 2 (May 1987): 347–375.

Phillips, Kevin. *The Emerging Republican Majority.* New York: Anchor, 1969.

Polsby, Nelson. "The Institutionalization of the House of Representatives." *American Political Science Review* 62, No. 1 (March 1968): 144–168.

Pomper, Gerald. "Future Southern Congressional Politics." *Southwestern Social Science Quarterly* 44, No. 1 (1963): 14–24.

_____. "From Confusion to Clarity: Issues and American Voters, 1956–1968." *American Political Science Review* 66, No. 2 (June 1972): 415–428.

Poole, Keith T. "Dimensions of Interest Group Evaluation of the U.S. Senate, 1969–1978." *American Journal of Political Science* 25, No. 1 (February 1981): 49–67.

Poole, Keith T., and Steven Daniels. "Ideology, Party and Voting in the U.S. Congress, 1959–1980." *American Political Science Review* 79, No. 2 (June 1985): 373–399.

Poole, Keith T., and Howard Rosenthal. "The Polarization of American Politics." *Journal of Politics* 46, No. 4 (November 1984): 1061–1079.

_____. "A Spatial Model for Legislative Roll Call Analysis." *American Journal of Political Science* 29, No. 2 (May 1985): 357–384.

_____. "Patterns of Congressional Voting." *American Journal of Political Science* 35, No. 1 (February 1991): 228–278.

_____. *Congress: A Political-Economic History of Roll Call Voting.* New York: Oxford University Press, 1997.

Prendergast, William B. *The Catholic Voter in American Politics.* Washington, D.C.: Georgetown University Press, 1999.

Prothro, James A., Ernest Q. Campbell, and Charles W. Grigg. "Two-Party Voting in the South: Class vs. Party Identification." *American Political Science Review* 52, No. 1 (March 1958): 131–139.

Purdum, Todd. "California G.O.P. Faces a Crisis as Hispanic Voters Turn Away." *New York Times* (December 9, 1997): A1.

Rae, Nicol C. *The Decline and Fall of the Liberal Republicans from 1952 to the Present.* New York: Oxford University Press, 1989.

Ramirez, Ricardo. "Patterns of Mobilization: A Longitudinal Analysis of Latino Political Participation in California." Paper presented at the Annual Meeting of the American Political Science Association, San Francisco, August-September 2001.

Reiter, Howard L. "The Building of a Bifactional Structure: The Democrats in the 1940s." *Political Science Quarterly* 116, No. 1 (spring 2001): 107–129.

Rohde, David W. *Parties and Leaders in the Postreform House.* Chicago: University of Chicago Press, 1991.

_____. "Electoral Forces, Political Agendas and Partisanship in the House and Senate." In *The Postreform Congress,* edited by Roger Davidson, 27–47. New York: St. Martin's Press, 1992.

_____. "Parties and Committees in the House: Member Motivations, Issues, and Institutional Arrangement." *Legislative Studies Quarterly* 19, No. 3 (August 1994): 341–360.

Rosenbaum, David E. "In with the Ideologues, on with Deadlock." *New York Times* (January 21, 1996): D5.

Rossiter, Clinton. *Parties and Politics in America.* Ithaca: Cornell University Press, 1960.

Rubin, Richard L. *Party Dynamics: The Democratic Coalition and the Politics of Change.* New York: Oxford University Press, 1976.

Rumbaut, Ruben G., Nancy Foner, and Steven J. Gold. "Immigration and Immigration Research in the United States." *American Behavioral Scientist* 42, No. 9 (June/July 1999): 1258–1263.

Rusk, David. *Cities Without Suburbs,* second edition. Washington, D.C.: The Woodrow Wilson Center Press, 1995.

Salmore, Barbara G., and Stephen A. Salmore. *Candidates, Parties, and Campaigns: Electoral Politics in America,* second edition. Washington, D.C.: Congressional Quarterly Press, 1989.

Samuelson, Robert J. *The Good Life and Its Discontents.* New York: Vintage Books, 1997.

Schaffer, William R. "Party and Ideology in the U.S. House of Representatives." *Western Political Quarterly* 35, No. 1 (March 1982): 92–106.

_____. "Rating the Performance of the ADA in the U.S. Congress." *Western Political Quarterly* 42, No. 1 (March 1989): 33–51.

Schantz, Harvey L. "Inter-Party Competition for Congressional Seats: the 1960s and 1970s." *Western Political Quarterly* 40, No. 2 (June 1987): 373–383.

Schattschneider, E. E. *The Semisovereign People.* New York: Holt, Rinehart, and Winston, 1960.

Schickler, Eric, and Andrew Rich. "Controlling the Floor: Parties as Procedural Coalitions in the House." *American Journal of Political Science* 41, No. 4 (October 1997): 1350–1375.

Schlesinger, Joseph A. "The New American Political Party." *American Political Science Review* Vol. 79, No. 4 (December 1985), 1152–1169.

Schmitt, Eric. "Temporary Coalition Against Trade Bill Crosses Party and Ideological Lines." *New York Times* (May 24, 2000): A15.

Schneider, Jerold E. *Ideological Coalitions in Congress.* Westport, Conn.: Greenwood Press, 1979.

Schraufnagel, Scot. "Measuring Legislative Contentiousness in the United States Congress (1953–2000)." Paper presented at the Annual Meeting of the Southern Political Science Association, Atlanta, Ga., November 2001.

Schwab, Larry M. *Changing Patterns of Congressional Politics.* New York: Van Nostrand, 1980.

Schwarz, John E., and Barton Fenmore. "Presidential Election Results and Congressional Roll Call Behavior: The Cases of 1964, 1968, and 1972." *Legislative Studies Quarterly* 2, No. 4 (November 1977): 409–420.

Shannon, W. Wayne. *Party, Constituency and Congressional Voting: A Study of Legislative Behavior in the United States House of Representatives.* Baton Rouge, La.: Louisiana State University Press, 1968.

Shapiro, Isaac, and Robert Greenstein. *The Widening Income Gap.* Washington, D.C.: Center on Budget and Policy Priorities (September 4, 1999).

Sinclair, Barbara Deckerd. "Political Upheaval and Congressional Voting: The Effects of the 1960s on Voting Patterns in the House of Representatives." *Journal of Politics* 38, No. 2 (May 1976): 326–345.

_____. "Determinants of Aggregate Party Cohesion in the U.S. House of Representatives, 1901–1956." *Legislative Studies Quarterly* II, No. 2 (May 1977): 155–175.

_____. "Party Realignment and the Transformation of the Political Agenda: The House of Representatives, 1925–1938." *American Political Science Review* 71, No. 3 (September 1977): 940–953.

Sinclair, Barbara. *Congressional Realignment 1925–1978*. Austin, TX: University of Texas Press, 1982.

_____. *Legislators, Leaders and Lawmaking*. Baltimore: The Johns Hopkins University Press, 1995.

_____. "Evolution or Revolution? Policy-Oriented Congressional Parties in the 1990s." In *The Parties Respond*, third ed., edited by L. Sandy Maisel, 263–285. Boulder: Westview Press, 1998.

Smith, Eric R. A. N., Richard Herrera, Cheryl L. Herrera. "The Measurement Characteristics of Congressional Roll-Call Indexes." *Legislative Studies Quarterly* XV, No. 2 (May 1990): 283–295.

Smith, Steven S. "The Consistency and Ideological Structure of U.S. Senate Voting Alignments, 1957–1976." *American Journal of Political Science* 25, No. 4 (November 1981): 780–795.

Smith, Steven S., and Gerald Gamm. "The Dynamics of Party Government in Congress." In *Congress Reconsidered*, seventh edition, edited by Lawrence C. Dodd and Bruce I. Oppenheimer, 245–268. Washington, D.C.: Congressional Quarterly Press, 2001.

Snyder, James M., Jr. "Committee Power, Structure Induced Equilibria, and Roll Call Votes." *American Journal of Political Science* 36, No. 1 (February 1992a): 36–39.

_____. "Artificial Extremism in Interest Group Ratings." *Legislative Studies Quarterly* XVII, No. 3 (August 1992b): 319–345.

Snyder, James M., and Tim Groseclose. "Estimating Party Influence in Congressional Roll-Call Voting." *American Journal of Political Science* 44, No. 2 (April 2000): 193–211.

Stanley, Harold W. *Voter Mobilization and the Politics of Race: The South and Universal Suffrage*. New York: Praeger, 1987.

Stevenson, Richard W. "Seeking Common Ground on Federal Tax Cut." *New York Times* (July 25, 1999): 18.

Stonecash, Jeffrey M. "Working at the Margins: Campaign Finance and Party Strategy in New York Assembly Elections." *Legislative Studies Quarterly* XIII, No. 4 (November 1988): 477–493.

_____. "Political Cleavage in Gubernatorial and Legislative Elections: The Nature of Inter-Party Competition in New York Elections, 1970–1982." *Western Political Quarterly* 42, No. 1 (March 1989): 69–81.

_____. "Split Constituencies and the Impact of Party Control." *Social Science History* 16, No. 3 (fall 1992): 455–477.

_____. "The Pursuit and Retention of Legislative Office in New York, 1870–1990: Reconsidering Sources of Change." *Polity* XXVI, No. 2 (winter 1993): 301–315.

_____. "Chickens and Eggs, Money and Votes. What's the Question and Does it Matter?" Paper prepared for the conference on campaign finance sponsored by the Committee for the Study of the American Electorate, Washington, D.C., July 29–30, 1994.

_____. "Political Cleavage in State Legislative Houses." *Legislative Studies Quarterly* XXIV, No. 2 (May 1999): 281–302.

_____. *Class and Party in American Politics.* Boulder: Westview Press, 2000.

_____. "A Double-Edged Sword: Party Dilemmas in Mobilizing Electoral Bases in U.S. House Elections." In *The State of the Parties,* edited by John Green and Rick Frommer. Lanham, Md.: Rowman and Littlefield, forthcoming, 2002a.

_____. "The Trend That Never Happened: Incumbent Vote Percentages in House Elections." Manuscript, Department of Political Science, Syracuse University, January 2002b.

Stonecash, Jeffrey M., and Anna Agathangelou. "Trends in the Partisan Composition of State Legislatures: A Response to Fiorina." *American Political Science Review* 91, No. 1 (March 1997): 148–155.

Stonecash, Jeffrey M., Mark D. Brewer, and Mack D. Mariani. "Northern Democrats and Polarization in the U.S. House." *Legislative Studies Quarterly* forthcoming, 2002.

Stonecash, Jeffrey M., Mark D. Brewer, Mary P. McGuire, R. Eric Petersen, and Lori Beth Way. "Class and Party: Secular Realignment and the Survival of Democrats Outside the South." *Political Research Quarterly* 43, No. 4 (December 2000): 731–752.

Stonecash, Jeffrey M., and Sara E. Keith. "Maintaining a Political Party: Providing and Withdrawing Party Campaign Funds." *Party Politics* 2, No. 2 (July 1996): 313–328.

Stonecash, Jeffrey M., and Nicole Lindstrom. "Emerging Party Cleavages in the U.S. House of Representatives." *American Politics Quarterly* 27, No. 1 (January 1999): 58–88.

Stonecash, Jeffrey M., and Mack D. Mariani. "Republican Gains in the House in the 1994 Elections: Class Polarization in American Politics." *Political Science Quarterly* 115, No. 1 (spring 2000): 93–113.

Stonecash, Jeffrey M., and Andrew Milstein. "Parties and Taxes: The Emergence of Distributive Issues, 1950–2000." Presented at the 2001 Midwest Political Science Association Meetings, Chicago, Illinois, April 2001.

Sundquist, James L. *Dynamics of the Party System: Alignment and Realignment of Political Parties in the United States.* Revised edition. Washington, D.C.: The Brookings Institution Press, 1983.

Suro, Roberto. *Strangers Among Us: How Latino Immigration is Transforming America.* New York: Alfred A. Knopf, 1998.

Taylor, Andrew. "The Ideological Development of the Parties in Washington, 1947–1994." *Polity* XXIX, No. 2 (winter 1996): 273–292.

Teaford, Jon C. *City and Suburb: The Political Fragmentation of Metropolitan America, 1850–1970.* Baltimore: Johns Hopkins University Press, 1979.

_____. *The Twentieth-Century American City,* second edition. Baltimore: Johns Hopkins University Press, 1993.

Texiera, Ruy A., and Joel Rogers. *America's Forgotten Majority: Why the White Working Class Still Matters.* New York: Basic Books, 2000.

Timpone, Richard J. "Mass Mobilization or Government Intervention? The Growth of Black Registration in the South." *Journal of Politics* 57, No. 2 (May 1995): 425–442.

Tufte, Edward R. "Determinants of Outcomes of Midterm Congressional Elections." *American Political Science Review* 69, No. 3 (September 1975): 812–826.

Turner, Julius. *Party and Constituency: Pressures on Congress.* Baltimore: Johns Hopkins Press, 1951.

Turner, Julius, and Edward V. Schneier. *Party and Constituency: Pressures on Congress.* Revised Edition. Baltimore: Johns Hopkins Press, 1970.

Uchitelle, Louis. "The American Middle Class; Just Getting By." *New York Times* (August 1, 1999): Sec.3, 1.

United States Bureau of the Census. *Statistical Abstract of the United States, 1974.* Ninety-Fifth Edition. Washington, D.C., 1974.

_____. *Statistical Abstract of the United States, 1985.* 105th Edition. Washington, D.C., 1985.

_____. *Statistical Abstract of the United States, 1990.* 110th Edition. Washington, D.C., 1990.

_____. "Voting and Registration in the Election of November 1988." Current Population Reports, Series P–20–440. Washington, D.C., 1989.

_____. "Voting and Registration in the Election of November 1992." Current Population Reports, Series P–20–466. Washington, D.C., 1993.

_____. "Voting and Registration in the Election of November 1996." Current Population Reports, Series P–20–504.Washington, D.C., 1998.

United States Commission on Civil Rights. *The Voting Rights Act: Ten Years After: A Report of the United States Commission on Civil Rights.* Washington, D.C., January 1975.

United States Immigration and Naturalization Service. *Statistical Yearbook of the Immigration and Naturalization Service, 1998.* Washington, D.C.: U.S. Government Printing Office, 2000.United States Congress. *Congressional Directory,* Sixty-Sixth Congress, First Session. Washington, D.C.: U.S. Government Printing Office, July 1919.

United States Congress. *Congressional Directory,* Seventy-Sixth Congress, Third Session. Washington, D.C.: U.S. Government Printing Office, January 1940.

United States Congress. *Congressional Record.* Permanent edition. Sixty-Sixth Congress, First Session, Volume 58, Part 3, July 22, 1919. Washington, D.C.: U.S. Government Printing Office.

United States Congress. *Congressional Record.* Permanent edition. Seventy-Sixth Congress, Third Session, Volume 86, Part 1, January 10, 1940. Washington, D.C.: U.S. Government Printing Office.

Vandoren, Peter M. 1990. "Can We Learn the Causes of Congressional Decisions from Roll-Call Data?" *Legislative Studies Quarterly* XV, No. 3 (August 1990): 311–339.

Waldinger, Roger. "Immigration and Urban Change." *Annual Review of Sociology* 15 (1989): 211–232.

Wilcox, Clyde, and Aage Clausen. "The Dimensionality of Roll-Call Voting Reconsidered." *Legislative Studies Quarterly* XVI, No.3 (August 1991): 393–405.

Wilson, James Q. "Realignment at the Top, Dealignment at the Bottom." In *The American Elections of 1984*, edited by Austin Ranney, 297–311. Washington, D.C.: American Enterprise Institute, Published by Duke University Press, 1985.

Wright, John R. "Interest Groups, Congressional Reform, and Party Government in the United States." *Legislative Studies Quarterly* XXV, No. 2 (May 2000): 217–235.

Zimmerman, Joseph F. "Election Systems and Representative Democracy: Reflections on the Voting Rights Act of 1965." *National Civic Review* 84, No. 4 (fall-winter 1995): 287–309.

Index

Printed in the United States
66629LVS00004B

9 780813 398433